Tonga

WORLD BIBLIOGRAPHICAL SERIES

General Editors:
Robert G. Neville (Executive Editor)
John J. Horton

Robert A. Myers   Hans H. Wellisch
Ian Wallace   Ralph Lee Woodward, Jr.

John J. Horton is Deputy Librarian of the University of Bradford and was formerly Chairman of its Academic Board of Studies in Social Sciences. He has maintained a longstanding interest in the discipline of area studies and its associated bibliographical problems, with special reference to European Studies. In particular he has published in the field of Icelandic and of Yugoslav studies, including the two relevant volumes in the World Bibliographical Series.

Robert A. Myers is Associate Professor of Anthropology in the Division of Social Sciences and Director of Study Abroad Programs at Alfred University, Alfred, New York. He has studied post-colonial island nations of the Caribbean and has spent two years in Nigeria on a Fulbright Lectureship. His interests include international public health, historical anthropology and developing societies. In addition to *Amerindians of the Lesser Antilles: a bibliography* (1981), *A Resource Guide to Dominica, 1493-1986* (1987) and numerous articles, he has compiled the World Bibliographical Series volumes on *Dominica* (1987), *Nigeria* (1989) and *Ghana* (1991).

Ian Wallace is Professor of German at the University of Bath. A graduate of Oxford in French and German, he also studied in Tübingen, Heidelberg and Lausanne before taking teaching posts at universities in the USA, Scotland and England. He specializes in contemporary German affairs, especially literature and culture, on which he has published numerous articles and books. In 1979 he founded the journal *GDR Monitor*, which he continues to edit under its new title *German Monitor*.

Hans H. Wellisch is Professor emeritus at the College of Library and Information Services, University of Maryland. He was President of the American Society of Indexers and was a member of the International Federation for Documentation. He is the author of numerous articles and several books on indexing and abstracting, and has published *The Conversion of Scripts and Indexing and Abstracting: an International Bibliography*, and *Indexing from A to Z*. He also contributes frequently to *Journal of the American Society for Information Science, The Indexer* and other professional journals.

Ralph Lee Woodward, Jr. is Professor of History at Tulane University, New Orleans. He is the author of *Central America, a Nation Divided*, 2nd ed. (1985), as well as several monographs and more than seventy scholarly articles on modern Latin America. He has also compiled volumes in the World Bibliographical Series on *Belize* (1980), *El Salvador* (1988), *Guatemala* (Rev. Ed.) (1992) and *Nicaragua* (Rev. Ed.) (1994). Dr. Woodward edited the Central American section of the *Research Guide to Central America and the Caribbean* (1985) and is currently associate editor of Scribner's *Encyclopedia of Latin American History*.

VOLUME 217

Tonga

Martin Daly

Compiler

CLIO PRESS
OXFORD, ENGLAND · SANTA BARBARA, CALIFORNIA
DENVER, COLORADO

British Library Cataloguing in Publication Data

Daly, Martin
Tonga. – (World bibliographical series; v. 217)
1. Tonga – Bibliography
I. Title
016.9′9612

ISBN 1–85109–293–5

ABC-CLIO Ltd.,
Old Clarendon Ironworks,
35A Great Clarendon Street,
Oxford OX2 6AT, England.

———

ABC-CLIO Inc.,
130 Cremona Drive,
Santa Barbara,
CA 93117, USA.

Designed by Bernard Crossland.
Typeset by Columns Design Ltd., Reading, England.
Printed in Great Britain by print in black, Midsomer Norton.

THE WORLD BIBLIOGRAPHICAL SERIES

This series, which is principally designed for the English speaker, will eventually cover every country (and some of the world's principal regions and cities), each in a separate volume comprising annotated entries on works dealing with its history, geography, economy and politics; and with its people, their culture, customs, religion and social organization. Attention will also be paid to current living conditions – housing, education, newspapers, clothing, etc. – that are all too often ignored in standard bibliographies; and to those particular aspects relevant to individual countries. Each volume seeks to achieve, by use of careful selectivity and critical assessment of the literature, an expression of the country and an appreciation of its nature and national aspirations, to guide the reader towards an understanding of its importance. The keynote of the series is to provide, in a uniform format, an interpretation of each country that will express its culture, its place in the world, and the qualities and background that make it unique. The views expressed in individual volumes, however, are not necessarily those of the publisher.

VOLUMES IN THE SERIES

Contents

Contents

Introduction

Many older people in Britain may have had the same first experience of
Tonga as I did: seeing Queen Sālote in an open carriage as the rain
poured down on the coronation procession of Queen Elizabeth II in
London in 1953, beaming with joy. 'Where in the world is Tonga?',
many may have asked, a question asked so forcefully by her classmates
in the United States that Samantha Fisk, going to Tonga with her
anthropologist mother, wrote a delightful book for them under that very
title (item no. 20).

The Kingdom of Tonga, about 1,800 km north of New Zealand and
about 800 km east of Fiji, consists of three main groups of islands, with
three outliers to the north and one to the south spread over about
900 km, between 15° and 22° south and 173° and 175° west. While
Tonga is just to the east of the 180° meridian, the International Date
Line was adjusted so that Tonga is to its west, and thus within the same
day as New Zealand and Fiji; however, Samoa, although almost due
north, is to the east of the line and thus twenty-four hours behind
Tonga. Tonga time is Greenwich Mean Time plus thirteen hours, one
hour ahead of New Zealand and Fiji, and Tonga thus has the best claim,
despite some creative claims by others, to be the first country in the
world to see in the new Millennium. From such cartographic quirks
does fame come.

Tonga consists of about 150 islands. Of these, according to the 1996
census, forty-one are currently inhabited, though some with no resident
population are farmed for their produce from neighbouring islands. The
census gives the total area of the inhabited islands as 648.78 sq.km and
the total population as 97,446. The main island of the southern group,
Tongatapu, on which is situated the capital and seat of government,
Nuku'alofa, and the main ports of entry by air and sea, contain two-
thirds of the population (66,212), a figure that has been steadily
growing as people have moved there from outer islands. A short
distance to the south east is 'Eua (population 4,924). The seventeen

islands of the central Ha'apai group have a population of 8,148, showing a steady decrease over twenty years. The thirteen islands of the Vava'u group to the north have 15,779, remaining steady. The figures for the three northern outliers are: Niuafo'ou 735, Niuatoputapu 1,161 and Tafahi 122; these are decreasing slightly.

Many, visiting Tonga for the first time, have been captivated by the country and its people. Captain Cook, writing in his journal on his second voyage, when he visited Tonga in October 1773, noted 'Benevolent Nature has certainly been very bountifull to these isles . . . No one wants the common necessaries of life, joy and contentment is painted in every face; indeed how can it be otherwise, here an easy freedom prevails among all ranks of people, they injoy every blessing of life and live in a climate where the extremes of heat and cold is unknown'. So impressed was he by the people, misleadingly as it turned out, that he called their country the Friendly Islands. Some, on the other hand, found a picture of depravity and wickedness in the description of Tonga and the other Pacific islands given by Cook, and felt and responded to an evangelical call not to accept and enjoy but to change and convert.

Today's traveller or visitor will find Tonga a fascinating and subtle combination of a traditional Polynesian kingdom – the only one to survive the impact of colonialism in the 19th century and remain independent – and a thoroughly Christian country of a curiously 19th-century variety. It might be said that what the imperial powers could not achieve, the missionaries did. They did their work well. The Christian faith pervades the country, largely in its Methodist variety but with many churches and denominations represented, and with a strong Mormon presence. All meals start and finish with a grace, which is not just a formal phrase or two but a long, all-encompassing extempore prayer. Prayers will just as naturally be offered at the opening of a commercial building or a petrol station.

Older guidebooks and travellers' accounts describe arrival by ship, the line of trees gradually coming into view along the Nuku'alofa waterfront, then the low buildings, white wood with red tin roofs; or the journey up the spectacular channel to Neiafu in Vava'u, which has been described as the finest natural harbour in the world. Sadly there are no regular passenger shipping services to Tonga today. A few visitors arrive on their own yachts but most are likely to arrive by air, flying in to Fua'amotu airport on Tongatapu, noting what also struck Captain Cook: the neatness of the plantations on this largely agricultural island and the vivid blues and greens of the waters round the coast. The degree of shabbiness in Nuku'alofa, however, is also striking.

'The Kingdom of Tonga, ancient Polynesia' is the slogan on the tourist literature, and it is the survival of a Polynesian kingdom whose regime still affects many aspects of daily life which is so remarkable about Tonga, and which makes it unique, even if the amalgam of traditional and modern is sometimes a little uneasy. A 'compromise culture' it has been called, containing some of the best of both, and some of the less than best as well. Tonga is not paradise. No one's best interests are served by ignoring the problems – demographic, political, economic and environmental – which face Tonga as they do other small, isolated countries lacking significant natural resources other than their land, their seas and their people.

The islands

Given the small spread of the islands forming the Kingdom of Tonga, the differences in their geological structure and appearance are remarkable. Starting at the southern end, 'Eua is a series of raised limestone terraces on a volcanic base, a high island with dramatic cliffs, and some of the last remaining native forest in Tonga, where parrots may be seen. Tongatapu, the main island, an area of raised reef limestone on a volcanic base, is largely flat, rising gently from northwest to south and east, with rich and fertile soil. The Ha'apai group consists of two parallel chains. To the east is a line of low coral atolls, with poor, sandy soil. To the west is a line of volcanic islands, of which the cone of Kao is the highest point in Tonga (1,109 m) and Tofua is still active. The islands of the Vava'u group have a volcanic base and present a more varied aspect. To the north again, Niuafo'ou is an active volcano, a ring of land round a crater lake; the volcano last erupted in 1946 (item no. 133). Niuatoputapu is the eroded remnant of a large volcano, while Tafahi, a few kilometres to the north, is an extinct volcano cone. All these three have rugged shores on which landing is difficult. To the east of the whole chain is the Tonga Trench, with depths of over 10,000 m – some of the deepest ocean in the world.

Tonga's climate is sub-tropical rather than tropical, with winter temperatures never less than about 17°C and summer temperatures never warmer than about 33°C. Vava'u is noticeably warmer than Tongatapu. High humidity can make the months of December to March rather uncomfortable. These are the months of highest rainfall and also of cyclones. The last major cyclone, Isaac, was in 1982 but there have been others of less destructive effect since, most recently Cora in December 1998, which caused damage assessed at T$19.6 million to crops and buildings in Ha'apai, Tongatapu and 'Eua.

History

Historians of the Pacific used to place the settlement of the islands of Polynesia by their present peoples within the first millennium AD, but now it is generally accepted that the earliest archaeological remains place the first settlement of Tonga by the Lapita peoples at about 1,500 BC. Discoveries in the last twenty years of distinctive pottery made by the Lapita peoples (named after a site in New Caledonia where it was first found) have established this much earlier date for the movement of a people from south-east Asia, through Melanesia and into Polynesia. A comprehensive treatment of the whole topic, with a bibliography of all published references, is now available in P. V. Kirch's *The Lapita peoples* (item no. 73). From the archaeological record it seems that these people were largely shore-dwellers, living on fish and shellfish. Why the making of their distinctive pottery died out remains unclear.

The evidence, both archaeological and linguistic, indicates quite clearly that the Polynesian peoples, the Tongans among them, came from south-east Asia, and the efforts of Thor Heyerdahl to prove that they came from South America must be discounted. This is not to deny that there are many unanswered questions, as to the relationship between the Polynesians, and the Melanesians of Fiji, the Solomon Islands and other groups to the west and north, and as to the order in which the Lapita peoples settled the island groups of Polynesia and thus became the Polynesians whom we know today. But the basic direction of the movement and its approximate dating are now far better established than they were. Because the word Tonga means 'south' it is suggested that they may have come immediately from Samoa to the north, but Tongan legends tell of no migration, only of creation by the gods, among whom Maui fished up the islands from the bed of the sea.

The first phase of Tongan history of which oral records tell is the emergence of 'Aho'eitu as the first Tu'i Tonga probably about 950 AD. He was born, so legend tells, from the union between the sun god Tangaloa and a beautiful Tongan girl. The origin myth makes it clear that the Tu'i Tonga was a sacred king, as much priest as ruler, possessed of *mana* (presence, authority) and at the head of a society based on *tapu* (prohibition, hence probably the one Tongan word taken into English, taboo), which governed all behaviour and relationships within a highly structured society.

From 'Aho'eitu there is a record of a continuous line, oral until the coming of the Europeans and then written, until the thirty-ninth, Laufilitonga, who died in 1865. Long before then, however, in the early 15th century, a second royal line developed, the Tu'i Ha'atakalaua, taking on the temporal authority of the Tu'i Tonga and leaving him only with his sacred role. Early in the 17th century a third line developed, the Tu'i Kanokupolu, also a temporal line whose power had, by the time of European contact, become greater than that of the other two. The Tu'i Tonga title was absorbed by King George Tupou I on the death of Laufilitonga and the three lines were brought together by the marriage of Queen Sālote Tupou III to Tungī Mailefihi, so that all are embodied in the person of her eldest son, the present King Taufa'āhau Tupou IV.

Tonga was not a peaceful place during the reigns of the early Tu'i Tongas, some of whom met violent deaths. The earliest recorded stories tell of the tenth, in the 12th century. The eleventh, Tu'itātui, built the Ha'amonga trilithon, one of the most remarkable sights in Tonga today, made of three huge stones each weighing forty tonnes and five metres high which, whatever its other purposes, served as an astronomical marker for the passing of the seasons. This was also the period of the building of the *langi*, massive stone terraced tombs which may be seen around the old capital of Mu'a.

The first sighting of Tonga by Europeans was in 1616 when the Dutch explorers Schouten and Le Maire visited briefly the far northern islands of Niuatoputapu and Tafahi. The first visit to Tongatapu was by Abel Tasman in 1643. The first significant visit, however, had to wait for over a century, when Captain James Cook visited 'Eua, Tongatapu and Nomuka on his second voyage in 1773-74 and, for a much longer period on his third voyage in 1777, Nomuka, Ha'apai, Tongatapu and 'Eua. Cook's virtues as a captain, a navigator, a cartographer and an observer, a man of humanity and of learning, have been written about often and need no repetition here. Suffice it to say that his journals, and the printed accounts of his voyages, which had enormous circulation and influence, offer a sympathetic, comprehensive and informed account of the islands that he visited, the Tongans whom he met, and their way of life, and all serious study of Tonga must begin with him. I have been navigated round the harbour at Nuku'alofa by a sailor using Cook's chart, which he said had never been bettered.

However, for some the picture of the Pacific Islands presented by Cook and other explorers was not one of paradise but of depravity. For Protestants, inspired by the evangelical revival of the 18th century, and later for Catholics, Tonga was a mission field. In 1796 the London Missionary Society equipped the ship *Duff* to place missionaries in Tonga and other islands. Ten were left in Tonga but the mission was a disaster. They were all men of great zeal but little formal education and the strategy of reaching Tongans for the Christian faith by teaching them their trades was quite impractical. Some were killed, and within a few years all those left were withdrawn.

Introduction

They had arrived at a time of increasing unrest within Tonga, of rivalries between chiefs in the three island groups which was to culminate in a long period of civil war. In the meantime the Christian presence was re-established, this time by the Wesleyan Missionary Society which first sent Walter Lawry, from 1822-23, and then John Thomas and John Hutchinson and their wives, who arrived in 1826. In 1831 the young chief Taufa'āhau was baptised, taking the Christian name of George. He gained authority in Vava'u, and on the death of the Tu'i Kanokupolu in 1845 he assumed that title and thus became the ruler of a united Tonga as King George Tupou I.

The achievements of his long reign (he died in 1893, aged ninety-six) were without parallel in the Pacific, although some opposition and disaffection continued until about 1860. Whether he called upon and used the expertise of his missionary advisers, and in particular his Prime Minister for many years, Shirley Baker, to work to his own ends, or whether Baker directed him, is a matter of debate, with Rutherford (item no. 128) and Lātūkefu (item no. 120) presenting different aspects of the question. However, by the end of his reign George I had united his kingdom, given Tonga codes of laws, culminating in the Constitution of 1875 which established personal freedoms and transformed the old chiefs into new nobles, and had above all kept Tonga independent by playing off one European power against another by a series of treaties which ensured that Tonga never became a colony. Baker even imported for the King from New Zealand the palace which is still occupied by the royal family today, as an appropriate European trapping of authority, and devised a flag and coat of arms.

There were many European residents and traders who mocked what they saw as the pretensions of the King and Shirley Baker. Baker eventually had to be expelled, after an attempt to assassinate him, and it was after this, and the King's death, that in 1900 Britain imposed a Treaty of Protection and Friendship by which a British Agent and Consul was appointed, who was not to interfere in internal affairs but was to advise the king on all foreign affairs, and on local and financial policy as requested.

The achievements and status of King George I are summed up by Rutherford in his *Friendly Islands: a history of Tonga* (item no. 92): 'The Kingdom of Tonga was his own creation and the independence, prosperity and well being of his people his lifetime care. He was the greatest Tongan of his own and probably any other century'. Yet Tonga was not as well-founded as it might seem, and the reign of his great-grandson King George Tupou II, who did not have the same gifts, was less happy. Since 1890 the government had fallen into administrative and financial chaos. Rivalries emerged. The King alienated many by vacillating between two possible wives, and his choice made him so unpopular that for a time he could not leave the palace without an armed guard. His government had to borrow money from traders, and King and parliament were set against each other. Such was the concern both of foreign residents in Tonga and the British government that Britain imposed a supplementary treaty in 1905, further restricting Tonga's independence, and enforced a change of ministers. And yet the affair of the Tonga ma'a Tonga kautaha (item nos. 141 and 142) showed that the power of the British consul was limited and could not totally override the King and his government. The rest of the reign saw a greater degree of unity and some economic progress.

Even so, the early years of the reign of his daughter, Queen Sālote Tupou III, who succeeded at the age of eighteen in 1918, were far from easy. From a later perspective her long reign, ending in 1965, was seen as a golden age of stability, of the recovery of those important elements of Tongan tradition which had been unnecessarily lost: a pride in being truly Tongan together with a careful acceptance of that which was best and most appropriate from the West, and quiet progress in the economy, health and education. The definitive account of the reign is Dr Wood-Ellem's biography (see item no. 136). The early years of Sālote's reign were distinctly unsettled, but her attempt to bring together the divided churches (item no. 171), her presence in the villages, her work during the Second World War when many American troops were based in Tonga, exposing it for the first time to Western culture on a large scale, and much else, including her presence in London in 1953, gave her people a new self-confidence in the value of their own Tongan identity, while ensuring that Tonga was a stable unit within the region and the British Commonwealth. An important part of this was her concern, with the help of Western scholars such as Elizabeth Bott (item nos. 208 and 221) working with her and with other Tongans, to record Tongan tradition and history. Her death prompted the deepest grief in Tonga.

For sixteen years Queen Sālote had been assisted as Prime Minister by her son, who succeeded her as King Taufa'āhau Tupou IV. A law graduate from the University of Sydney, he saw that Tonga could not remain protected from the larger world, that it needed investment in health and education, in transport and communications and an economy based less on subsistence agriculture than on industry and commerce. All of this, he knew, would need external funding through development aid and loans.

Early in his reign, in 1970, Tonga achieved full independence from Britain, within the British Commonwealth. Earlier, in 1968, surface oil seepages raised hopes of commercially exploitable oil, which it was hoped would fund Tonga's development, but after much exploration none was found. However, much was done in the early years of the reign: a hotel was built, a radio station and newspaper started, and a bank established. But, with a population growing through improved health care, pressure on the limited land resources increased. No longer could every young man receive the tax allotment to which he was entitled. Many, encouraged by the government, emigrated to New Zealand, Australia and the United States, seeing that as the only answer to economic problems, and the considerable literature on the inter-related themes of population, migration and remittances and their impact on the Tongan economy (item nos. 311-33) demonstrates their crucial importance to Tonga today. At the same time it is perhaps both ironic and inevitable that Tonga has not been able to establish an export-led economy based on small-scale industry and on tourism, and that the success of vanilla and of squash, and the potential for kava and for fish, suggest that the local resources of land and sea remain Tonga's best hope. Yet the King remains indefatigable, even now at the age of eighty, in his efforts to improve his kingdom and the lot of his people, taking initiatives and pursuing opportunities whenever they present themselves. Now it seems that he is himself laying more emphasis on the agricultural sector. In his Christmas message for 1998 he spoke of market gardens being established on land bought by the government in Hawai'i and California, and of a new variety of watermelon which could be grown in Tonga for the Japanese market.

The reign has seen considerable concern over the issue of the distribution of land, in part related to calls for greater democracy and accountability. However, the extraordinary national celebrations for the King's eightieth birthday in July 1998, the days of feasting and dancing, of church services, concerts and displays, the decorated archways erected over every main road in Nuku'alofa, the presence of distinguished visitors from around the Pacific, all served to demonstrate that the monarchy is still at the heart of the Tongan polity.

Political system

Tonga is a monarchy, the only Polynesian monarchy to survive, and the monarch does not only reign but also rules. The role of the monarch is set within the parliamentary system established by the Constitution of 1875, but this does not give sovereignty to a democratically elected parliament in the Western style, and significant tensions have appeared in the last decade.

The Constitution provides for a sovereign and a Privy Council. The monarch is both head of state and head of government, and appoints the Prime Minister and all members of the Cabinet. (The monarch with the

Cabinet forms the Privy Council.) Tonga has only had three Prime Ministers in the past fifty years: from 1949-65, the present King when he was Crown Prince during the latter part of the reign of his mother Queen Sālote; from 1965-91, the present King's brother Prince Fatafehi Tu'ipelahake; and since 1991, Baron Vaea, who it is said wishes to retire soon. Until mid-1998 the Minister for Foreign Affairs and for Defence was the present Crown Prince Tupouto'a. He resigned after holding the post for twenty-five years and the post is now held by his youngest brother Prince 'Ulukālala-Lavaka-Ata. All members of the Cabinet sit in the single-chamber legislature, along with nine Nobles' Representatives elected by the Nobles from among the thirty-three of them, and nine Peoples' Representatives elected by universal suffrage. There are no political parties as such. A group, loosely formed, calling itself the Pro-Democracy Movement, has emerged in the last ten years, led by some of the Peoples' Representatives who have been elected with large majorities. In October 1998 they chose as their new name the Tonga Human Rights and Democracy Movement. They call for greater ministerial accountability, and at times have suggested that cabinet ministers should be drawn from among elected representatives rather than appointed by the King. However, they are bound by no common ideology and have at times fallen out among themselves, and there is little apparent feeling that the monarchy should become subservient to parliament, let alone that it should be replaced by a republic. Most calls for reform are set within the limits of the present system. The fact remains that the King, through his Cabinet and with the usual support of the Nobles' Representatives, can always obtain a majority in the legislature if necessary; but also that some Tongans who have travelled or lived abroad, and are aware of other styles of government, increasingly question aspects of the present system.

At a constitutional convention in January 1999 the Tonga Human Rights and Democracy Movement proposed two major changes in the Constitution: the right of the King to rule only as honorary head of state and under direction of Cabinet; and the election of all thirty members of the Legislative Assembly, who would then choose Ministers of the Crown. The effect of these changes would be radically to transfer the exercise of political authority in Tonga.

Foreign relations

At a time when many of the Pacific island countries have been united in their opposition to the continuing French colonial presence in the Pacific, and in particular to their nuclear tests, Tonga has followed a resolutely independent path of friendship to all, as is the stated aim of its foreign policy. Membership of the British Commonwealth is central, and there is a personal friendship between the British and Tongan royal families. Tonga participates fully in all the regional organizations of the South Pacific and is associated with some of the subsidiary agencies of the United Nations, such as the World Health Organization, although it is not a member of the United Nations itself, its population being too small. However, this may change. In January 1999 the King was in New York discussing possible membership with the Secretary-General.

Tonga has until recently been in a minority in the South Pacific in maintaining diplomatic relations with Taiwan, but in a sudden and unexpected move in October 1998 terminated these and established relations with the People's Republic of China (item no. 277). In an interview in the December 1998 issue of *Matangi Tonga*, Princess Pilolevu, the King's daughter and Chair of TongaSat, puts the need for this change in the wider context of developing business opportunities with China, particularly the use by China of some of Tonga's orbital satellite slots, and even suggested that it might open China to Christian evangelism by Tongans.

The economy

To economists accustomed to near-balanced national accounts, the Tongan economy must appear precarious in the extreme. For 1997 imports were valued at close to T$90 million and exports at under T$20 million, producing a balance of payments deficit of around T$70 million. Tonga now has what is classified by economists as a MIRAB economy, in which the main elements are migration, remittances and bureaucracy. It is only the large volume of remittances from Tongans now living overseas, in recent years almost equal to the value of the export of goods and services, together with overseas aid, which has funded the value of imports fuelled by a rising standard of living. It is likely that a considerable part of the money received by families from their kin overseas has been spent directly on the construction of houses, on cars and on other imported consumer durables, as well as on food, much of which is imported. The scale of remittances is shown by a survey in 1984 in which, in the sample area, ninety per cent of households received remittances, totalling twenty-six per cent of household income. There are plenty of signs of apparent prosperity, at least in Nuku'alofa where the number of vehicles has increased so much in recent years that there are now traffic jams at busy periods.

Yet the position is precarious, and foreign currency reserves have recently fallen to alarmingly low levels. Tonga faces all the problems of a small group of islands nearly 2,000 km from its nearest potential major market, New Zealand, with high shipping costs and services that are not always reliable. Tonga is a primarily agricultural country which before European contact produced more than enough staple foods for all (albeit with a population of probably no more than 20,000) with surpluses the size of which amazed early explorers when presented on ceremonial occasions such as the *'inasi* (first fruits) for the Tu'i Tonga. Indeed the volume of food, whether presented for ceremonies or for feasts, can still amaze the visitor today. On the whole Tongan dietary problems are more of being overweight than of malnutrition, though diet may not always be well-balanced. Coconut oil and copra, the flesh of the coconut, used in the production of soap and margarine, were in the 19th century and remained for long the main export crop. Attempts to diversify and develop new export crops (coffee, cotton and sugar) were made in the 19th century but never became significant, though a little coffee is still grown today. By the 1970s the world price of copra had fallen so low that the trade became unremunerative, and efforts, financed by overseas aid, to develop the export of both copra and bananas largely came to nothing. In recent years two significant new export crops have been developed. The first was vanilla, largely grown in Vava'u and commanding a good price in the world market if of good quality. More recently has come squash (pumpkin) for the Japanese market, which Tonga can supply for a short period at the end of the year when there are no other suppliers. Much land has been turned over to squash production, sometimes to the detriment of the production of staple foods for domestic consumption, and some people have grown very rich through this trade. But another factor affecting all agricultural production, domestic or export, is the weather. Tonga is prone both to hurricanes, which can devastate crops for many years, and to drought, which can greatly reduce yields. 1998 was a year of low rainfall and poor crops. Squash export quotas to Japan were not filled, and the volume exported was sharply reduced. The drought has also sharply reduced the amount of fruit and vegetables exported to New Zealand. A new fumigator recently installed at the airport so that produce can meet stringent New Zealand standards is lying unused for most of the time because there is no export produce to be treated.

Yet there are hopes for agricultural exports. The world price of copra is now rising and traders are again buying in the market. The potential for the export of kava to Germany and the United States for the production of a natural tranquilizer is great. One American company was reported at the end of 1998 as wanting to buy twenty tonnes of kava a week, a demand that Tonga could not meet, although a first shipment of 1,000 kg was sent in October. New crops are being explored, such as limu tanga'u, a seaweed for which there is a good market in Japan. But many growers produce in the short term and take profits for immediate consumption. There is too little capital investment in agriculture, and supplies are not consistent enough to meet regular demand from export markets.

There have been attempts to start small businesses producing for export and a Small Industries Centre, developed outside Nuku'alofa, was hailed as a model for small Pacific island countries. However, the distances over which raw materials (largely wool for knitwear and leather for coats) had to be imported and the finished goods then exported militated against success, and it seems unlikely that this can be a significant part of the answer to Tonga's problems.

Commercial fishing has yet to produce significant exports, while Tonga imports considerable quantities of tinned fish. Prospects may be improving and the Ministry of Fisheries anticipates exports of T$50 million by 2000, with new fishing boats coming into service.

Tourism, as in many such countries, has been seen as a generator of employment as well as an earner of foreign currency, but it has never developed in Tonga to the extent hoped. Tonga could never be a large-scale tourist destination such as Fiji or Hawai'i: there are neither the facilities nor the transport links, and standards have not always been what today's tourists expect. Tonga's hope for tourism has to rest on smaller groups with particular specialist interests such as yacht cruising, which is being developed in Vava'u, diving and deep-sea fishing. It seems that tourism is at present in a state of some crisis. In December 1998 the four largest hotels in Nuku'alofa were all saying that rates of occupancy were so low that they might have to close before the end of 1999, when Tonga is working to bring a large, though inevitably brief, influx of visitors, for the Millennium.

Other sources of foreign income have been more successful, though some have been controversial. For a while Tonga was selling protected-person passports in places such as Hong Kong, though that was challenged as being unconstitutional and has now ceased. It is said that this produced T$40 million. Tonga has most successfully exploited the satellite slots above it, in partnership with overseas interests, and TongaSat is now paying significant sums to the government, estimated at T$10 million to date.

Society

Traditional Tongan society is highly stratified and its inter-relationships often complex. The extensive literature on rank and status and on social relationships as they have been observed (item nos. 173-222) bears witness to the fascination of the subject to scholars over the 200 years since Captain Cook recorded his observations.

At its simplest, below royalty is a clear and sharp distinction, based on birth and thus on inherited rank, between *tu'a* (commoners) and *'eiki* (chiefs). This extends to three levels of language, for monarch, nobles and commoners. In pre-European times the distinction was absolute. Not only did *tu'a* have no rights in this life: only *'eiki* could reach the afterlife in Pulotu. While King George I's Code of Laws of 1862 removed from the chiefs the right to demand exactions from commoners, and the Constitution of 1875 transformed the chief into a parliamentary noble, this did nothing to affect social relationships and ranking, and the stratification remains. Rank (acquired by birth) and status (acquired by achievement) are not always identical, and the literature on the relationship between one and the other, and on how rank is acquired and transmitted, is highly technical. Every Tongan needs to know where he or she stands in the social order, and for a Tongan child, part of the process of growing up is become skilled (*poto*) in knowing one's place in society and operating within it. This has now been well demonstrated by Helen Morton in her widely-acclaimed book *Becoming Tongan* (item no. 175).

The picture now, however, is not as clear as it once was. There is a growing number of commoners, better educated than some nobles, holding senior positions in government and business. The reciprocal relationship of nobles and commoners, each with both obligations and responsibilities, has on occasions been a one-way process. Concepts of democracy and of equal political rights are seen to be valid elsewhere but not in Tonga by some. Rank still remains central, and it is necessary to be aware of this in any attempt to understand Tongan society today.

Kava

Kava occupies such an important place in Tongan society, and in life generally, that it merits a section on its own (item nos. 223-30). Kava is a drink made from the pounded root of the kava plant (*Piper methysticum*), mixed with water. The taste is slightly peppery and muddy, and for most non-Tongans it is an acquired taste. Its chemical composition is alkaloid; it is an anaesthetic and analgesic, and its effect is gently soporific. It is not, as is sometimes stated, alcoholic, nor does it have the same effect. As noted above in the section on agriculture, it is in increasing demand in the United States and Europe as the basis of a natural tranquilizer.

The social drinking of kava, without any ceremony, in informal groups or in kava clubs in every village is central to the daily life of most Tongan men (not usually women). Here information is shared and matters of common concern are discussed long into the night.

However, a formal kava ceremony, when kava is ceremonially mixed and shared on major occasions such as the conferring of a title on a noble, is also a deeply significant social ritual. The strict arrangement of seating in the circle, the gifts which accompany the kava, and the order of precedence signified by the sequence in which the kava is distributed to each person present, all ratify and affirm the hierarchies of Tongan society. As Urbanowicz writes in his paper on kava (item no. 223), kava is 'a seal on all occasions . . . a model of Tongan society'. Others have interpreted the kava ceremony at a deeper level, from a psychoanalytical viewpoint (item no. 225), seeing it as resolving some of the tensions inherent in Tongan society from its mythic beginning. Others still, as Christians, have seen it as a powerful prefiguring of Holy Communion. The altar in the Roman Catholic cathedral in Nuku'alofa is in the form of a giant kava bowl. However, at whatever level it is interpreted, or simply observed and experienced, to witness a major kava ceremony is to see the traditional Tongan society made visible.

The essence of Tonga

How, then, can one sum up the essence of this complex society? What can be identified as its governing principles as they can be seen by observers from outside?

The ability to adopt and absorb without losing its essential character seems to be a continuing thread running through Tongan history. For all the Western influences which have deeply affected it, Tonga, 200 years after the first significant European contact, is still remarkably distinct. The present Deputy Prime Minister and Minister of Education, Dr Kavaliku, identifies 'ofa, love, as the principal characteristic feature of Tongan society (item no. 203). All aspects of life in Tonga, at its ideal best, are governed by 'ofa. Of course not all relationships in Tonga reach this ideal. Yet the very fact that, at the end of the cynical 20th century, this can be recognized as an ideal is significant. Tongans may disagree strongly about almost everything – politics, religion, the family or business. They are, it has been observed, highly litigious, often ready to go to court against each other. Yet, as Marcus records in investigating litigation and succession disputes (item no. 265), the use of lawyers to avoid direct confrontation allows harmonious relations to resume after a case, whichever way the verdict may go.

The proliferation of churches of different denominations is very apparent: even a small village may contain two or three. But they all work together when necessary, for instance if labour is required for a new building. Western and traditional medicine co-exist, and indeed Clare Parsons, writing about this (item no. 244), sees the maintenance of harmony in relationships as central not just to health but to life generally. Christianity and concepts of evil spirits co-exist too. Both the causes of and the remedies for illness are seen as complementary, more than exclusively the domain of only one system of belief and knowledge. Tongan graves are decorated with all sorts of Western material such as bottles and fabrics (item no. 401) which might be thought incongruous and inappropriate to Western eyes. Yet why should they be? At a celebration both the police silver band or one of the many school brass bands may appear, and also traditional dance and music troupes playing in very much the way observed by Captain Cook. Tonga has learnt and taken much from the West, not all to the good, but the West has not yet swamped or transformed Tonga. Perhaps it is because Tonga is a largely homogeneous society, with no alienation of land and no significant immigration, that it has been able both to adopt and to retain, and to become a truly 'compromise culture'.

Alongside this ability to adopt and absorb is the fact that traditionally no Tongan stands alone, living a purely private, individual life. Life is lived as part of a wider network of extended family and kin. It has been stated that the 'we' is more important than the 'I' in Tonga. Thus, you do not save money for yourself first, but for the needs of your kin, your village or your church. There is no social security in Tonga. The care of the elderly is the welcomed responsibility of those who can support them. It can be more difficult where the owner of a small shop is expected to give goods or credit to his kin, or where a businessman or farmer is trying to accumulate capital to develop their business. For the non-Tongan the fact that a Tongan is seldom alone can be difficult to appreciate. To go for a walk or read a book on your own is simply not done. Some younger Tongans, particularly if brought up overseas, may find it less easy to live in this way. But to anyone spending any time in Tonga the sense of the strength of the communal is palpable. This is 'ofa in practice.

How far this may all survive into the 21st century must remain an open question. A younger generation increasingly exposed to the values of Western individualism may find it less easy to hold the balance. Many of the writers whose works are featured in this bibliography are concerned with one aspect or another of this situation. The system may seem to some, both inside and outside, to be something of an anachronism. Others may feel that, without characteristics such as these, Tonga would no longer be Tonga.

Knowledge of the best that is Tongan is one way to ensure that the best survives. Social change is inevitable – societies are dynamic, not static, and no society can now isolate itself from the rest of the world. F. O. Kolo, in his paper on the myth of indigenous authenticity in *Tongan culture and history* (item no. 93), notes, 'After all the years of teaching us that we are primitive and have an inferior culture to that of the Europeans, all of a sudden we are told our culture is beautiful, that we should go back and live by it'. He calls for scholars to list all available Tongan articles of historical significance, to collect all written materials produced by non-Tongans such as early descriptions by traders, navigators and others, and to collect articles by scholars on all Tongan subjects. It is hoped that this bibliography may contribute to this process, and thus to the well-being of Tonga within a wider world.

Scope and arrangement of the bibliography

It would be almost impossible to do now what Philip Snow set out to do thirty years ago in his *A bibliography of Fiji, Tonga and Rotuma* (item no. 440): to provide a complete listing of all material, not only books and academic papers but also newspaper articles. Far too much has been published since for this to be even conveniently listed, let alone annotated. However, this is not, in any case, the aim of this series. I have attempted, as far as possible, to follow the brief given me by the publisher, and to give preference to more recent books, commercially published and generally available, and to include older and more specialist material only where necessary. However, in the case of Tonga, in many subject areas, few if any recent books have been published, and the bulk of the literature is contained within papers in academic journals. For example, recent general works of synthesis have been published on the Lapita people (item no. 73) and on Tongan history (item no. 95) and art (item no. 387). On the other hand, virtually all of the large literature on the complex matter of Tongan social structure, status and rank is to be found in papers in academic journals or collected volumes and it has thus been necessary to cover these more fully. The same applies to the subjects of population and migration. At the same time standard monographs on some subjects, though now old, have not been superseded. The standard work on the plants of Tonga was published in 1959 (item no. 65), and that on canoes of Oceania in 1936 (item no. 399).

It must be stressed that this bibliography is selective, and makes no claim to completeness. I have done my best to cover all significant works which I have been able to locate. However, I am aware of some works which I have not been able to find in any of the libraries available to me, and I have therefore not been able to include them. I have no doubt that I have missed works which others would have included, and that my judgement as to what should be included and what not may not be that of others. There are many books on the Pacific Islands generally, or on regions within it, which have brief sections on Tonga. These I have excluded unless it has been necessary to include them for want of anything more specialized.

I should also make it clear that I am not a professional scholar or bibliographer in the field of Pacific studies. My annotations attempt not to evaluate the validity of an argument but to offer a factual summary of what the author has written. Where I have offered my own comments, they have been largely confined to older works, relating the content to current conditions.

I have followed broadly the structure of sections suggested by the publisher for the series, but with some adaptations. For some sections which appear in other volumes in the series, little if anything has been written. Others, such as kava, seem important enough to warrant a section of their own.

Any attempt to review the whole literature on Tonga reveals one sad fact, that so little about Tonga is written by Tongans themselves – for example, fewer than ten PhD theses out of fifty-five listed here are by Tongans. First explorers and visitors such as Cook and Mariner, then missionaries and teachers such as Collocott, and in more recent times scholars from Europe, North America, Australia and New Zealand have made substantial contributions to the study of Tonga. Tongans will tell you that some of these authors have misunderstood aspects of their subjects, in some cases perhaps because they did not know the language themselves and had to work through interpreters, or because their informants had a partial view. For a small country of limited resources, it is not easy to train young scholars through to PhD standard with the prospect of an academic career and the opportunity to research, write and publish. The University of the South Pacific in Fiji, the university for the region, has done its best, through the work of the Institute of Pacific Studies, to encourage writing and make possible the publication of work by Pacific islanders, but much of this necessarily consists of brief papers in collected volumes. It is to be hoped that more Tongans in future will be encouraged and trained to interpret their remarkable country to the wider world.

A note on names and spelling

Tongan lacks some of the letters of the European alphabet. It has no j, r or b, using s, l and p instead. Further every syllable concludes with a vowel. Once this is understood, many names and words which seem unfamiliar become clear. Thus, Semisi is James, Sione is John, Kalonikali is Chronicle, kolisi is college, siupeli is jubilee.

Acknowledgements

My first thanks must go to Philip Snow, pioneer bibliographer of Tonga, for suggesting to the publisher that I might be able to prepare a volume on Tonga for this series. I have drawn much on his knowledge, resources and encouragement.

Work on this bibliography began with the library of books that my wife and I have collected for many years, but this is selective, is stronger on the old than on the new, and consists only of books. I could not have contemplated embarking on this undertaking without having available to me the superb library resources of my own institution, the School of Oriental and African Studies in the University of London. There are to be found many of the books and journals consulted, and listed here. I thank particularly Helen Cordell, herself author of the *Laos* volume in this series, for her help and encouragement. However, it became obvious at an early stage that it would be necessary to supplement the holdings of SOAS from one of the major academic libraries in the Pacific specializing in Pacific studies, and I am most grateful to Karen Peacock and her staff in the Pacific collection of the University of Hawai'i library for enabling me to spend a very productive week there, working through their fine collection.

Other libraries in the University of London have provided materials within their own specialist areas. A particularly rich source has been the library of the Institute of Commonwealth Studies, where Julie Evans provided much help. Other libraries were those of the Institute of Archaeology, the London School of Hygiene and Tropical Medicine, the Institute of Advanced Legal Studies, the Institute of Education and the Warburg Institute. Also in London, the library of the Natural History Museum provided access to material not found elsewhere.

While in Tonga in July 1998 for the celebrations of the eightieth birthday of His Majesty King Taufa'āhau Tupou IV, and also to gather local material, I was fortunate to meet some of the leading scholars currently working on Tonga, Adrienne Kaeppler, Jehanne Teilhet-Fisk, Eric Shumway and Elizabeth Wood-Ellem. I am grateful to them for their interest and encouragement. William Hamilton, Director of the University of Hawai'i Press, fellow-publisher and friend for many years, kindly made the arrangements for my visit to the University of Hawai'i library; all who work on the Pacific are indebted to him and his Press as the leading publisher of books and journals on the region.

Linda Crowl and Barbara Hauʻofa of the University of the South Pacific were helpful in many ways.

Having advised the publisher for several years on possible authors for volumes on Asia and Africa, it has been an interesting experience to turn to being an author myself, and I thank Dr Robert Neville and Julia Goddard for entrusting this volume to me and for their help and guidance as I have worked on it.

I am grateful to the Tongan High Commissioner in London, Akosita Fineanganofo, for her interest in the work and for arranging for me to obtain information in Tonga, where the Minister of Justice, the Hon. Tevita Tupou and the Acting Government Statistician, Seini Filiai, were particularly generous with their time and information.

My gratitude to His Majesty King Taufaʻāhau Tupou IV and to all the people of Tonga whom I have come to know over more than thirty years, and who have enabled me to know something of their kingdom, is so great that it is difficult to express it adequately.

My final, and greatest, debt is to my wife Diane Vahoi and to her late mother Agnes Tuʻifua. I have, I hope, learnt something of Tonga from what I have read, but I could never have come to know Tonga in the way that I have been privileged to do, without them. I hope that this bibliography may be, however inadequate, an attempt to return to them and to the people of Tonga something of what they have given me

Martin Daly
March 1999

Chronology

c.1500 BC	Probable first settlement of the Tongan islands by the Lapita people
c.950 AD	'Aho'eitu, first Tu'i Tonga
c.1200	Ha'amonga trilithon built by eleventh Tu'i Tonga, Tu'itātui
1616	Schouten and Le Maire, the first Europeans to find Tonga, visit Niuatoputapu and Tafahi
1643	Abel Tasman visits 'Eua, Tongatapu and Nomuka
1767	Captain Wallis visits Niuatoputapu
1773-74	Captain James Cook, on his second voyage, visits 'Eua, Tongatapu and Nomuka
1777	Captain James Cook, on his third voyage, visits Nomuka, Ha'apai, Tongatapu and 'Eua.
1781	Dom Francisco Mourelle discovers Vava'u
1787	La Pérouse visits Niuatoputapu
1797	First missionaries arrive on the *Duff*
1799	Three of the missionaries murdered
1800	Remaining missionaries leave
1805	The *Port-au-Prince* attacked, William Mariner adopted by Finau 'Ulakālala
1807	Siege of Nuku'alofa by Finau 'Ulakālala
1822	Walter Lawry arrives to re-establish the mission
1826	John Thomas arrives to take the place of Walter Lawry. Taufa'āhau becomes ruler of Ha'apai
1831	Taufa'āhau baptized, taking the name of George
1839	Taufa'āhau issues the Vava'u Code, the first written law in Tonga
1842	First Roman Catholic missionaries arrive
1845	George Taufa'āhau assumes the title of Tu'i Kanokupolo, becoming ruler of a united Tonga as King George Tupou I

1850	Second code of laws
1855	Treaty of friendship with France
1862	New code of laws, emancipating the people
1875	Granting of the Constitution
1876	Treaty with Germany
1879	Treaty with Britain
1890	Prime Minister Shirley Baker deported
1893	Death of King George Tupou I, accession of King George Tupou II
1900	Treaty of friendship and protection with Britain
1905	Supplementary agreement with Britain
1918	Death of King George Tupou II, accession of Queen Sālote Tupou III
1942	US forces arrive in Tonga
1946	Niuafo'ou devastated by volcanic eruption
1965	Death of Queen Sālote Tupou III, accession of King Taufa'āhau Tupou IV
1970	Full independence within the British Commonwealth
1975	Tonga Council of Churches seminar on land reform
1989	First shipment of squash to Japan
1990	Election returns candidates pledged to electoral reform and greater ministerial accountability

PhD Theses

Tsukamoto Akihisa. 'The language of Niuafo'ou island', Australian National University, 1988.

John Richard Baker. 'Transfer costs in the overseas and internal shipping services of Fiji and Tonga', Australian National University, 1974.

Muawia Barazangi. 'Three studies of the structure and dynamics of the upper mantle adjacent to a descending lithospheric slab. I. Lateral variations of seismic waves above the inclined earthquake zone of the Tonga Island Arc deep anomaly in the upper mantle: II. Propagation of seismic waves through and beneath the lithosphere that descends under the Tonga Arc: III. Late Cenozic evolution of the Great Basin, Western United States as an ensialic interarc basin', Columbia University, 1971.

Louise M. Bernstein. '*Ko e laupē* (It's just talk): ambiguity and informal social control in a Tongan village', University of California, Berkeley, 1983.

Arthur Cyril Cato. 'A survey of native education in Fiji, Tonga and Western Samoa, with special attention to Fiji', University of Melbourne, 1951.

W. F. Clark. 'Population, agriculture and urbanization in the Kingdom of Tonga', Michigan State University, 1975.

R. Cowell. 'The transformation of traditional Tonga: the significance of local identity with particular reference to the period 1799-1875, and its influence on modern Tonga', University of Adelaide, 1977.

Wendy Cowling. 'On being Tongan: responses to concepts of tradition', Macquarie University, Sydney, 1990.

H. G. Cummins. 'Missionary chieftain. James Egan Moulton and Tongan society, 1865-1909', Australian National University, 1980.

M. P. Dukes. 'On the nonexistence of anaphors and pronomials in Tongan', University of California, Los Angeles, 1996.

PhD Theses

T. S. Dye. 'Social and cultural change in the prehistory of the ancestral Polynesian homeland', Yale University, 1988.

M. Evans. 'Gifts and commodities on a Tongan atoll: understanding intention and action in a MIRAB economy', McMaster University, 1996.

A. R. Ewins. 'Tradition, politics and change in contemporary Fiji and Tonga', Australian National University, 1996.

Inoke Fakatene. 'The relationship between self concept and academic achievement of Tonga students at Liahona High School, Tonga', Brigham Young University, 1975.

Charles D. Fein. 'Some trace elements in lavas from the Lau islands, Tofua, Tonga and Tutuila, American Samoa', University of Hawai'i, 1971.

Christine Ward Gailey. '"Our history is written in our mats": state formation and the status of women in Tonga', New School for Social Research, New York, 1981.

Tamar Gordon. 'Inventing Mormon identity in Tonga', University of California, Berkeley, 1988.

Elizabeth Parks Hahn. 'The communication of Tongan traditions: mass media and culture in the Kingdom of Tonga, Polynesia', University of North Carolina at Chapel Hill, 1992.

J. B. Hardaker. 'Agriculture and development in the Kingdom of Tonga', University of New England, Armidale, 1975.

Phyllis Herda. 'The transformation of the traditional Tongan polity: a genealogical consideration of Tonga's past', Australian National University, 1988.

Adrienne Lois Kaeppler. 'The structure of Tongan dance', University of Hawai'i, 1967.

S. L. Kavaliku. 'Educational reorganisation for national development in Tonga', Victoria University of Wellington, 1966.

Helen Kavapalu. 'Becoming Tongan: an ethnography of childhood in the Kingdom of Tonga', Australian National University, 1992.

Debra Connolly Kirsh. 'Tourism as conflict in Polynesia: status degradation among Tongan handicraft sellers', University of Hawai'i, 1984.

S. Dektor Korn. 'To please oneself: local organization in the Tongan islands', Washington University, Missouri, 1977.

Sione Lātūkefu. 'Church and state in Tonga: the influence of Wesleyan Methodist missionaries in the political development of Tonga, 1826-1875', Australian National University, 1967.

Penelope A. Lavaka. 'The limits of advice: Britain and the Kingdom of Tonga, 1900-1970', Australian National University, 1981.

Janet Louise Luckcock. 'Thomas of Tonga, 1797-1881: the unlikely pioneer', Open University, England, 1990.

'Okusitino Māhina. 'The Tongan traditional history *Tala-e-Fonua*: a vernacular ecology-centred historico-cultural concept', Australian National University, 1992.

George Emmanuel Marcus. 'The ancien regime in the modern Kingdom of Tonga: conflict and change among the nobility of a Polynesian constitutional monarchy', Harvard University, 1975.

A. Maude. 'Population, land and livelihood in Tonga', Australian National University, 1965.

Barbara Burns McGrath. 'Making meaning of illness, dying and death in the Kingdom of Tonga', University of Washington, 1993.

C. Morgan. 'Competing circuits in the Vava'u social economy', Australian National University, 1985.

E. J. Morton. 'A descriptive grammar of Tongan (Polynesian)', Indiana University, 1962.

Keith L. Morton. 'Kinship, economics and exchange in a Tongan village', University of Oregon, 1972.

E. G. Olson. 'Conflict management in congregation and community in Tonga', University of Arizona, 1993.

Claire D. F. Parsons. 'Sickness experience and language: aspects of Tongan and Western accounting', Waikato University, 1981.

Michael Pietrusewsky. 'The physical anthropology of early Tongan populations: a study of the bones and teeth and an assessment of their biological affinities based on cranial comparisons with eight other Pacific populations', University of Toronto, 1969.

Jens Poulsen. 'A contribution to the prehistory of the Tongan islands', Australian National University, 1967.

C. Guy Powles. 'The persistence of chiefly power and its implications for law and political organization in Western Polynesia', Australian National University, 1979.

Shivaji Ramalingam. 'The mosquito fauna of Samoa and Tonga and its relation to subperiodic Bancroftian filariasis', University of California, Los Angeles, 1965.

S. Deacon Ritterbush. 'Sometimes the "native" knows best. A discourse on contextualization, indigenous knowledge and the implications of culture in sustainable commercial farm development for the Kingdom of Tonga', University of Hawai'i, 1993.

Garth Rogers. '*Kai* and *kava* in Niuatoputapu: social relations, ideologies and contexts in a rural Tongan community', University of Auckland, 1975.

Noel Rutherford. 'Shirley Baker and the Kingdom of Tonga', Australian National University, 1966.

Seth Martin Schmerzler. 'Attitudes towards environmental conservation in the Kingdom of Tonga: observed behavior and implications of environmental education', University of California, Santa Barbara, 1991.

'Asinate Samata. 'Education and national development in Tonga: a critical policy review', University of Queensland, 1995.

F. V. Sevele. 'Regional inequalities in socio-economic development in Tonga: a preliminary study', University of Canterbury, Christchurch, 1973.

Cathy B. Small. 'Women's associations and the pursuit of wealth in Tonga: a study in social change', Temple University, 1987.

D. H. Spennemann. "Ata 'a Tonga mo 'ata 'o Tonga: early and late prehistory of the Tongan islands', Australian National University, 1989.

C. J. Stevens. 'The political ecology of a Tongan village', University of Arizona, 1996.

S. L. Taifu'i. 'The role of accounting in the developing economy of the Kingdom of Tonga', University of Wollongong, 1996.

R. R. Thaman. 'The Tongan agricultural system with special emphasis on plant assemblagies', University of California at Los Angeles, 1978.

C. Urbanowicz. 'Tongan culture: the methodology of an ethnographic reconstruction', University of Oregon, 1972.

Elizabeth Wood-Ellem. 'Queen Sālote Tupou III and Tungi Mailefihi: a study in leadership in twentieth-century Tonga (1918-1941)', University of Melbourne, 1981.

The Country and Its People

1 **The definition of authentic Oceanic cultures with particular reference to Tongan culture.**
Sione Lātūkefu. *Pacific Studies*, vol. 4, no. 1 (1980), p. 60-81.

Lātūkefu shows how Tongan culture has undergone radical changes, from a stratified society with a chiefly political system, abundant staple crops and simple living requirements, in which social organization and relationships played a significant part in the production and distribution of wealth. Relations between the classes were governed by the traditional values of *faka'api'api* (respect), *fatongia* (obligation) and *mateaki* (loyalty). It was a well-integrated system, yet dynamic and full of potential for change. The influences of European explorers, traders, missionaries, tourists and others have been significant, as has the migration of Tongans overseas. The first areas to change were material culture, technology and economy. Western-style housing has largely superseded the traditional. Transport and the growth of the monetary economy have brought changes in diet. The principles of respect, obligation and loyalty still govern social relationships, but the Christian emphasis on the importance of family life has made the nuclear family more important. Yet traditional hospitality, lavish feasting to support king, government and church are still central to Tongan life. Traditional material culture and performing arts survive, though adapted to the needs of tourists. The language has taken in many European words and thought patterns have changed with formal education. However, Lātūkefu sees all this as evidence of the strength of Tongan culture, ready to adopt what it finds best from outside while in no way affecting its distinct identity. Looking ahead, he believes that traditional values will continue to be ascribed willingly to church and state, though significant reforms will be needed in the parliamentary and land tenure systems. All new influences accepted into Tongan culture will be made to work in a Tongan setting and become accepted as a genuine part of it. Nearly twenty years later this prediction seems to hold up remarkably well, though with some strains.

2   **The Far East and Australasia.**
    London: Europa Publications, 1969- . annual.
    The 28th edition, for 1997, of this standard reference guide provides much information
    on Tongan history, including recent political developments, the economy, some key
    statistics, the constitution, politics and government, religion, media, finance and
    education. While compressed, it is perhaps more comprehensive than the broadly
    similar *Pacific Islands Yearbook* (item no. 11).

3   **Finding treasure in Tonga.**
    Lyn Greenall.   Nuku'alofa: Friendly Islands Bookshop, 1996. 151p.
    2 maps.
    The author, an Australian, came to know Tonga when her husband was appointed
    external auditor to the Free Wesleyan Church. This meant long visits, and much travel
    around the islands. She writes about Tonga and the life of its people with enthusiasm
    and affection, dealing particularly with the schools, hospital and church. She states
    that she lost her heart in Tonga, that she is 'most content when there'. She admits the
    need to adapt to a different way of life, where the community is more important than
    the individual, where being is more important than doing. But she does not disguise
    the converse, the lack of privacy, the limited and dilapidated medical and educational
    facilities, and the noisy nights. Greenall adds, 'I also found magnificent music, kind
    people, balmy weather, a slower pace of life, a Christian ethos, a lack of materialism
    and technology'; this may in some respects be a little too idealistic.

4   **Friendly island.**
    Patricia Ledyard.   Sydney: Pacific Publications, 1974. 2nd ed. 252p.
    The second edition of Patricia Ledyard's general description of her early years in
    Tonga was published in the same year as her *'Utulei, my Tongan home* (item no. 19)
    and covers some of the same ground. First published in 1956, it ranges more widely
    over Tonga beyond Vava'u and forty years later still conveys her early enchantment
    and wonder at Tonga, the attraction of its islands and the life of its people.

5   **Gentle people: into the heart of Vava'u, Kingdom of Tonga,
    1781-1973.**
    Donna Gerstle.   San Diego, California: Tofua Press, 1973. 65p. map.
    bibliog.
    Donna Gerstle arrived in Vava'u in 1971 to work for the US Peace Corps, and was
    captivated by the quiet, communal, caring quality of life, which was unlike anything
    she had known. Her little book tries to convey the essence of Vava'u and its people,
    with an introduction full of her own enthusiasm, followed by a history woven round
    extracts from the writings of Tongans, visitors and explorers, from the Spaniard
    Maurelle in 1781 to Queen Sālote.

6   **The happy isles of Oceania: paddling the Pacific.**
    Paul Theroux.   London: Hamish Hamilton, 1992. 541p. 14 maps.
    Paul Theroux seems not to have been happy as he travelled what he called the happy
    isles of Oceania with his collapsible kayak. He seems not to have been able to judge
    their peoples by any standards other than his own. He did not like Nuku'alofa, where
    he spent some days waiting for an interview with the King. He found the place scruffy

and unfriendly. But he loved Vava'u for its peace and beauty, finding some serenity staying on small uninhabited islands. Nevertheless some of his observations on Tonga ring true, even if he dwells more on the frustrations than the joys and even if his experience may have been limited. We must accept that this was what he found, and his account is vivid and interesting.

7 Ko e me'akai faka-Tonga/Tongan food.

Tupou L. Pulu. Anchorage, Alaska: National Bilingual Materials Development Center, 1981. 100p.

The purpose of this book, produced by the migrant Tongan community in Alaska, is to help Tongans away from home to prepare their traditional food in a healthy way, as their forefathers did, usually baked or roast, never fried or boiled. Pulu describes the many uses of the coconut, the preparation of the 'umu (earth oven), the main types of food plants, and the preparation and cooking of fruit and vegetables, fish, shellfish, crabs, pigs, chickens, whales, turtles, fruit bats and birds. The text is in both Tongan and English.

8 The new Friendly Islanders: the Tonga of King Taufa'ahau Tupou IV.

Kenneth Bain. London; Sydney; Auckland, New Zealand: Hodder & Stoughton, 1993. 207p. 2 maps.

Bain first went to Tonga in 1953 as Secretary to Government, when it was still a British protectorate and not yet fully independent, and he wrote an earlier book, *The Friendly Islanders* (1967), about the Tonga of that time. Wanting to know how much had changed, he returned in 1991 to see what had happened to the people and the kingdom he knew then. Tonga still seems to him a 'steadfast anachronism'. As he writes of his meetings with the King, with politicians, teachers, business people and others he reveals, with a light touch, something of the spirit of Tonga today. He shares the vision of many in Tonga in relation to the lack of accountability by government and the lack of leadership by nobles. He believes that the two things necessary to take Tonga intact into the next century are change in the attitude to privileged status and reform of the structures and tools of government; given these changes, there would be an even chance of survival intact. As the King writes in his foreword, Bain 'has again been a close observer looking in from outside'. Bain's book offers an informed general view of Tonga in transition.

9 Obscure kingdoms.

Edward Fox. London: Hamish Hamilton, 1993. 240p.

The title of this book came one night to Edward Fox, a bored newspaper reporter in West Virginia; it is an attempt to report fleeting glimpses of the universal model of kingship in some of its infinite variety of forms. He visited Tonga, for him the 'distant kingdom', in 1987. He describes seeing the King in public, obtaining a personal interview with the King and attending the opening of parliament, and goes on to sketch the historical background. He contrasts this with the King Louis XIV, who wrote 'The majesty of kings largely consists in not allowing themselves to be seen'. Tonga is too small for the King to hold himself apart, yet the respect due to him is just as great. Largely Fox's observations ring true, though his statement that if it were not for British protection, there would be no monarchy in Tonga must be questioned.

10   **The Pacific islands: politics, economics and international relations.**
     Te'o I. J. Fairbairn, Charles E. Morrison, Richard W. Baker, Sheree A.
     Groves.   Honolulu, Hawai'i: International Relations Program,
     East-West Center, 1991. 170p. 23 maps. bibliog.

This book aims to provide a succinct account of trends, issues and recent developments affecting the Pacific islands in the fields of politics, economics and international
relations. The authors note that the Pacific island region, traditionally regarded as a
haven of calm and tranquility, entered a less settled phase in the 1980s, reflecting the
emergence of a more complex world. The book provides basic information on each of
the island countries and covers political structures and issues, prospects and constraints
on their economic development, the state of regional cooperation, and major issues
and themes in the field of political and international relations. Appendixes provide
brief profiles and maps of each of the twenty-one countries, and list major intergovernmental regional organizations. The comparative information makes it possible
to relate Tonga to its neighbours in terms of resources and development as at the end
of the 1980s.

11   **Pacific islands yearbook.**
     Suva: Fiji Times, 1994. 17th ed. 767p.

Sections on general Pacific island topics in this standard regional reference book, first
published in 1932 (and not in fact published annually), are followed by data on each
country (twenty-eight pages on Tonga) in standard format on salient facts relating to
the government and the economy. Government departments and major office holders
and ministers are listed, and each of the islands is described. It is not correct that a
new hotel has recently been completed near the airport: at the time of writing this
bibliography five years later it is still incomplete.

12   **Raising a few eyebrows in Tonga.**
     Elizabeth P. Hahn.   In: *The humbled anthropologist: tales from the
     Pacific.*   Edited by Philip R. DeVita.   Belmont, California:
     Wadsworth Publishing Company, 1990, p. 69-76.

In this light but telling little essay Hahn writes of her arrival in Tonga knowing no
one, and nothing about the culture, of initial misunderstandings and of eventual
progress in comprehending and relating to Tongans. Her motif is the Tongan gesture
of the raised eyebrows, which simply means an affirmative but which she had taken to
mean something quite different. She realized that she had already come to know an
astonishingly large amount about everyday Tongan life and interaction.

13   **Socio-economic study of the Kingdom of Tonga.**
     Elizabeth S. Udui.   Honolulu, Hawai'i: Pacific International Center for
     High Technology Research, 1989. 226p. map.

This study was undertaken as part of the background preparation for a possible open
cycle ocean thermal energy conversion project in Tonga, for which no suitable sites
were in fact found. However, the general survey of Tonga conveniently brought
together much information covering climate and geological background, the economy,
power, water and waste disposal, history and government, human resources, education
and health, banking and financial concerns, transport, communications and construction.
To these are appended lists of government ministers and officials, and contacts in

ministries. Detailed information is presented in thirty tables covering aspects of population, economic activity, government revenues, trade, education and energy. Thompson's book *The climate and weather of Tonga* (item no. 22) is reprinted as an appendix.

14 Tin Can Island: a story of Tonga and the swimming mail man of the South Seas.

Charles Stuart Ramsay, Charles P. Plumb.   London: Hurst & Blackett, 1938. 320p. 4 maps.

The far northern island of Niuafo'ou is famous for its tin-can mail. Because there was no safe anchorage for mail steamers, the mail was sealed in large tins and taken out by swimmers. The most famous of them was Charles Stuart Ramsay, an Englishman who went out to Niuafo'ou in the 1920s as a copra trader. Here he tells of his amazing exploits with the mail but of much more too. He became deeply involved in the island and writes with much affection of it and the daily lives of its people. The book is illustrated with many of Ramsay's own photographs.

15 Tonga.

James Siers.   Wellington: Millwood Press, 1978. 128p. 5 maps.

Siers' book offers an attractive selection of photographs of the Tongan people, their islands and their way of life, with a brief introduction. He captures faces particularly well, and some of his aerial views are spectacular. Although not as glossy as Eckert's book (item no. 16) and now slightly outdated in parts, it still presents a rounded portrait of Tonga and the Tongans. Some old historic photographs are also included, among them one of King George Tupou I.

16 Tonga: the Friendly Islands.

Fred J. Eckert.   Fredericksburg, Virginia: Burgess Books, 1993. 112p. map.

This is, writes the Crown Prince of Tonga, 'a delightful book that truly captures the beauty, warmth and tranquility of the Kingdom of Tonga'. Eckert was the American ambassador to Tonga. His colour photographs portray the beauty of the scenery, people in their daily lives, their homes and churches, their crafts and feasts. He covers 'Eua, Ha'apai and Vava'u as well as Tongatapu. Like every picture book it shows only the best and the most picturesque. Not all of Tonga is quite like this all the time, but it is the Tonga which most visitors will imagine or remember. A brief introduction describes the kingdom, its history and something of what he calls its truly special way of life.

17 Tonga pictorial: a tapestry of pride/Kupesi 'o Tonga: ko e makatu'unga 'o e Laukau.

Donna Gerstle, Helen Raitt.   San Diego, California: Tofua Press, n.d. (c.1974). 101p. map. bibliog.

The authors describe their book as 'a photographic narrative – though by no means comprehensive – of the story of Tonga: showing how the myriad, complex elements of her past evolved and became interwoven into the tapestry of life that this small but proud Polynesian Kingdom reveals today as her own'. Chapters cover life and seafaring, art and creative expression, political structure and its evolution, the gods and religion, and Tonga today. The illustrations are a mixture of old prints and modern photographs and are captioned in both Tongan and English. This is an affectionate portrait by two people who knew Tonga well. Although some of the photographs are now a little dated, the essential portrait remains of interest.

18 Tongan place names.
Edward Winslow Gifford. Honolulu, Hawai'i: Bernice P. Bishop Museum, 1923. 258p. 2 maps. (Bernice P. Bishop Museum Bulletin, no. 6).

From the records of the Tongan Lands Office, Gifford collected 4,776 place-names for more than 8,200 locations. For each name he provides the place to which the name applies, the individual island and the group, the nearest village, the name of the landlord, the meaning of the name and other data. His purpose was not just to collect and explain names but to contribute to the study of the movement of peoples within the island groups of Tonga. By analysing different occurrences of the name he suggests for example that Tongatapu was more closely tied to Vava'u than to Ha'apai. Samoan names are most prevalent in Tongatapu, reflecting Samoan marriage into the Tu'i Kanokupolo line.

19 'Utulei, my Tongan home.
Patricia Ledyard. London: Robert Hale, 1974. 192p. map.

Sailing up Vava'u harbour in the early 1950s to take up a one-year appointment as a teacher, Patricia Ledyard saw a house by the waterside which immediately captivated her. It was 'Utulei. A few months later she married the Scots doctor Farquhar Matheson who lived there, and moved in. She writes simply but movingly and with great affection about the ordinary events of daily life: bringing up their own daughter and their adopted Tongan daughter; the house and the garden; Farquhar's work in the hospital; and the sights, history and legends of Vava'u. But there were extraordinary events too: the first time she met Queen Sālote; her break with the Methodist missionaries who ran the school and whom she found narrow and arrogant; a devastating hurricane; the death of Queen Sālote; and the death of Ledyard's husband. The book's narrative ends with Tongan independence in 1970, and expresses Ledyard's confidence for the future despite very real problems. Ledyard still lives in 'Utulei today, and from this book one can understand why she never left. It is illustrated with many of her own photographs.

20 Where in the world is Tonga?
Samantha J. Fisk. Carson, California: KIN Publications, 1996. 56p. map. bibliog.

When Samantha Fisk was first taken to Tonga by her mother at the age of nine, she did not even know where it was, and the culture shock of arriving in an island whose winter was California's summer, with no television, and where almost everything was unfamiliar, was obviously great. Her mother told her it would be like the Polynesian village at Disney World. But on this and subsequent visits she came to know Tonga well and to love the country and people. Her account was written after her first visit and redrafted when she was sixteen. She describes through the eyes of a child Limu Havea's Sunrise guesthouse that became home from home, which was, as she soon came to realize, not at all like Disney's Polynesian village. She writes about the sights of Tongatapu, going to school, feasts and funerals, customs and crafts. Her text, with many of her mother's photographs, is a delightful introduction to Tonga.

21   **A world of islands.**
     June Knox-Mawer, photographs by Peter Carmichael.   London:
     Collins, 1968. 78p. 4 maps.

June Knox-Mawer lived in Fiji, where her husband was a judge whose jurisdiction
covered much of the south-west Pacific. This enabled her to come to know well the
islands of which she writes, Fiji, the Gilberts, the Ellices and Tonga. Her section on
Tonga starts with the coronation of the present king in 1967, the Western-style
Christian service in the royal chapel which she contrasts with the traditional royal
kava ceremony. Here, as elsewhere, she has a perceptive eye for the similarities and
the differences, 'a mixture which seems strange to no one except the outsider'. The
monarchy is totally Tongan, yet the monarch lives in a palace straight from 19th-
century New Zealand. Nuku'alofa is 'a mixture of English Victoriana, South Seas and
Wild West'. The picture is perhaps a little too idyllic, and also dated. Tongans have
problems too, and it is only part of the picture to write that 'the Tongans seem to have
acquired the perfect *modus vivendi*, a gentle confluence of sociable life and everyday
work on the land and the sea'. She captures something of the spirit of Tonga behind
the obvious, and the photographs are not just of tourist highlights but of daily life
which few other than Tongans would see.

Geography and Environment

22 **The climate and weather of Tonga.**
C. S. Thompson.   Wellington: New Zealand Meteorological Service,
1986. 60p. 6 maps. bibliog. (New Zealand Meteorological Service
Miscellaneous Publications, no. 188 [5]).

This report is based on data obtained from the New Zealand Meteorological Service
which began observations at Nuku'alofa in 1881. It describes the general weather
pattern in the South Pacific, the incidence of cyclones and their variability and gives a
case-study of cyclone Isaac in 1982. It sets out the normal trade wind pattern and tabulates
directional percentages for each of the island groups for each month, as well as rainfall and air temperatures, evaporation and soil water balance, and sea temperature.

23 **The environment of Tonga: a geography resource.**
Wendy Crane.   Lower Hutt, New Zealand: Wendy Crane Books, 1992.
165p. 58 maps.

This is a textbook for secondary schools in Tonga, but is also for anyone interested in
the geography and environment of the kingdom. Chapters cover air and weather; the
sea; land formation and geology (with information on each permanently inhabited
island); soil formation and structure; water; plants; animals and coast life. Each page
is filled with information, examples, exercises and suggested activities. Many drawings, diagrams and maps illustrate the text. Tongan legends are told, and linked to
modern scientific knowledge. The overall theme is the vulnerability of such a small
country, the inter-relationship of everything in the environment, and the need to care
for it and keep its balance.

24 **Geography of Tonga.**
T. F. Kennedy.   Nuku'alofa: Government Printer, 1958. 89p. 6 maps.

This textbook for schools in Tonga describes concisely and simply the main features
of the geography of Tonga, amplifying the even briefer introduction in Wood's book
(item no. 94). Kennedy covers the geological formation of the high volcanic islands of
the Western chain and the low coral and limestone islands of the eastern chain: some,

such as 'Eua and Vava'u, are quite high and rugged and others, such as Tongatapu and the Ha'apai islands, much lower. He sets out the main facts that a school child would need to know, on weather and climate; soils; the different types of native and introduced vegetation; types of crops; areas under cultivation and yields; timber and fishing; population and employment; daily life in villages and towns; internal and external communications; and patterns of imports and exports. Much has naturally changed. Copra and bananas are no longer the main exports, and a monthly steamer has been replaced by daily air services. But the book can still serve as an introduction to the basic geographical facts if the reader is alert to the ways in which it is now out of date.

25 The geography of Tonga: a study of environment, people and change.
E. A. Crane. Auckland, New Zealand: Heinemann Educational Books, 1979. 76p. 12 maps.

This school textbook assists in understanding the physical, economic and social processes that mould the lives of Tongans. It sets out the relationships of climate, soil, relief, plants and animals and examines man and his relationship to the environment. Chapters cover the natural environment (land and sea, vegetation and climate); produce from soil and sea; buying and selling; people and places (with sections on migration and on Nuku'alofa); tourism; and the current of change. There are many photographs, but some are not clearly reproduced.

26 Geology and offshore resources of Pacific island areas – Tonga region.
Edited by David W. Scholl, Tracy L. Vallier. Houston, Texas: Circum-Pacific Council for Energy and Mineral Resources, 1985. 488p. maps. bibliog. (Circum-Pacific Council for Energy and Mineral Resources Earth Science Series, vol. 2).

This volume reports the results of an international survey sent to investigate the energy and mineral resources of the south-west Pacific, particularly the potential for petroleum. The papers provide information on the regional framework, geology, tectonic evolution and resources potential of the Tonga Ridge and immediately adjacent regions. Introductory papers describe the basic geology of the Tonga Ridge, rising from the Tonga Trench. Twenty-seven specialist papers then examine: submarine geology and geophysics of bordering basins and ridges; framework geology; and resource synthesis. All papers are accompanied by maps and charts.

27 Geology of 'Eua, Tonga.
J. Edward Hoffmeister. Honolulu, Hawai'i: Bernice P. Bishop Museum, 1932. 114p. 5 maps. bibliog. (Bernice P. Bishop Museum Bulletin, no. 96).

Rising to nearly 1,000 feet at the centre, with cliffs falling 400 feet sheer to the sea on the eastern side, with its tropical rain forest and even its little river (the only one in Tonga), 'Eua is quite different from all Tonga's other islands and the most dramatic in the Kingdom. This report of a scientific expedition reconstructs the complex geological history of 'Eua, with its series of six limestone terraces on a volcanic base. There are detailed analyses of the rocks and rock structure, of the corals from the elevated limestones with the species listed and tabulated for each terrace, and of the Eocene Foraminifera of the limestone. There are almost 100 photographs of the landscape and rock structures.

28   **Geology, petrography and geochemistry of the volcanic islands of Tonga.**
       W. B. Bryan, G. D. Stice, A. Ewart.   *Journal of Geophysical Research*, vol. 77, no. 8 (1972), p. 1,566-85.

The authors outline the at least nine centres of active volcanism in Tonga, some of which are submarine and may raise temporary islands above the sea. They survey and map the geological structure of those which are or once were active: Fonualei, Late, Kao, Tofua and 'Eua. They analyse the petrography and geochemistry of each and tabulate their findings. They do not include Niuafo'ou, though still active, as the relationship of this volcano to the rest is uncertain.

29   **The Kingdom of Tonga: action strategy for managing the environment.**
       Robert Thistlethwaite, David Sheppard, Netatua Prescott.   Apia, Western Samoa: South Pacific Regional Environment Programme, 1993. 112p. map. bibliog.

An environmental management plan for Tonga was set up in 1989-90. Review and revision of it culminated in this action strategy, intended to take a fresh look at programmes for the protection of the Tongan environment and for sustainable development. A general introduction to the environmental setting of Tonga covers land, agriculture, and forest, marine, water, mineral and energy resources, population and education. There are summary statistics on the economic performance of the different sectors of the economy. The report then examines specific environmental constraints and issues. Eleven specific action strategies are then set out, each with specific goals and achievements. These include environmental education; sewage disposal; climate change; hazardous chemicals; renewable energy; biological diversity; marine and land resources; and drinking water. Action has been taken in the years since on some of these.

30   **Nuku'alofa: a study of urban life in the Pacific islands.**
       A. C. Walsh.   Wellington; Sydney; London: A. H. & A. W. Reed, 1972. 48p. 5 maps.

While Nuku'alofa has changed greatly since the early 1970s, little has been written about it as a town, and this school textbook shows much that is recognizable today. Part of Nuku'alofa's growth is still the result of migration from outer islands, and Walsh describes the life of a migrant family from Ha'apai, houses and the way people live in them, and employment. The government coconut processing factory has long since disappeared, and fewer residents of Nuku'alofa are probably now employed in agriculture while employment in shops, hotels and restaurants has grown. Walsh also describes 'play, pageantry and prayer', where there has been less change, and sets out some of the problems which Tonga faced then, some of which still apply.

31   **Pacific 2010: urbanisation in Polynesia.**
John Connell, John P. Lea.   Canberra: National Centre for
Development Studies, Australian National University, 1995. 161p.
4 maps. bibliog.

Although small by world standards, urban development in the South Pacific presents
challenges and problems as severe as any. This study focuses on three Polynesian
countries, Tonga being one. It examines the difficulties of providing adequate urban
infrastructure and services. In Nuku'alofa (population now about 34,000), as in other
towns in the Pacific, problems of water supply, sanitation, waste disposal and the supply
of low-cost housing already cause concern. There are few skilled urban managers and
planners. The authors describe the colonial heritage and the development of towns
from the 19th century; the particular problems caused by the land tenure system;
population; rural-urban and overseas migration; the general economic scene; and
trends in employment. They believe that urban planning must be developed and that in
Tonga urban land tenure must be reconsidered and the quality of housing improved.
There are problems with urban waste management and pollution, and the water supply
and sewage systems need to be modernized. The authors conclude that there has been
no shortage of technical advice for the countries, but that the time has now come to
reconsider land tenure, general responsibility for urban affairs, the improvement of
urban services, and the integration of their management and delivery in the context of
an urban plan. New forms of urban local government should be established in
Nuku'alofa and elsewhere in Polynesia to obtain funding for and carry out the necessary
works. The relevant issues are political, social and institutional as well as technical.

32   **Pollution sources survey of the Kingdom of Tonga.**
Richard H. Chesher.   Noumea: South Pacific Commission, 1984. 110p.
9 maps. bibliog. (SPREP/Topic Review, no. 19).

A survey was made in 1984 of pollution sources in Tonga. Sewerage discharge from
tourist facilities and destructive fishing techniques with resultant coral death were
identified as the most acute environmental problems. Other chronic hazards included
the use of lead in paints used for water catchment systems, increasing pesticide use,
siltation of harbour environments and the construction of causeways without culverts
for water circulation. Report sheets on many of the individual hazards are reproduced.
The report recommends a restriction on hazardous chemical imports, an improved
solid waste system, oil spill prevention and environmental impact statements. It also
notes beneficial steps which have already been taken.

33   **Recovering from a tropical cyclone in Tonga.**
Jennifer Wendt.   Auckland, New Zealand: Longman Paul, 1987. 20p.
4 maps. (Focus on the Pacific).

Cyclones hit the islands of Tonga regularly, but cyclone Isaac in 1982 was one of the
worst for many years. This book for children describes how it developed and shows
with vivid colour photographs the damage it caused, and how reconstruction began.

34 **Soils of the Kingdom of Tonga.**
    G. E. Orbell. Wellington: New Zealand Soil Bureau, 1983. 47p.
    bibliog.

This booklet describes the kinds of soils that are found in Tonga, how they have been
formed, where they occur in the landscape, their good and bad features, and the crops
most suited to them. It has the practical aim of alerting Tongans to the value of their
soils and to the need to protect and preserve them wisely. It is fully illustrated with
diagrams and colour photographs, and describes the soils of each of the island groups
in turn.

35 **Some perspectives on natural disaster vulnerability in Tonga.**
    James Lewis. *Pacific Viewpoint*, vol. 22, no. 2 (1981), p. 145-62.

Lewis examines the history of disasters in Tonga, listing over the previous century
twenty-eight hurricanes, twenty-two earthquakes of moderate magnitude or greater,
five periods of drought, four volcanic eruptions and three known tsunamis. There are
five active volcanic islands, two inhabited. Yet Tongan folklore and legend seem to
make no reference to the concept of natural disasters. Lewis examines early records
from the colonial period as well as more recent events to view their effects and the
changes they brought about. Structures built with modern techniques have often suf-
fered more than the traditional and there are many examples of inappropriate relief
aid. Lewis believes that the cycle of relief, dependency, vulnerability and relief must
be broken and that local coping mechanisms should reduce dependence on international relief aid.

36 **Tonga Trench.**
    Russell W. Raitt, Robert L. Fisher, Ronald G. Mason. In: *The crust of
    the earth*. New York: Geological Society of America, 1955, p. 237-54.
    (Special Paper, no. 62).

An expedition in 1952-53 conducted probably the first survey of the Tonga Trench
using modern techniques. The trench reaches depths of about 10,800m, and is associated with a line of volcanoes and earthquakes. This paper describes and charts its
topography, identifies its geological layers and gives an assumed structure section, and
concludes that the trench is relatively young. There is a fully detailed fold-out chart of
the bathymetry of the area.

37 **Tongan soils: site characteristics and management practices.**
    L. M. Potter. Armidale, Australia: South Pacific Smallholder Project,
    University of New England, 1986. 40p. 8 maps. bibliog. (Occasional
    Paper, no. 7).

In 1985 a survey was undertaken to discover whether the fertility of Tongan soils was
declining, as perceived by some Tongans. Thirty samples were taken from two sites in
Tongatapu, nine from one site in Ha'apai and ten from one site in Vava'u. The paper
sets out the detailed chemical composition of each sample, and concludes that in some
areas soil nutrient status and physical condition, particularly water-holding capacity,
are declining. Fallow periods to restore fertility are becoming rarer under the pressure
of population growth and more intensive cash cropping.

Tourism and Travel Guides

38   **A cruising guide to the Vava'u island group in the Kingdom of Tonga.**
Clearwater, Florida: The Moorings, 1992. 20p. 9 maps.
The Vava'u island group offers some of the finest sailing in the Pacific, and this booklet, produced by a yacht charter company in Neiafu, within the group, provides a detailed guide to the waters of Vava'u and to forty-two specific anchorages. It is organized around a large fold-out chart and eight detailed charts. These provide depths, notes on navigation and indications of hazards. The text describes each anchorage, and gives general information on the weather, currents, Tongan customs and environmental protection.

39   **The Kingdom of Tonga.**
Nuku'alofa: Friendly Islands Bookshop, no date. 1 sheet.
This single-sheet map provides in separate panels a small-scale map of the whole group at about 45 miles to the inch, and detailed maps of each island group at about 2 miles to the inch. These show principal villages, roads, airports and places to be visited, but not relief. Inset in each panel is information on the island or group, and general information on some aspects of Tonga and its life – myths, history, traditions, feasts, kava, dancing etc.

40   **Pacific tourism as islanders see it.**
Edited by Freda Rajotte, Ron Crocombe.   Suva: The Institute of Pacific Studies, University of the South Pacific, 1980. 171p. 9 maps. bibliog.
Most writing about tourism in the Pacific is from a foreign perspective. This book presents the viewpoints of twenty-four Pacific islanders, from Hawai'i to New Zealand. It is not a research study but a collection of experiences and viewpoints from the inside looking out. Tourism is supposed to bring economic benefits to small isolated island communities with few natural resources, but the balance sheet, in both the economic and socio-cultural fields, is by no means always clear. Much that tourists need has to be imported, and foreign investors often take much of the profit. Tourists

may disturb the very society that they come to see. This book offers brief case-studies and local experiences. There are two papers on Tonga. 'The social and cultural impact of tourism in Tonga' discusses the benefits in terms of employment in hotels and guest houses, in the production and sale of Tongan handicrafts and in arranging dances, feasts and ceremonies. On the other hand, problems of prostitution and begging are growing. 'The development of a small tourist enterprise' describes the successful tourist facility of 'Oholei Beach, how it began and how it is run by 'Osika Kami and his family. It might be seen as a good model for a country where tourism is on a small scale and not for the mass market, and uses only local resources. A further short note describes the work of a group of Tongans in the Fijian tourist industry.

41 South Pacific handbook.
David Stanley.   Chico, California: Moon Publications, 1996. 6th ed. 914p. 143 maps. bibliog.

Fifty-four pages of this hefty travel guide to the South Pacific are devoted to Tonga. General articles on its history, politics, economy and daily life are followed by sections on accommodation, transport, and on each island group in detail. The listings and ratings for hotels, restaurants, resorts, entertainment, etc., seem reliable, but the scene changes quickly; for example, two good new Italian restaurants were established in Nuku'alofa in 1998. Stanley also erroneously states that a turtle was given by Captain Cook and lived in the grounds of the palace until recent years; it was in fact a tortoise, but this may arise from a difference between English and American usage.

42 Tonga: a Lonely Planet travel survival kit.
Deanna Swaney.   Hawthorn, Victoria, Australia: Lonely Planet Publications, 1994. 2nd ed. 198p. 23 maps.

Deanna Swaney obviously knows Tonga well and has produced a useful and practical visitors' guide, in the inimitable style of the Lonely Planet series. She provides basic facts about the country – a thorough introduction to its history, briefer sections on geography, climate, government, economy and much more, including social protocol for visitors and some basic Tongan phrases. The heart of the book consists of a series of sections on the different island groups and individual islands: how to travel, what to see, where to stay, where to eat, all dealt with in considerable detail. There seems to be no island, however remote, that Swaney has not visited. The whole book has been greatly expanded and updated from the first edition in 1990, and she notes how much things have changed in only five years. Inevitably a few facts are now out of date, as hotels and restaurants open and close, and the colour photographs might have shown more of the daily life of Tongans and not only attractive scenery. But this book contains a wealth of information clearly presented in a conveniently compact format.

43 Tongatapu, island tour guide.
Nuku'alofa: Government Printer, 1990. 2nd ed. 40p. map.

This handy booklet informs visitors to Tongatapu, the main island of Tonga, of the main sights and scenic spots that they should expect to see. It describes twenty-nine principal sites, in Nuku'alofa and around the island, from the Royal Palace to the Small Industries Centre, and sets these out in relation to the four main eras of Tongan history. In addition to buildings there are natural features such as the blow-holes at Houma and archaeological sites such as the royal tombs at Mu'a. The booklet gives a list of telephone numbers for hotels, restaurants and tourist facilities. Inevitably some of the information is not now fully up-to-date.

44 Tourism in Tonga revisited: continued troubled times?

Charles F. Urbanowicz. In: *Hosts and guests: the anthropology of tourism*. Edited by Valese L. Smith. Philadelphia: University of Pennsylvania Press, 1989, p. 105-17.

Urbanowicz sees tourism in Tonga as really starting in 1966, when large numbers of cruise ships began to arrive. In this study, a continuation of work which he began in the early 1970s, he examines the impact of tourism on the Tongan economy and the problems associated with the advent of mass tourism. He admits that his perspective, covering eighteen years, is not very positive. He records tourist arrivals by ship and by plane between 1958 (1,779 tourists) and 1988 (55,694), producing earnings of T$11,000,000. The government has promoted and invested in tourism. Yet the industry exacerbates Tonga's economic problems, particularly the need for additional imported foodstuffs, and increases local prices. Urbanowicz foresees a decrease in cruise ships, which did indeed happen after this article's publication. The tourist's experience is often unhappy, with the deliberate creation of a 'phony folk culture' often not even wholly Tongan. Tongans may survive large-scale tourism, but will they still be Tongans? Urbanowicz concludes that tourism must be properly controlled if it is to make a positive contribution to Tonga, although in fact for many reasons mass tourism has not developed in Tonga to the extent that he feared.

45 A walking tour of Neiafu, Vava'u.

Pesi Fonua, Mary Fonua. Neiafu, Tonga: Vava'u Press, 1981. 48p. 2 maps.

Neiafu, the quiet capital of the northern island group of Vava'u, retains a traditional charm which is now less easy to find in bustling Nuku'alofa. This booklet describes five walks, one round Neiafu itself and four round other parts of this attractive island. Sites, their tradition and history, are described. Times are given for the sections of each walk.

Travellers' Accounts

46   An account of the natives of the Tonga islands, in the South Pacific Ocean, with an original grammar and vocabulary of their language, compiled and arranged from the extensive communications of Mr. William Mariner, several years resident in those islands.
John Martin.   London: John Murray, 1817. Volume I, 460p. Volume II, 528p.

On 29 November 1806 the ship *Port-au-Prince* anchored off the island of Lifuka in the Ha'apai group. The crew was initially welcomed but was later attacked. Many were killed and the ship burnt, but Mariner escaped and was taken under the care of the chief, Fīnau 'Ulukālala, who adopted him as his son. Mariner then spent four years in Tonga, became fluent in the language and travelled throughout the islands. On his return to England he met John Martin, a doctor and amateur anthropologist, who wrote the book from their conversations. As Martin puts it in his introduction, all previous accounts of Tonga had been written from the outside: this was the first from the inside, though he ignores Vason (see item no. 47). It offers a wealth of information on every aspect of life – political and social organization, medicine, music and much else – and is a valuable source for the history of the time. It also provides the first thorough account of the Tongan language, with a 60-page grammar and a 216-page vocabulary. The work was enormously popular and went into a second edition the next year and a third in 1827 in a smaller format with some additional material, a map and two pages of specimens of Tongan music. Cook's scientific account and Mariner's personal narrative together give a basis for the study of Tonga. Local reprints are available in Tonga today.

47   An authentic narrative of four years' residence at Tongataboo, one
     of the Friendly Islands in the South-Sea by --- who went thither in
     the Duff, under Captain Wilson, in 1796.
     Anon. (George Vason).   London: Longman, Hurst, Rees & Orme,
     1810. 234p. map.

George Vason was one of the first groups of missionaries who arrived in the *Duff* in
1797. However, attracted by the Tongan way of life and by the locals' kindness, he
left the missionaries to live with Mulikiha'amea, the last of the Tu'i Ha'atakalaua
royal line. He slipped easily into Tongan ways: pleasure and idleness replaced the
regular Christian life of the missionary. Vason's original intention to keep contact
with his fellow missionaries was quickly forgotten. He explains: 'I began to dislike the
means of grace, I never visited the brethren, found delight in the company, manners
and amusements of the natives; and soon took too large a part in them.' He began to
wear Tongan rather than European dress; he was given a Tongan wife and an estate
and lived completely as a Tongan. The idyll did not last. After the death of his protector
he was caught up in civil war, fled to Vava'u, and was glad to seize the opportunity of
a visit by a missionary boat in 1801 to escape and return to England. Vason's story, a
spiritual apologia for his weakness, is the first account by a European to live in Tonga
as a Tongan, predating Mariner's by several years. His account of the events of the
period and his descriptions of Tongan life, ceremonies, dance and music, though perhaps tinged with moralizing regret, are of interest because observed for the first time
from the inside. Looking back, he compared 'the comforts of civilized life, a well-
ordered government and the holy duties and services of revealed religion' with the
'precarious subsistence, uncertain safety, corrupt conduct and savage violence' of
Tonga. He nevertheless writes of Tonga with obvious warmth, even if he came to
regret his years there.

48   Journal of a cruise among the islands of the western Pacific,
     including the Feejees and others inhabited by the Polynesian negro
     races, in Her Majesty's Ship Havannah.
     John Elphinstone Erskine.   London: John Murray, 1853. 488p. map.

After the pacification of New Zealand the colonial authorities turned their attention to
regular inspection of the neighbouring islands; the first resultant cruise was that of
Erskine in 1849. There was no missionary or colonial intent; the object was simply to
observe and record. After the disturbances described by Mariner early in the century,
the three island groups of Tonga were now united under King George Tupou I, who
had converted to Christianity and whom Erskine met in Ha'apai. In Vava'u, Ha'apai
and Tongatapu he found churches well established, with impressive buildings, schools
and many knowledgeable and devout believers. Erskine was genuinely interested in
Tongan culture and tradition and records some chiefs as telling him that 'they had
never been treated so like chiefs by any strangers'. He also comments unfavourably on
the intolerance of the Wesleyan missionaries towards the newly established Catholic
mission, and on their narrow-minded attitude to Tongan culture and their dictatorial
approach to chiefs and people. He describes the geography and navigation of the
islands, summarizes their recent history, and closely observes the Tongan way of life,
their beliefs, their language and even their sense of humour.

49 **The journals of Captain James Cook on his voyages of discovery: the voyage of the *Resolution* and *Adventure* 1772-1775.**
Edited by J. C. Beaglehole.   Cambridge, England: Cambridge University Press for the Hakluyt Society, 1961. 1,021p. 25 maps. bibliog.

Behind the printed editions of Cook's voyages (item no. 53) lie his own journals, definitively edited for the Hakluyt Society by Beaglehole. In a long and detailed introduction Beaglehole describes the plans for the second voyage, the ships, the crews and the route which Cook followed. He examines the surviving manuscripts, printed editions and graphic records, maps and drawings. He annotates the text of the journals with explanations, background information and variant readings, based not only on his studies but also on his own travels along Cook's route. Many of the original artists' illustrations, upon which the later engravings for the printed editions were based, are reproduced. It was during this second voyage that Cook first visited Tonga, staying at 'Eua and Tongatapu in October 1773 and Nomuka in Ha'apai in June 1774. His descriptions of the Tongan people, their language, way of life and society were based on brief observation, and he may not have understood everything fully, but he depicts a near idyllic state in which all lived easily and happily together; so impressed was he that he dubbed Tonga the Friendly Islands.

50 **The journals of Captain James Cook on his voyages of discovery: the voyage of the *Resolution* and *Discovery* 1776-1780.**
Edited by J. C. Beaglehole.   Cambridge, England: Cambridge University Press for the Hakluyt Society, 1967. Part One, 718p. 15 maps. Part Two, 928p. map.

The general arrangement of Beaglehole's edition of Cook's third voyage follows that of the second (item no. 49), with a full introduction, annotated text and illustrations. The first of the two volumes prints Cook's own journal, the second the journals of some others who sailed with him. During this voyage Cook spent over two months in Nomuka and Ha'apai, Tongatapu and 'Eua, and was able to write far more fully about Tonga and the Tongans than on his second voyage. He continued to be impressed and delighted, considering his visit a period, 'during which time we lived together in the most cordial friendship'. He called Tonga 'a humane and peacable nation' in comparison with what he was told of Fiji. He was concerned with what he could give them, as well as with the supplies he could obtain, and was keen that trade should be fair. Little can have escaped his observant eye and these journals are a rich source of information on every aspect of Tongan life at the time. The journals of his colleagues provide some further information, including word lists, and generally reinforce Cook's own favourable view of Tonga. 'They are in every respect almost as perfectly civiliz'd as it is possible for mankind to be', wrote Anderson (who accompanied Cook and died on the third voyage) of the Tongans.

51 **A missionary voyage to the Southern Pacific Ocean, performed in the years 1796, 1797, 1798 in the ship Duff, commanded by Captain James Wilson, compiled from the journals of the officers and the missionaries . . .**
James Wilson.   London: T. Chapman, 1799. 420p. 7 maps.

Where Cook showed the way and described the islands of the Pacific and their peoples, missionaries followed. In 1796 the London Missionary Society equipped the ship *Duff* to take a first group of missionaries to settle and work in Tahiti and Tonga. It arrived in Tonga in April 1797, to leave seven missionaries, returning in August after visiting the Marquesas and Tahiti. The missionaries' journals from April to August, printed in the book, are of interest as the first account by Europeans who attempted to live in Tonga, setting up home, growing crops, preaching and generally trying to learn about the country and its people. They are supplemented by Wilson's own description of Tongatapu. When the time came for the *Duff* to leave they felt vulnerable: 'Our work is great, our strength is small, very weakness itself'. The mission was not to succeed and in 1800 they had to abandon Tonga. But the account of their arrival and their first few months is an important first chapter in the history of Christian missions in Tonga.

52 **Narrative of the United States exploring expedition, during the years 1838, 1839, 1840, 1841, 1842. Volume III.**
  Charles Wilkes.   Philadelphia: Lea & Blanchard, 1845. 438p. map.
Captain Wilkes arrived in Tongatapu in 1840 to find civil war between what the missionaries called the Christian and Devil's parties. King George, the Christian king backed by the missionaries, had arrived from Vava'u with 800 warriors to attempt to destroy the heathen opposition and assert his authority over all Tonga. Wilkes found Tongatapu far from the 'perfect garden' described by earlier explorers. Because of the civil war it was now 'entirely neglected'. Wilkes attempted to mediate, but without success, and came to the view that the arrogance and insensitivity of the missionaries, in their attempts at conversion, were in part to blame, though at the same time he admired their educational and agricultural work. He also admired the physique and character of the Tongans, comparing them favourably with the Maoris of New Zealand and the Fijians. He comments bitterly on how troublesome the mosquitoes were, making sleep very difficult. They can still be a problem today.

53 **A new, authentic and complete collection of voyages round the world, undertaken and performed by royal authority. Containing an authentic, entertaining, full, and complete history of Captain Cook's first, second, third and last voyages, undertaken by order of his present majesty for making discoveries in geography, navigation, astronomy &c. in the southern and northern hemispheres.**
  George William Anderson.   London: Alex. Hogg, 1784. 656p. 28 maps.
The serious study of Tonga began with Cook, and his work remains the starting point for any student of Tonga. Though earlier explorers touched upon parts of Tonga and wrote brief accounts, Cook was the first to present an extensive, detailed and scientifically based account, which had an enormous impact in its time and remains an unsurpassed source today. On his second voyage Cook spent only a few days each in Tongatapu, 'Eua and Nomuka, but on his third voyage he spent over two months in 1777 in Nomuka and Lifuka (Ha'apai) and in Tongatapu. He genuinely admired much of the Tongan way of life and liked the Tongans he met. He was interested in and mostly impressed by what he saw, and recorded his observations in meticulous detail. The maps and charts which he drew as navigator and cartographer are still useful today. Many editions of his voyages were published in his lifetime and after his death, and these are listed in the bibliography by Beddie (item no. 439). The advantage of the particular edition here cited is that the accounts of the three voyages, as well as those of others before him, are printed in one volume.

54 **Voyage in search of La Pérouse performed by order of the Constituent Assembly, during the years 1791, 1792, 1793 and 1794.**
M. Labillardiere.   London: John Stockdale, 1800. Volume I, 487p. map. Volume II, 449p.

In 1787, on a voyage to Australia, the French explorer La Pérouse visited Niuatoputapu, passed Vava'u and briefly stood off Tongatapu. After his disappearance an expedition was mounted under Admiral d'Entrecasteaux to try to find him, and the published account by the ship's naturalist, Labillardière, represents the next extended account of Tongatapu after Cook. D'Entrecasteaux's crew arrived in March 1793, made their base at Pangaimotu island, and stayed about two weeks. As a naturalist the author had a particular interest in flora and fauna but he also observes the social system, relations between chiefs and people, crafts and ceremonies. Memories of Cook, though not all fond, were strong; for example, Labillardière describes how two hatchets given by Cook to Fatafehi were brought to be sharpened. The charms of the women and frequent thefts by the men were particularly noted. Three detailed plates show a wide range of Tongan artefacts, but a general view of Tongatapu is ludicrously inaccurate in showing an island consisting of ranges of rolling hills. An appendix gives a vocabulary of about 300 Tongan words.

55 **The voyages of Abel Janszoon Tasman.**
Andrew Sharp.   Oxford: Clarendon Press, 1968. 375p. 27 maps.

Schouten and Le Maire were the first Europeans to visit any part of the Tongan islands, Niuatoputapu and Tafahi in 1616, but Tasman was the first European to visit the main islands of Tonga, in 1643. He called at 'Eua, Tongatapu, Nomuka, Tofua, Kao and Late. His journals, here reprinted in this modern edition with explanatory notes, describe the islands and the people, with views of how the islands appear from the sea, and drawings. Tasman's visit was brief, but the work is of interest as the first description of these islands. Charts and maps are also reproduced.

Flora and Fauna

56 An annotated checklist and keys to the mosquitoes of Samoa and Tonga.
Shivaji Ramalingam. *Mosquito Systematics*, vol. 8, no. 3 (1976), p. 298-318.

This paper represents the first systematic account of mosquitoes from Tonga. It identifies eight species belonging to the genera *Culex* and *Aedes*. All the species are described in detail and their locations in each island group surveyed are tabulated. There are descriptive keys to the adults, pupae and larvae. The author admits that current knowledge of the mosquito fauna of Tonga is extremely fragmentary as only a few of the islands have been surveyed.

57 Birds of Fiji, Tonga and Samoa.
Dick Watling, illustrated by Chloë Talbot-Kelly.   Wellington: Millwood Press, 1982. 176p. 68 maps. bibliog.

The first ornithological observations in the region were made in Tonga on Cook's second voyage, but serious study only began in the early 19th century. The author first outlines the history of the birds of the region and describes the composition of the avifauna in its ecological setting; the appearance of species in breeding and moult stages; and the geographical features of the region. Each species of land and sea bird is then described in terms of English, Latin and indigenous name; size; identification; flight; voice; food; breeding; habitat and range, together with general remarks, a distribution map, and illustrations in colour.

58 The butterflies of the Tonga islands and Niue, Cook Islands, with the descriptions of two new subspecies.
Jacqueline Y. Miller, Lee D. Miller.   Honolulu, Hawai'i: Bishop Museum Press, 1993. 24p. map. bibliog. (Bishop Museum Occasional Papers, no. 34).

The authors first list collectors and students of the butterflies of Tonga, from Banks and Solander, who sailed with Cook, to the present day. For Tonga they list thirteen taxa, each of which is then described in detail, with monochrome photographs. They find that much of the current butterfly fauna of Tonga is closely related to that of Fiji and Samoa, and that most Tongan butterflies owe their presence in Tonga to dispersal or accidental introduction. Because of the paucity of research they expect that the list is far from complete.

59 The cicadas of the Fiji, Samoa and Tonga islands, their taxonomy and biogeography (Homoptera and Cicadoidea).
J. P. Duffels. London; New York; Copenhagen; Cologne: E. J. Brill, 1988. 108p. 8 maps. bibliog. (Entomonograph, vol. 10).

Duffels describes twenty-four cicada (sub)species for Fiji, Samoa and Tonga and illustrates them in the larval stage and in the exuviae. However, only two of these species occur in Tonga. Duffels goes on to provide a general introduction to the biogeography of the cicadas of the south-west Pacific. A brief geological history of the region, and its relationship to the early geography of the islands and the development of life on them, is added by A. Ewart. This contains a summary of the geological evolution of the Tonga islands.

60 The ethnobotany of Tonga: the plants, their Tongan names, and their uses.
W. A. Whistler. Honolulu, Hawai'i: Bishop Museum Press, 1991. 155p. map. bibliog.

Whistler carried out ethnobotanical surveys of Tonga between 1987 and 1990. From his visits, interviews with Tongans and surveys of existing literature he produced an alphabetical checklist of the Tongan names of about 620 plants, with information on their uses, particularly in the medicinal field. Appendixes list the Tongan plant names given by Yuncker (item no. 65) and by Churchward in his dictionary (item no. 154) which Whistler was unable to substantiate. There is an index of scientific names.

61 A field guide to the birds of Tonga.
Douglas Cook. Nuku'alofa: Government Printer, 1984. 56p.

A booklet describing the sea, shore and land birds of all the islands of Tonga. For each species the author provides details of English, Latin and Tongan name; size; field marks; voice; and location and habitat. He also includes a black-and-white drawing adapted from the colour plate in Watling's *Birds of Fiji, Tonga and Samoa* (item no. 57).

62 Fish names of Western Polynesia: Futuna, Niue, Samoa, Tokelau, Tonga, Tuvalu, Uvea, outliers.
Karl H. Rensch. Canberra: Archipelago Press, 1994. 311p. map. bibliog.

Rensch has used his own field notes, manuscript sources and dictionaries to compile this list, and includes obsolete names not in current usage. He has not attempted to equate local names with established scientific taxonomy. The alphabetical listing gives the local name; the name of the relevant language; a translation or description; the scientific name, where known; and the source of information. For Tonga this is usually Churchward's dictionary (item no. 154) or the paper by Vaea and Straatmans (item no. 359). The work ends with a Latin finder list.

63 **Flowers of the Pacific island seashore – a guide to the littoral plants of Hawai'i, Tahiti, Samoa, Tonga, Cook Islands, Fiji and Micronesia.**
W. Arthur Whistler. Honolulu, Hawai'i: University of Hawai'i Press, 1992. 154p. bibliog.

From his own field trips Whistler records the 120 species of plants found on the shores of Polynesia, 87 of which are found in Tonga. He groups the plants into trees, shrubs, herbs, vines, and grasses and sedges, and in a table shows which is found in which country, and whether it is native or introduced. Within each group he arranges the plants in alphabetical order of Latin name. For each species he gives the name in English and in the vernaculars of the countries in which it occurs; precise botanical description; geographical range; habitat; and medical and commercial use. Each plant is illustrated with a colour photograph. The book could be used as an attractive and handy field guide as well as for academic reference.

64 **On the diet of pigs foraging on the mud flats of Tongatapu: an investigation in taphonomy.**
Dirk H. R. Spennemann. *Archaeology in New Zealand*, vol. 37, no. 2 (1994), p. 104-10.

One of the most remarkable sights in Tongatapu is pigs burrowing for food on the mud flats and reef flats off the coast. The author was concerned to establish what they ate from the sea to supplement the household scraps and vegetation which make up their normal diet. From an analysis of their excreta he established that, while they ate a few molluscs, they ate large numbers of small mud crabs but that, given the fragility of the remains of the crabs, they would be unlikely to survive in the archaeological record.

65 **Plants of Tonga.**
T. G. Yuncker. Honolulu, Hawai'i: Bernice P. Bishop Museum, 1959. 283p. (Bernice P. Bishop Museum Bulletin, no. 220).

Botanists before Yuncker had visited Tonga and published reports, but this book gives the first comprehensive listing. Over 750 species and varieties are classified by family and genus. Yuncker provides the Latin name, description and location of each, with remarks where appropriate, and the Tongan name where known. It should be noted that Whistler (item no. 60) says that some of these are wrong. There are indexes of Latin and Tongan names, and some photographs.

66 **Psocoptera of the Tongan archipelago.**
I. W. B. Thornton. In: *Pacific Insects Monograph 37*. Honolulu, Hawai'i: Department of Entomology, Bishop Museum, 1981, p. 106-35.

Thornton collected and recorded thirty-five species of psocoptera in the Tongan islands, eight for the first time. For each he gives a description based on his specimens; location; details of references in the literature; and a line illustration. He shows that the Tongan fauna can be regarded largely as an extension of that of Fiji.

67   **A revision of the *Aedes scutellaris* group of Tonga (Diptera: Culicidae).**
Yiau-min Huang, James C. Hitchcock.   *Contributions of the American Entomological Institute*, vol. 17, no. 3 (1980), p. 1-107. 9 maps. bibliog. (Medical Entomology Studies XII).

This paper describes the three new species and one new subspecies of mosquito in Tonga, and presents information on their type-data, distribution, bionomics, medical importance and taxonomy. The male, female, pupa and larva of the four species are illustrated in twenty-nine detailed figures. Their role in the transmission of filariasis and dengue viruses is discussed.

Prehistory and Archaeology

68 **Archaeological discoveries on Niuatoputapu island, Tonga.**
Garth Rogers. *The Journal of the Polynesian Society*, vol. 83, no. 3
(1974), p. 308-48.

Rogers discusses the importance of Niuatoputapu as a highly attractive settlement for
the bearers of Lapita-style pottery. He documents a large collection of potsherds and a
few stone tools found there. Analysis shows that the pottery was made locally. He
describes a field survey of some seventy archaeological structures divided into eight
types, and relates them to geological features and to oral history. Technical appendices
give an analysis of the sand tempers used in a sample of the sherds (William R.
Dickinson) and an account of the source of obsidian (Graeme Ward) – probably
Tafahi.

69 **Archaeology of Tonga.**
W. C. McKern.   Honolulu, Hawai'i: Bernice P. Bishop Museum, 1929.
124p. 48 maps and plans. (Bernice P. Bishop Museum Bulletin, no. 60).

Early European explorers and travellers noted the most obvious of the spectacular and
impressive archaeological remains in Tonga: the *langi* (royal tombs), the Ha'amonga
trilithon (an arch of three huge stones), mounds and fortifications. Basil Thomson
wrote a short paper on the most important of these ('Notes upon the antiquities of
Tonga', *Journal of the Anthropological Institute*, vol. XXXII [1902], p. 81-88), but
McKern's was the first systematic description, based on his own fieldwork carried out in
1920-21. He also conducted limited excavations of tombs and kitchen middens and
found pottery, the dating and significance of which were only realized by Poulsen and
others forty years later (item no. 71).

70 **Changing gender roles in Tongan society: some comments based on archaeological observations.**
Dirk H. R. Spennemann. In: *Tongan culture and history.* Edited by Phyllis Herda, Jennifer Terrell, Niel Gunson. Canberra: The Journal of Pacific History, 1990, p. 101-09.

Spennemann considers what the archaeological record can reveal about the respective roles of men and women in Tonga in prehistoric and historic times. Whereas most studies on gender roles have been concerned with rank and power, Spennemann concentrates on the life and work of ordinary people. He examines skeletal remains of men and women in order to deduce, from wear on bones and joints, the tasks that each undertook. Women were mostly involved, he deduces, in gardening work, tapa (bark-cloth) production and shellfishing. Men were concerned with the building of houses and canoes, making weapons and ornaments and fishing. He also summarizes what early European observers saw of the roles of men and women, and suggests how Christian values affected the role of women, which is still changing.

71 **Early Tongan prehistory: the Lapita period on Tongatapu and its relationships.**
Jens Poulsen. Canberra: Department of Prehistory, Research School of Pacific Studies, The Australian National University, 1987. Volume I, 307p. map. bibliog. Volume II, 205p. 4 maps. (Terra Australis, no. 12).

After McKern's work in 1920-21 (item no. 69) there was some limited excavation in Tonga in the 1950s, but Poulsen's fieldwork in 1963-64 led to the next significant major advance, with his establishment of a chronology for what had by then come to be known as Lapita pottery. Named after a site in New Caledonia this type of pottery spread through the south-west Pacific between 1200 BC and 200 AD. This pushed back the date of the earliest settlement in Tonga much further than had been thought, implying Polynesian communities springing from a common ancestral culture which entered from the west in the first millennium BC. Poulsen cites the earliest Tongan find to 1050-820 BC, suggesting that Tonga and Samoa were settled roughly contemporaneously from Fiji. Volume I of his work contains the text, Volume II the supporting maps, tables and illustrations.

72 **Ethno-archaeology and the development of Polynesian fishing strategies.**
P. V. Kirch, T. S. Dye. *The Journal of the Polynesian Society*, vol. 88, no. 1 (1979), p. 53-76.

Drawing on Dye's work on current fishing practices in Niuatopatapu (item no. 355), the authors examine what can be learnt of fishing practices in prehistoric times, using both archaeological and linguistic evidence to reconstruct and interpret Lapita fishing strategies. Excavated remains of fish suggest a concentration on inshore resources, with fishermen probably mostly using nets and spears rather than hooks.

73 **The Lapita peoples: ancestors of the Oceanic world.**
Patrick Vinton Kirch. Cambridge, Massachusetts; Oxford: Blackwell Publishers, 1997. 353p. 9 maps. bibliog.

In this general synthesis Kirch brings together and reviews the many publications on the Lapita peoples, who first settled the Pacific about 3,000 years ago and who left their distinctive pottery as evidence of their existence and diffusion, from their first appearance in the Bismarck archipelago as far as Tonga and Samoa in the east. Kirch himself has undertaken much of the work in this field since 1966, particularly in Tonga (item nos. 72, 74 and 77). He draws upon archaeological, linguistic and genetic evidence in reconstructing their progress. He uses three sites, one of these being Niuatoputapu (Tonga), to describe in detail the societies which made Lapita pottery, their patterns of settlement, economy, ecology and diet. An appendix lists all major Lapita sites, among them two on Tongatapu, two in the Ha'apai group and one on Niuatoputapu. A bibliography of about 400 items lists all published references to the Lapita peoples and related topics to date.

74 **Monumental architecture and power in Polynesian chiefdoms: a comparison of Tonga and Hawaii.**
   P. V. Kirch. *World Archaeology*, vol. 22, no. 2 (1990), p. 206-22.

Kirch contrasts the role of monumental architecture in the late prehistorical and early historical politics of Tonga and Hawai'i. He compares their style of chiefdoms; examines the various forms of mounds which are the most prominent field monuments in the Tongan archaeological landscape; and charts and classifies those with and without stone facings. He takes Niuatoputapu as a particular example, where mounds have been well investigated and can be related to the land segments of known local chiefs. The Hawai'ian archaeological landscape is very different, with temples rather than burial mounds. Kirch finds that the two cases illustrate variations in the role of monuments within highly stratified chiefdom societies.

75 **Myths and history: some aspects of history in the Tu'i Tonga myths.**
   'Okusitino Māhina. In: *Tongan culture and history.* Edited by Phyllis Herda, Jennifer Terrell, Niel Gunson. Canberra: The Journal of Pacific History, 1990, p. 30-45.

The author discusses the content of the Tu'i Tonga myths – specifically, what they actually mean within the Tongan social context or within the wider West Polynesian culture complex in which Tongan society was a specific socio-cultural development. These are accounts of actual situations and events that took place in Tongan prehistory, though many scholars believe that they are of no use in attempting to reconstruct prehistoric Tongan society. The study is based on both oral and written sources and considers social change and the place of social liberalism in relation to the dominance of the ruling order. The origin myth of 'Aho'eitu yields insights into some social, economic, mental, political and ethical aspects of the prehistory of Tonga, and suggests a move from mythologism to theism. Four main periods in Tongan prehistory are identified. The myths reveal the major chiefly lineages struggling for supremacy throughout Tonga; some of the developments in this process are set out in chart form. The author claims that these observations on some aspects of history in the Tu'i Tonga myths confirm that they can be used as historical sources.

76 **Myths, legends and volcanic activity: an example from northern Tonga.**
   Paul W. Taylor. *The Journal of the Polynesian Society*, vol. 104, no. 3 (1995), p. 323-46.

Believing that many myths and legends may be based on real events, Taylor examines a legend common to several of the outlying northern islands of Tonga. This concerns the exploits of the last of the apparently native devils of Tonga, who were said to have removed the centre of the island of Niuafo'ou and, on being chased, dropped it to form the separate island of Tafahi, with a period of darkness ended by an impromptu sunrise. Taylor relates this to records of volcanic activity and to wind patterns and suggests a volcanic eruption, possibly less than 3,000 years ago, as the basis for the legend.

77 **Niuatoputapu: the prehistory of a Polynesian culture.**
Patrick Vinton Kirch. Seattle, Washington: Burke Museum, 1988. 298p. 34 maps. bibliog. (Thomas Burke Memorial Washington State Museum Monograph, no. 5).

Kirch conducted archaeological excavations in Niuatoputapu in 1976, and some of the key findings were incorporated in his 1984 monograph *The evolution of the Polynesian chiefdoms* (item no. 86). This is the definitive archaeological report, providing much of the detailed evidence for his more general conclusions about the nature of Tongan political and social systems. Kirch describes the material culture (Lapita pottery, adzes, fishing gear, tools and ornaments) and the fauna (mammals, birds and fish) revealed by excavations, and reconstructs from them changes in technology and in subsistence patterns, bringing the evidence together to produce a sequence of prehistoric periods and of the development of the Tongan maritime chiefdom. He sees in Niuatoputapu a microcosm of much that is characteristic of the whole of Polynesia. The work is fully illustrated with photographs, diagrams and drawings.

78 **Samoa and Tonga.**
Janet M. Davidson. In: *The prehistory of Polynesia.* Edited by Jesse D. Jennings. Cambridge, Massachusetts; London: Harvard University Press, 1979, p. 82-109. 3 maps. bibliog.

Davidson, who has herself excavated in both countries, surveys the closely related archaeology of Samoa and Tonga in the light of new evidence, obtained from the dating and analysis of Lapita pottery of the first settlements in the region, established a little over 3,000 years ago. She records the main types of remains and reviews the literature relating to earlier excavations, drawing new conclusions from the data where appropriate. She points out that, in contrast to the earlier period, there is still little known of the post-Lapita period, which extended from probably about 300 AD until the beginning of the period of oral record about 1,000 years ago.

79 **Sand tempers in indigenous Lapita and Lapitoid Polynesian plainware and imported protohistoric Fijian pottery of Ha'apai (Tonga) and the question of Lapita tradeware.**
William R. Dickinson, Richard Shatler Jr, Rob Shortland, David V. Burley, Thomas S. Dye. *Archaeology in Oceania*, vol. 31, no. 2 (1996), p. 87-98.

Some scholars have suggested that Lapita pottery from sites in Polynesia and Melanesia may have been used as tradeware, and may not have been manufactured where it was found. From the detailed examination of the sands used in its composition, the writers of this paper conclude that large deposits of Lapita pottery found at two sites in the Ha'apai group were made where they were found. This is significant for the study of early settlement patterns and skills in Tonga.

80 **Settlement patterns and Tongan prehistory: reconsiderations from Ha'apai.**
David V. Burley. *The Journal of the Polynesian Society*, vol. 103, no. 4 (1994), p. 379-411.

Burley addresses the problem of settlement patterns, settlement forms and their transformation, covering a period from the colonization of Tonga about 3,200 years ago to the late 19th century. His discussions and conclusions focus on archaeological data from the Ha'apai group. He sees a continuity of settlement patterns for the first 1,000 years, a dispersed pattern then emerging, with a return to more nucleated settlement in more recent years as a consequence not so much of the civil wars, as generally believed, as of the later constitutional policies of land reform implemented by King George Tupou I. These, however, led to a village structure which was considerably different from the earlier aggregations of a chief and his followers. Burley relates his findings to what is generally agreed about the sequence of archaeological periods in Tonga.

81 **The temple of Faleme'e: archaeological and anthropological considerations of a pre-Christian god-house on the island of Ha'ano, Kingdom of Tonga.**
David V. Burley. *New Zealand Journal of Archaeology*, vol. 16 (1994), p. 55-67.

Pre-Christian religious beliefs and practices in Tonga are incompletely documented and poorly understood. Burley excavated a stone enclosure and corner posts of a pre-Christian god-house on an island in Ha'apai. He identifies this as a temple to Hikule'o, one of the three principal deities within the Tongan pantheon and deity of the Tu'i Tonga lineage.

82 **Tonga, Lapita pottery, and Polynesian origins.**
L. M. Groube. *The Journal of the Polynesian Society*, vol. 80, no. 3 (1971), p. 278-316.

In this contribution to the debate about the significance of Lapita pottery in the study of Polynesian origins, Groube proposes a crucial role for Tonga. He examines both the archaeological and the linguistic evidence for the relationship between Fiji, Samoa and Tonga, partly drawing on his own excavations in Tongatapu. On the strength of a long technical discussion of radiocarbon dating and of the stratigraphy of excavation sites he suggests that the generally accepted sequence of dating of Lapita pottery in Tonga needs to be revised. He concludes that Polynesians became Polynesians sometime near the middle of the first millennium BC after over 500 years of isolation in the remote archipelago of Tonga: 'The Polynesians, therefore, did not strictly come from anywhere: they *became* Polynesians, and the location of their becoming was Tonga'.

83 **Tonga malohi: Tongan fortifications in Western Polynesia.**
Kimi Papa. *Archaeology in New Zealand*, vol. 37, no. 1 (1994), p. 44-57.

Papa lists the recorded fortifications of Tonga and examines the excavation records, setting them in their historical context and discussing how far their styles, some rectangular and some circular, were indigenous or influenced by Fijian styles. He also examines fortifications elsewhere in Western Polynesia supposedly built by Tongans, and concludes that the Tongan history of fort building is long and probably has its own independent origins.

History

General Pacific

84 **The Cambridge history of the Pacific islanders.**
Edited by Donald Denoon with Stewart Firth, Jocelyn Linnekin,
Malama Meleisea, Karen Nero.   Cambridge, England: Cambridge
University Press, 1997. 518p. 24 maps. bibliog.

For one hundred years the Cambridge histories have set standards of international
collaborative scholarship, with chapters written by leading specialists in their fields.
The newest Cambridge history covers the Pacific. The editors state that it is 'for
readers who seek an introduction to the experiences of the people of this vast and
ill-defined region. We seek to provide clear and reliable first words, not to lay down
the last word'. A first chapter on ways to approach the history of the Pacific is followed
by twelve more, covering a period from prehistory and the first human settlement to
the Pacific of today. Each chapter is thematic and covers the whole of the region.
Thus, although some information on Tonga is included in most, it would not be easy
to follow the history of Tonga, or of any one country, alone and for Tonga there is
little on significant political and economic developments since independence. The
book is more useful in breaking down the insularity and identifying common themes
throughout the Pacific than in providing a cohesive history of each constituent part.

85 **European vision and the South Pacific.**
Bernard Smith.   New Haven, Connecticut; London: Yale University
Press, 1985. 2nd ed. 370p. bibliog.

The voyages of Cook and those who followed him opened the eyes of Europeans to
new landscapes and civilizations, portrayed by the artists who accompanied them.
Smith examines the way in which the artists, mindful of the social conventions and
intellectual attitudes of their time, depicted what they saw. Pacific islanders were first
seen as noble savages but later, under missionary influence, came to be portrayed as
unredeemed and ugly. Landscapes were both familiar and exotic. In the illustration of

Cook's landing at 'Eua, Tongans were depicted in classical dress and poses, to show that the event was worthy of portrayal in a suitably serious style. Some suggested even that the clue to the origin of art and civilization was to be found not in classical Greece and Rome but in the islands of the Pacific. Smith shows how the artists' first sketches were often altered for the final painting to fit such concepts. His book reproduces many of the illustrations of explorers and missionaries to demonstrate the attitudes of those who first explored Tonga and the other islands.

86 The evolution of the Polynesian chiefdoms.
Patrick Vinton Kirch. Cambridge, England: Cambridge University Press, 1984. 326p. 19 maps. bibliog.

Though derived from a common ancestral Polynesian society, the thirty-eight major Polynesian archipelagos and islands evolved different types of social and political systems. Kirch first reconstructs the broad outlines of ancestral Polynesian society and proceeds to analyse the major processes (technological, environmental, demographic, social and political) that led to change. He then takes three case-studies, of which Tonga is one. Tonga, Kirch argues, demonstrates a high degree of hierarchical stratification and differentiation in social status and rank, which was present in all Polynesian societies from the beginning but which survives to this day in Tonga more than in most others. Despite the lack of permanent watercourses, the unusually fertile soils of the islands of Tonga made possible an intensive level of agriculture which could support a considerable population. His examination of the genealogies of the sacred Tu'i Tonga and related secular lines, alongside oral tradition, archaeological evidence and records of inter-island trade and tribute, provides a comprehensive picture of the Tongan social and political order up to the time of European contact.

87 A history of the Pacific from the Stone Age to the present day.
Glen Barclay. London: Sidgwick & Jackson, 1978. 264p. 6 maps. bibliog.

This history of the Pacific for the general reader provides a summary running briskly from earliest human occupation (though with no mention of Lapita pottery and the consequent revisions to settlement dates) to the mid-1970s. It is written from a New Zealand perspective. Tonga is covered at appropriate points, but it would not be possible to construct a satisfactory outline of the history of Tonga from these references alone. The chronological table of events from 100 AD to 1977 is inadequate for Tonga, omitting many key events, and an illustration from Tasman's voyage of 1643, captioned as of Fiji, is of Tonga.

88 A history of the Pacific islands.
I. C. Campbell. Christchurch, New Zealand: University of Canterbury Press, 1989. 239p. 8 maps. bibliog.

Campbell presents a synoptic history of the region, intending his book to be an introduction, making accessible to a non-specialist readership the richness of the many specialized works on the subject. His concern is with broad themes and with general outlines: the original peoples and their migrations, the coming of the Europeans as explorers, traders, missionaries and colonizers, and the attainment of political independence by some of the island countries, though still not by all. However, the islands are now increasingly locked into a world economic system of dependency, with a loss of control and also of traditional social processes. Campbell puts the islanders in the centre of his picture, not merely as passive victims of what is called 'the fatal impact'.

89 **The people from the horizon: an illustrated history of the Europeans among the South Sea Islanders.**
Philip Snow, Stefanie Waine.   Oxford: Phaidon, 1979. 296p. map. bibliog.

Philip Snow and Stefanie Waine (his daughter, born in Fiji) have a broad canvas: the relationship over 450 years between Europeans and the peoples of Micronesia, Melanesia and Polynesia, set in an ocean occupying one third of the world's surface. They describe for the general reader the impact of discoverers; explorers; early residents; traders and whalers; missionaries; settlers and planters; colonial administrators; artists and writers; the two world wars which the Western powers brought to the Pacific; nuclear testing; and political independence. This is more of an account of the Europeans in the Pacific than of the islanders themselves. The unique situation of Tonga is well outlined. The text is inevitably brief and general: there is no space to go into issues in depth. It is the wealth of illustrations, many from rare and unfamiliar sources, which makes the book an attractive introduction to this subject.

90 **Tides of history: the Pacific islands in the twentieth century.**
Edited by K. R. Howe, Robert C. Kiste, Brij V. Lal.   Honolulu, Hawai'i: University of Hawai'i Press, 1994. 475p. 4 maps.

The authors of this collective volume present an analysis, from a variety of perspectives, of the nature of the social, political, economic and cultural experiences of the Pacific island peoples in late colonial and contemporary times. The three sections cover colonization (in Polynesia by Britain, Germany, Australia, New Zealand and France); moves towards decolonization during and after the Second World War; and what the authors call 'uncertain times', in which they examine themes since independence, with the consolidation of some themes originating in the 19th century and the advent of new forces. In a concluding essay Lal rejects the earlier versions of the fatal impact theory and emphasizes the positive role of the islanders in responding to European contact. Yet this is in danger of being overstated. Island economies are still today much in the hands of foreigners and political independence is limited, though perhaps less so in Tonga than elsewhere. Self-reliance is now impossible, and the islands cannot return to the past with its customs and traditions. This book does not set out the history of each Pacific country in any detail, and Tonga is covered less than some others, but the conclusion is as valid for Tonga as for any: that bridging the gap between past and present without losing the essence of their nation's being is the agonizing question for any Pacific island leader or thinker.

General Tonga

91 **Exchange patterns in goods and spouses: Fiji, Tonga and Samoa.**
Adrienne L. Kaeppler.   *Mankind*, vol. 11, no. 3 (1978), p. 246-52.

Kaeppler believes that the motivation for exchanges between Fiji, Tonga and Samoa, usually of canoes and pottery for which there is ethnographic evidence, has not been understood, and she examines other objects, and social relationships involved in their movement. Her viewpoint is Tonga-centric. She sees both Fiji and Samoa as 'spouse givers' to Tonga, and suggests that the exchange of goods was directly related to patterns of exchange of spouses. She examines Tonga's relationship with Fiji and Samoa as an extension of its social principles of kinship and rank, and relates this to the dynastic concerns of the Tu'i Tonga line. She describes the ceremonial goods obtained from Samoa and Fiji, normally in the specialized context of weddings and funerals, and suggests that they may be in part responsible for the distinctive quality of the Tongan cultural and social system. It should be noted that her conclusions have been challenged by Claessen (item no. 102).

92   **Friendly Islands: a history of Tonga.**
Edited by Noel Rutherford.   Melbourne; Oxford; Wellington; New York: Oxford University Press, 1977. 297p. map. bibliog.

The need for a full, scholarly history of Tonga was first met by this book, in which fourteen scholars, four of them Tongan, each wrote on their specialized field, from the creation myth, prehistory and oral traditions to the Tonga of the mid-1970s, though the long and crucial reign of Queen Sālote Tupou III was perhaps too close for dispassionate analysis at the time of writing. Society and culture are described alongside political history. A select bibliography covers primary (both manuscript and printed) and secondary sources.

93   **Historiography: the myth of indigenous authenticity.**
F. O. Kolo.   In: *Tongan culture and history.*   Edited by Phyllis Herda, Jennifer Terrell, Niel Gunson.   Canberra: The Journal of Pacific History, 1990, p. 1-11.

Kolo discusses the view that there can never be a genuine European history of Tonga without a genuine cultural understanding of Tongan society, and compares aspects of Tongan and Western institutional tradition. Before the coming of schools the process of learning was one of socialization and the critical faculty was undeveloped, and to some extent this continues today. Kolo believes that European historians of Tonga have a responsibility to understand the language thoroughly and to 'feel' the culture and values of the people, and he criticizes Wood's history of Tonga (item no. 94) for failing to do this. If a real indigenous history is to emerge he looks to the development of a European intellectual tradition in Tonga, but doubts that this is realistic. The best that can be hoped for, Kolo believes, is a compromise history which is sensitive to indigenous values and culture. Oral tradition and myth should not go by the name of history. He concludes, 'Historical perspectives of Pacific islanders should therefore be regarded as complementary to Western academic history. All for the better'.

94   **History and geography of Tonga.**
A. H. Wood.   Nuku'alofa: Government Printer, 1932. 109p. 7 maps.

This brief introduction was originally prepared for use in Tongan schools in 1932. It remained of such value that it was reprinted in 1972 and is still available in Tonga today. Wood presents an outline of the history of Tonga from the origins of the people, through the rise and fall of the three royal lines, the beginnings of European contact from 1616, the period of civil war to 1826 and the development of modern Tonga to the present, i. e. the early 1930s. He then describes the geography of Tonga; the position and geological foundation of each island group; climate; animal and plant life; imports and exports; population; and the system of government and law. All statistics are of course now of historic interest only, and the section on prehistory is particularly out of date: the serious reader must look to more recent books. Another drawback is the book's use of the older form of spelling, e. g. Togatabu for Tongatapu. Yet, within its considerable limitations, it can still be a useful place for newcomers to Tonga studies.

95   **Island kingdom: Tonga ancient and modern.**
     I. C. Campbell.   Christchurch, New Zealand: Canterbury University
     Press, 1992. 257p. 3 maps. bibliog.

Campbell's theme is the continuity of Tongan history. Tongan culture, he maintains, adapted what it found to its advantage from Fiji, from Samoa and then from Europeans, but always retained its independence and integrity, at least until recent times when it became increasingly dependent on aid donors for development funds. Now it faces pressures from over-population and from changing social, political and economic aspirations; these forces, Campbell believes, are as powerful as any of the internal or external pressures of the past. This is the most accessible and up-to-date introduction to Tonga's history, a concise yet comprehensive survey from Tonga's origins to the 1990s.

96   **Oral traditions: an appraisal of their value in historical research in
     Tonga.**
     Sione Lātūkefu.   *The Journal of Pacific History*, vol. 3, no. 2 (1966),
     p. 135-43.

Historians have differed in their perception of the value of oral traditions. However, in a society such as Tonga where they are of great importance, they cannot be ignored, though their use requires a good knowledge of the language and culture, and often tact and patience with those who tell them. Lātūkefu tells of his early years as a Tongan historian and his problems in obtaining and evaluating oral traditions as well as in reconciling conflicting versions. He relates different oral traditions concerning the birthplace of King George Tupou I, the civil wars of 1825-26, and the destruction of the houses of the pagan gods to illustrate his theme. He concludes that oral traditions, carefully examined, can make a valuable contribution to the understanding of the history of Tonga. This is significant given that, for the larger part of Tongan history until the last 200 years of so, there are no written records.

97   **Pathways to the Tongan present/'Uuni hala ki Tonga he kuonga ni.**
     Kurt Düring.   Nuku'alofa: Kurt Düring, 1990. 204p. 4 maps.

This book (in Tongan and English) prints a selection of over 400 historic photographs taken between 1867 and 1970 by two German traders settled in Tonga, Eduard Becker and August Hettig, with brief text for each in both Tongan and English. They offer a vivid picture of traditional Tongan life, of the activities of European missionaries, traders and settlers, and the impact of these on one another. Many are rather fuzzy, but all are evocative of a Tonga which, despite many changes, remains remarkably and immediately recognizable.

98 **The practice of Tongan traditional history: *tala-ē-fonua*, an ecology-centred concept of culture and history.**
'Okusitino Māhina. *The Journal of Pacific History*, vol. 28, no. 1 (1993), p. 109-21.

Māhina examines the ecology-centred concept of cultural and historical thinking in Tonga. He does this through an analysis of a *lakalaka* (traditional dance) in which Queen Sālote sets her eldest son, the present King Taufa'āhau Tupou IV, within the context of the three main kingly titles. He formulates a conservative theory of Tongan society by weaving it into an artistic harmony of theme and form based on the operation of celestial objects which are important to navigation. Groups within society, like the gravitational force holding celestial objects in place, are held by boundaries which, if destroyed, signal the destruction of the surreal and the actual, the literal and the symbolic, in such verse, and this is illustrated from the Tongan origin myth and other episodes in Tongan history.

99 **Rivals and wives: affinal politics and the Tongan ramage.**
Aletta Biersack. In: *Origins, ancestry and alliance: explorations in Austronesian ethnography.* Edited by James L. Fox, Clifford Sather. Canberra: Department of Anthropology, Research School of Pacific and Asian Studies, The Australian National University, 1996, p. 237-79.

Biersack's essay is an extended examination of the structure of Tongan origins that has as its 'root' the Tu'i Tonga, covering succession within the title system over more than 150 years. The 'branches' of the origin structure are graded according to relative proximity to the original root, and Biersack considers the way in which relationships are ranked. She sees Tongan history as driven by the rivalry between matrilateral and patrilateral half-brothers. Political status acquired through father and personal status through mother can produce for a person complex and contradictory positions within a social and political field. She traces in detail the way in which this works through to the present king, who is emblematic of the fact that in Tonga centralization is achieved historically and horizontally, through marriage, rather than structurally and vertically, through descent. The analysis, developing her own earlier work (item no. 176) and that of Bott (item no. 208), Wood-Ellem (item no. 137), and others, presupposes considerable knowledge of the subject.

100 **Tongan historiography: shamanic views of time and history.**
Niel Gunson. In: *Tongan culture and history.* Edited by Phyllis Herda, Jennifer Terrell, Niel Gunson. Canberra: The Journal of Pacific History, 1990, p. 12-20.

Gunson, like Kolo in this volume (item no. 93) considers how far the writing of Pacific islands' history should be left to islanders. The island historian may have better insight into language and tradition but may be influenced by social, religious or educational constraints. Any Tongan historiography must begin with the 'living tradition', usually Methodist and Tupou-dynasty oriented. But Tongan history must be freed from modern associations. Most of it has clear associations with art and religion, in what Gunson calls a shamanic context. He believes that the oldest layer of religious belief and practice in Polynesia is shamanism, that shamanism was the most pervasive religious influence in Tonga until the introduction of Christianity, and that Tongan concepts of time and history are shamanic in origin. He sets out what he sees as traces of shamanistic beliefs and practice to be found in Tongan myth and history, in Tongan concepts of the universe, and also of time; this latter puts into question the historical value of linear genealogies. Gunson's thesis is suggestive, but it must be said that neither he himself nor others seem to have developed it subsequently.

101 The Tongan past.
Patricia Ledyard. Vava'u, Tonga: Matheson, 1982. 83p.

Patricia Ledyard has lived in Tonga for many years, and her personal knowledge and enthusiasm are evident in this brief introduction. She observes that, in writing about Tongan life before the Europeans came, one slips easily and constantly between the past and the present. She sketches the main facts and the broad themes of Tongan history, more fully for earlier periods than for the last seventy years.

102 Tongan traditions – on model-building and historical evidence.
Henri J. M. Claessen. *Bijdragen tot de Taal-, Land- en Volkenkunde*, vol. 144, no. 4 (1988), p. 433-44.

Claessen's purpose is to discuss whether the models that have been applied to explain the relations between Tonga, Samoa and Fiji are tenable in the light of both earlier and recent data. Some scholars have identified a regular exchange of spouses and prestige goods between the three countries, with Tonga as the hub; Claessen, however, believes that the exchange of prestige goods was restricted in Samoa. He notes the records of trading links and examines marriages, particularly between the Tu'i Tonga line and Samoa, and concludes that there was never any 'circulating connubium' or structural relationship between the noble families of these islands.

103 The Treaty of Friendship and Tongan sovereignty.
Sione Lātūkefu. In: *Sovereignty and indigenous rights: the Treaty of Waitangi in international context.* Edited by William Renwick. Wellington: Victoria University Press, 1991, p. 83-88.

Lātūkefu tells briefly the story of Tonga's treaty relationship with Britain. Britain refused King George Tupou I's request for a treaty recognizing Tonga's independent sovereignty because it could not consider elevating Tonga to a position of equality by officially recognizing it. Lātūkefu tells how the king and Shirley Baker negotiated a treaty with Germany in 1876 to force Britain to follow suit in 1879, though the treaty was not ratified by Tonga until 1881. Following Germany's renunciation of her treaty rights in Tonga by the Samoa Convention of 1899, Basil Thomson came to Tonga in 1900 for King George Tupou II to sign the 1900 Treaty of Friendship and Protection with Britain which in fact curtailed full Tongan independence. Under duress the king agreed to a supplement to the treaty in 1905 which further increased British control. In retrospect, however, he sees the treaties as saving Tonga from potentially worse dangers, and relations improved steadily from the accession of Queen Sālote, leading to full independence in 1970.

Mission and church

104 **Christian confrontations in paradise: Catholic proselytizing of a Protestant mission in Oceania.**
Paul van der Grijp. *Anthropos*, vol. 88, nos. 1-3 (1993), p. 135-53.

While many in Europe in the 19th century saw Oceania as a sort of paradise on earth, the churches saw it as a field ripe for mission. Catholics and Methodists in Tonga shared the same aims but not the same ideology. Van der Grijp traces French concern at the success of Protestants in Tonga; and the beginning of the French mission; the opposition of the Methodists, led by John Thomas; the French missionaries' initial success, particularly in gaining the confidence of the Tu'i Tonga; and their disastrous involvement in the civil war which led to France forcing a treaty of friendship on Tonga in 1855 guaranteeing the same freedoms for Catholics as for Protestants. This did not prevent continued hostility and mutual accusations. Catholics were more tolerant than Methodists of many social customs, and believed that they were closer to the people. However, many Tongans did not understand or respect their poverty and made no distinction between Catholic and Methodist, while many Catholics showed little understanding of Tongan society and culture. However, the tensions lessened over time, and by the end of his reign King George Tupou I was showing benevolence to them and was even assigning high titles to Tongan Catholics.

105 **The diaries and correspondence of David Cargill, 1832-1843.**
Edited, with an introduction and annotations, by Albert J. Schütz.
Canberra: Australian National University Press, 1977. 255p. bibliog.
(Pacific History Series, no. 10).

David Cargill, one of the outstanding early Methodist missionaries to Tonga, was the first to have a university education. Unlike his colleagues he was a scholar and trained linguist who translated the Bible. In his journals can be read the story of his greatest success, the mass conversion of many thousands of Tongans in the 1830s. After a time in Fiji and back in England, he returned to Tonga in 1842 but was disappointed to find that many of his converts had reverted to their old ways. He died in Vava'u in mysterious circumstances. Schütz convincingly suggests that it was suicide through an overdose of laudanum, probably brought on by depression following a bout of dengue fever. Because of this, later generations of Methodists played down his achievements, but Schütz's edition reinstates his memory and re-establishes his reputation. The journals, with Schütz's annotations, provide a vividly authentic account of both the triumphs and tribulations of his life and work.

106 **'He can but die . . .': missionary medicine in pre-Christian Tonga.**
Dorothy Shineberg. In: *The changing Pacific: essays in honour of H. E. Maude.* Edited by Niel Gunson. Melbourne; Oxford; Wellington; New York: Oxford University Press, 1978, p. 285-96.

The early missionaries to Tonga brought some limited medical knowledge. They were hesitant to use this for fear that failure would weaken their position and because evangelization was their first priority. However, Shineberg shows that they did have some successes, not least because Tongans came to them as a last resort after the failure of their own medicines, when their condition could hardly get worse; she further argues that the practice of medicine advanced the Wesleyan cause in Tonga.

107 **In some sense the work of an individual: Alfred Willis and the Tongan Anglican mission 1902-1920.**
Stephen L. Donald.   Hibiscus Coast, New Zealand: ColCom Press, 1994. map. bibliog.

In 1902 Alfred Willis, who had recently resigned as the Anglican Bishop of Honolulu, responded to the request of former followers of the disgraced Prime Minister, Shirley Baker, and established the Anglican Church in Tonga. Although he believed that the Anglican Church should become the national church of Tonga, this was never achieved and Anglicans remain a small minority among Methodists and Roman Catholics. The book, though poorly proofread, offers a lively description of church life in Tonga at the time, based on the author's original research in Tonga and illustrated with archive photographs.

108 **Memoirs of Mrs. Margaret Cargill, wife of the Rev. David Cargill, A.M., Wesleyan missionary. Including notes on the progress of Christianity in Tonga and Feejee.**
David Cargill.   London: John Mason, 1855. 2nd ed. 348p.

David Cargill (for whose diaries and correspondence see item no. 105) was deeply devoted to his wife Margaret, who worked with him in his first period of ministry in Tonga in the 1830s, moved with him to Fiji and died there in 1840. 'Biography is always instructive and profitable', Cargill begins this memoir, a first-hand account of the triumphant progress of the Christian faith in Tonga in the 1830s. 'All who knew her, loved her; and Heathen as well as Christian, manifested the esteem in which they held her by the respect which they showed to her memory'. The memoir is in no way dispassionate or objective. It chronicles the mission and ministry which the Cargills shared, and reveals much of the way in which they themselves viewed it, and the Tongans for whom they worked.

109 **Messengers of grace: evangelical missionaries in the South Seas 1797-1860.**
Niel Gunson.   Melbourne; Oxford; Wellington; New York: Oxford University Press, 1978. 437p. 8 maps. bibliog.

Tonga today is a remarkable mixture of 19th-century Christianity and traditional Polynesian kingship and society. This state of affairs was the achievement of Protestant missionaries. Working from original records of the missionary societies, and journals of the missionaries themselves, Gunson describes their largely humble social origins in the 'mechanic class', for whom personal piety and practical skills were more important than formal education; the theological background of their calling; their selection and training; and their work in the islands of the Pacific, seen both as a paradise and a challenge. Gunson also gives a comprehensive biographical listing of all missionaries, both European and Polynesian. He brings vividly to life the missionaries whose legacy is so visible today in Tonga.

110 **Mormons in the Pacific: a bibliography.**
Compiled by Russell T. Clement.   Lae, Hawai'i: The Institute of Polynesian Studies, 1981. 239p.

This bibliography is based on holdings at the Hawai'i and Utah campuses of Brigham Young University and at the Church Historical Department. It lists 2,877 items in straight alphabetical order, with author, title (translated if not in English), biblio-graphical information and location. It provides a geographic/subject index and a name index. Over 100 items on Tonga are recorded, reflecting the scale of Mormon activity in Tonga.

111   **Motives and methods: missionaries in Tonga in the early 19th century.**
      Charles F. Urbanowicz.   *The Journal of the Polynesian Society,*
      vol. 86, no. 2 (1977), p. 345-63.

Tongan society is based on kinship, and Tongan politics is 'kinship writ large'. From this starting-point, Urbanowicz outlines the early history of Tonga, where rank was based on kinship ties and on status attained through achievement. With the introduction of Western material goods some chiefs sought to consolidate their authority. With the 1875 Constitution much of the inherent consensus and flexibility of aboriginal Tongan society was, Urbanowicz claims, 'ossified into a pseudo-Western framework'. He examines the other great influence in Tonga, Christianity, and how the early Wesleyan missionaries sought to convert the Tongans. They realized early that material goods diffused more rapidly than philosophical or theological systems, and that the success of their mission depended on such goods. Urbanowicz believes that it was by the systematic introduction of Western material goods along with Wesleyan theology that the Tongan body politic was restructured, moving from consensus to the rise of the individual chief, and particularly King George Tupou I. The Wesleyans were able to exploit the differences between chiefs, with a policy of divide-and-conquer and active involvement in politics, while some Tongans manipulated the system to their own advantage. Urbanowicz's conclusion is that the missionaries 'did not aid the Tongans in becoming first-class Tongans, but rather encouraged the Tongans to become second-class Victorians'. This might be thought to give inadequate credit to Tongans' sincerity in their faith and to their skill in remaining independent.

112   **Semisi Nau: the story of my life.**
      Edited by Allan K. Davidson.   Suva: Institute of Pacific Studies,
      The University of the South Pacific, 1996. 153p. map. bibliog.

One of the outstanding features of the Methodist Church in Tonga is the way in which, from the earliest days, Tongans themselves shared in the evangelization not only of Tonga but also of other islands in the region. While working in the Solomons Davidson found a notebook containing Nau's account of his life and work as a missionary in Ontong Java from 1905 to 1919. After finishing his work there, Nau returned to Tonga, where he died in 1927. Although Nau shared at times a sense of moral superiority over those he was seeking to convert, as was usual at that time, he does show a real interest in their customs and a commitment to living and working among them. The book allows Nau to speak for himself, while Davidson outlines in an introduction the broader context of his missionary work, information on the Tongan background of his early years and details of the troubled history of the Methodist church there towards the end of the 19th century.

113   **Thomas of Tonga, 1797-1881: the unlikely pioneer.**
Janet Louisa Luckcock.   Peterborough, England: Methodist
Publishing House, 1990. 196p. map. bibliog.

In this published version of a PhD thesis Luckcock seeks to rehabilitate John Thomas
from the attacks, by contemporary and modern writers, on his reputation after his
early successful years as the 'father founder' of the Methodist Church in Tonga. She
seeks to reveal the whole man, using papers, particularly his private and official
journals, neglected by others who have written on him. She chronicles his life from his
humble beginnings in England, his conversion, his call to and preparation for mission,
and his work in Tonga with its triumphs and its setbacks. In 1826 there were no
Christians in Tonga: by 1840 there were about 8,000. His strong convictions did not
make him an easy colleague but explain views which today might seem unduly narrow.
She examines in particular the charge made by Dillon that he actively instigated and
encouraged a holy war against heathens by King George I in 1837, in which men,
women and children were brutally killed. She concludes that Thomas was in fact the
mildest of men, who hated violence of any sort, and absolves him of Dillon's accusations,
which Dillon had his own motives for making.

114   **To live among the stars: Christian origins in Oceania.**
John Garrett.   Geneva; Suva: World Council of Churches in
association with the Institute of Pacific Studies, University of the South
Pacific, 1982. 412p. 37 maps. bibliog.

Garrett provides a comprehensive account for the general reader of Christian origins,
Roman Catholic and Protestant, in the Pacific islands. He shows how readily
Christianity was accepted by some islanders as a religion more powerful than their
own. It was a faith not only adopted but also adapted; once established in centres like
Tonga, it was spread more widely by Pacific islanders themselves than by European
missionaries. He describes the progress of Christianity for each country in detail, as
one part of the overall picture, up to about 1900. Later developments are summarized.
His conclusions about the strength of Christianity and its successful synthesis of the
gospel and local tradition may, however, be somewhat over-optimistic.

115   **Tonga and the Friendly Islands; with a sketch of their mission
history, written for young people.**
Sarah S. Farmer.   London: Hamilton, Adams, 1855. 427p. 2 maps.

Sarah Farmer wrote to encourage support among young people for the Methodist
mission in Tonga. Her story is of its progress and successes, as well as of much still to
be done. She concludes, 'Much is admitted to be yet imperfect in this Christian State;
but what has been done already fills our minds with wonder and adoring thankfulness'.
She lists some of the triumphs of the previous thirty years: idols abolished; the
Sabbath strictly observed; polygamy given up; education for all; a written language;
many able to read the Bible; Christian laws enforced; and land divided among the
people. She had not been to Tonga herself, but had clearly read widely, and had
spoken to people who had been there. The history of exploration and discovery she
takes from Cook, Mariner and other published sources. For more recent events she
relies on information from John Thomas and other missionaries. Her work brings
together what was known of Tonga, and in particular the progress of Christian mission
there, by the mid-19th century.

116   **Women of the *lotu*: the foundations of Tongan Wesleyanism reconsidered.**
Bonnie Maywald.   In: *Tongan culture and history.*   Edited by
Phyllis Herda, Jennifer Terrell, Niel Gunson.   Canberra: The Journal
of Pacific History, 1990, p. 118-33.

Maywald believes that an examination of women's participation in the cultural and religious exchanges of the early 19th century between Polynesians and Europeans is long overdue, though the male bias of much of the historical record makes this difficult. By setting women's writings, mostly personal and unofficial, alongside the mainstream historical traditions it is made clear that a different emphasis, and sometimes a complete reconstruction of events, is necessary. Maywald examines the conventional account of the foundation of Wesleyanism in Tonga in the 1820s, and suggests that the role of women has been understated. She examines the active role they played in connections between missionary families in Australia and the South Pacific, and suggests that they were central to efforts that led to a permanent Wesleyan presence in Tonga. She considers in particular the role of Sarah Thomas, wife of John Thomas, and that of Tongan chiefly women in assisting the work of the missionaries. *Lotu* is the Tongan word for worship, prayer, religion and especially Christianity.

Pre-1900

117   **The alleged imperialism of George Tupou I.**
I. C. Campbell.   *The Journal of Pacific History*, vol. 25, no. 2 (1990),
p. 159-75.

It has been said that for nearly fifty years, from the early 1820s to 1869, King George Tupou I was working towards an extension of his territory, first within Tonga and then beyond. Campbell suggests that the king was far too burdened with worries about internal disunity and staving off imperial designs from outside, that even his planned invasion of Fiji in 1862 was not what it appeared, and that there is little foundation for the allegations of imperialism. Campbell suggests that much of the evidence is dubious, coming from unreliable European sources. He examines the king's dealings with Uvea and with Samoa before turning to Fiji, where he believes that his record is one of restraint.

118   **As a prescription to rule: the royal tomb of Mala'e Lahi and 19th century Tongan kingship.**
David V. Burley.   *Antiquity*, vol. 68, no. 260 (1994), p. 504-17.

In the royal tomb of Mala'e Lahi in Ha'apai are buried the father, son and other members of the lineage of Taufa'ahau, who became King George Tupou I. In its scale, style and markings it incorporates a symbolic claim for pre-eminent status and power. Burley examines the historical and archaeological contexts of the tomb within the realm of 19th-century Tongan culture and political machinations. The tomb illustrates the role of monumental architecture in establishing political legitimacy in chiefdom local societies. Burley provides a brief summary of the development of Tongan kingship from the arrival of the Lapita peoples about 3,300 years ago to the final consolidation of the three Tuʻi lines by King George I in 1875. He records the history of the site from its construction in 1820, describes and illustrates its present state, relates it to similar structures, and describes its role in the consolidation of power in the 19th century.

119   **Burial structures and societal ranking in Vavaʻu, Tonga.**
P. V. Kirch.   *The Journal of the Polynesian Society*, vol. 89, no. 3 (1980), p. 291-308.

Kirch tests the hypothesis that the size and complexity of a burial structure reflect the societal rank or status of the person buried, by examining some protohistoric funerary monuments in Vavaʻu for which evidence about the interred chief exists. He documents six burial sites from the late 18th century, representing the three hierarchical groups of Tongan society. He shows how the sites were related to the socio-political system within which they were constructed, and examines some implications. He finds that the degree of elaboration of the tombs seems not to correlate closely with the status of the interred chief. Relative socio-political status may not necessarily reflect societal rank.

120   **Church and state in Tonga: the Wesleyan Methodist missionaries and political development, 1822-1875.**
Sione Lātūkefu.   Canberra: Australian National University Press, 1974. 302p. 3 maps. bibliog.

King George Tupou I and the Wesleyan missionaries between them transformed Tonga during the 19th century, and it was in the missionaries' interests to claim credit for political developments as well as for spiritual progress. Lātūkefu's purpose is to assess critically and objectively the part played by the missionaries in the political development of Tonga, culminating in the Constitution of 1875. He concludes that they played a significant part in advising and assisting King George, but that they did not initiate political change and that in the final analysis the greatest credit for the transition to constitutional monarchy was due to the King. The King may have sought advice and relied heavily on it but he alone made the final decisions. Lātūkefu outlines the history of Tonga before the reestablishment of the mission in 1826, and examines in more detail the following crucial fifty years and the respective roles of King, missionaries, traders and external influences. Appendixes provide the full texts of the key documents, from the 1839 Code of Vavaʻu to the 1875 Constitution.

121   **The demise of the Tuʻi Kanokupolu Tonga 1799-1827.**
I. C. Campbell.   *The Journal of Pacific History*, vol. 24, no. 2 (1989), p. 150-63.

Campbell offers a detailed and technical analysis of the complexities of Tongan politics in the period, and the relationship of the three principal titles which made up royal authority, sacred and secular, through the period of civil war. With the advent of Christianity the office of Tuʻi Tonga had been degraded and the old ideology had failed. Campbell concludes that King George Tupou I based his authority not on the title of Tuʻi Kanokupolu but on an ideology of kingship, of submission to authority and of peace brought by the missionary John Thomas and his colleagues.

122   **The diversions of a Prime Minister.**
Basil Thomson.   Edinburgh, London: William Blackwood, 1894.
407p. map.
After the fall and exile of Shirley Baker in 1890 the British High Commissioner for
the Western Pacific sent a member of his staff, Basil Thomson, to sort out the chaos in
Tonga. Though only twenty-nine, he felt little daunted at working with a king now
over ninety. Thomson found the finances in a disastrous state, with £15,000 in liabilities
and arrears of pay, taxes uncollected, few reliable records and only £2,000 in the
Treasury. He found the administration and the courts to be in disorder, and a general
distrust of government. He had himself appointed Assistant Premier, a member of the
Privy Council and a magistrate, and set about reform. Within a year he had achieved
much. He had brought order to the finances, established some harmony between the
warring churches and rewritten Baker's unintelligible code of laws. In this book he
writes of his year in Tonga in a tone part affectionate and part sardonic. He had little
time for Shirley Baker or for most missionaries, too concerned with money, 'burning
with a zeal that drove out all considerations of policy and caution'. He felt the
Constitution of 1875 to be quite inappropriate for Tonga, and believed it to be
inevitable that Tonga would fall under some sort of British control, as did happen after
his departure and the death of King George. His view of what he called 'the brief
turmoil of Tonga and its turgid politics' is hardly dispassionate, but the book is a key
document for the period.

123   **An early public war of words in Pacific politics: Tonga, 1860-1890.**
Ralph D. Barney.   *The Journal of the Polynesian Society*, vol. 83,
no. 3 (1974), p. 349-60.
The first newspaper in Tonga was established in the late 19th century, and Barney
describes a verbal war which involved several of them, and their quite sophisticated use
in influencing public opinion regarding relations between Europeans, who argued for
relief from what they felt were excessive local restrictions, and the government. The
laws of King George Tupou I, advised by Shirley Baker, formalized government to the
extent that taxes became necessary. Barney traces the disputes over this matter which
lasted for thirty years. The government established its first newspaper, *Fetu'u 'o Tonga*
(Star of Tonga) in 1862, but it may only have survived for one issue. Barney describes
the other newspapers which followed, their role in the disputes about the authority of
Shirley Baker and attempts by the government to control press freedom through a newspaper regulation act, a sedition act and libel laws. With the expulsion of Shirley Baker,
the usefulness of the newspapers waned, and they died as quickly as they had been born.
It was not until 1963 that the government established *The Tonga Chronicle* (item
no. 422), but this was not, though so stated, Tonga's first newspaper.

124   **Early Tonga as the explorers saw it, 1616-1810.**
Edwin N. Ferdon.   Tucson, Arizona: The University of Arizona Press,
1987. 339p. map. bibliog.
Ferdon provides a thematic digest of what early European visitors recorded of Tongan
culture, drawing on the writings of explorers and residents, principally Schouten and
Le Maire; Tasman; Wilson; Labillardière; Vason; and, above all, Cook and Mariner.
His themes are: Tongans and their dwellings; social organization and government;
kava; religion; daily life from birth to death; recreation; the quest for food; trade and
transportation; and war and peace. He reproduces illustrations from some of the early
books, and adds a glossary of Tongan terms and a bibliography.

125   **Gender relations in Tonga at the time of contact.**
      Caroline Ralston.   In: *Tongan culture and history.*   Edited by
      Phyllis Herda, Jennifer Terrell, Niel Gunson.   Canberra: The Journal
      of Pacific History, 1990, p. 110-17.

As part of a wider study of gender relations in Polynesia as a whole, Ralston here sets
out what can be discerned about the position of women in relation to men in early
contact Tonga, c. 1770-1810. Most early visitors commented on the respect and high
regard afforded to Tongan women, who could do many things denied to women
elsewhere in Polynesia. She analyses not only the social niceties, as the Europeans
understood them, enjoyed by Tongan women, but also the legitimate secular and spiritual
influence and power they wielded, their social, domestic, economic, political and
spiritual roles. She believes that notions of hierarchy and kinship relation were more
central to Tongans' systems of belief and action than consideration of maleness and
femaleness.

126   **Imperialism, dynasticism, and conversion: Tongan designs on
      'Uvea (Wallis Island), 1835-42.**
      I. C. Campbell.   *The Journal of the Polynesian Society,* vol. 92, no. 2
      (1988), p. 155-67.

The religious transformation of Wallis Island in the 1840s witnessed the French navy
supporting Catholics and Tongan canoes and warriors supporting Protestants. It seems
likely that Tongans were using religious conversion for a political purpose, the
inclusion of Wallis Island in the revival of the ancient Tongan maritime empire.
Campbell describes events from the arrival of Tongan teachers from Niuatoputapu in
1835, and their conflicts with the French. In the end Catholicism triumphed, but
Campbell traces the subtle interplay of factors, many connected with Tongan politics,
which meant that, whichever version of Christianity prevailed, Wallis would lose its
independence.

127   **King George Tupou I of Tonga.**
      Sione Lātūkefu.   In: *Pacific islands portraits.*   Edited by J. W.
      Davidson, Deryck Scarr.   Canberra: Australian National University
      Press, 1970, p. 55-75. map.

Of all the men and women who lived in the islands of the Pacific between the early
19th and the early 20th century, King George I of Tonga, the first Christian monarch
of the united kingdom, is particularly significant. Lātūkefu's succinct paper sketches
the main points of his long and eventful life and reign, which ensured that Tonga,
alone of all the Pacific islands, never lost its independence and its monarchy.

128   **Shirley Baker and the King of Tonga.**
      Noel Rutherford.   Melbourne; London; Wellington; New York:
      Oxford University Press, 1971. 202p. map. bibliog.

King George Tupou I and his Prime Minister for part of his reign, the Methodist
missionary Shirley Baker, between them gave Tonga its Constitution of 1875, ensured
its legitimacy in the eyes of the colonial powers and maintained its independence.
Rutherford tells the remarkable story of the relationship between the two men, of
Baker's uncertain background, his role first as a missionary and then as a political
adviser to the king, his increasing unpopularity, the attempt on his life and his final

fall and deportation by the British government. Whatever the respective strengths of the two men, their achievement laid the foundation for Tonga's constitutional and international position today. Baker's motives may sometimes have been dubious and directed by his own self-interest, but the king came to rely on him, and Rutherford's verdict is that the alliance between the two was 'perhaps moved by humbug and an eye for the main chance but nevertheless productive of lasting benefit to Tonga'.

129 State and economy in Polynesia.
Henri J. M. Claessen. In: *Early state economics.* Edited by
Henri J. M. Claessen, Pieter van de Velde. New Brunswick, New
Jersey; London: Transaction Publishers, 1991, p. 291-325. (Political
and Legal Anthropology Series, vol. 8).

Claessen describes and compares the economic systems of two early states in 18th-century Polynesia, Tahiti and Tonga, setting out each in some detail and drawing on the accounts of early European observers. For Tonga he sets out the socio-political superstructure based on an agrarian economy, the exchange of goods and services and the provision of food and goods by commoners to chiefs on ceremonial occasions. There was also long-distance trade and exchange with Fiji and Samoa. Claessen find that the greater part of the state's income consisted of food, goods and services, which was normally sufficient to enable the rulers to fulfil their obligations. Initially the arrival of Europeans did not change the economic pattern very much. Only after the introduction of firearms and Christianity did Tongan society begin to change fundamentally.

130 The Tonga-Samoa connection 1777-1845.
Niel Gunson. *The Journal of Pacific History,* vol. 25, no. 2 (1990),
p. 176-87.

The links between Tonga and Samoa are ancient. Though the two island groups are distinct in customs and languages, intermarriage brought their two royal families close to each other, and contacts were frequent. Gunson examines the relationship until the coming of Christianity. He argues that, after the expulsion from Samoa of the fifteenth Tu'i Tonga, parts of Samoa remained within the Tongan sphere of influence, with Samoans paying tribute. Tonga became involved in internal Samoan wars and dominated affairs in part of Samoa. Tongan chiefs would only have been involved in Samoan politics when Samoan chiefs related to them by marriage or traditional alliances called on them for support. This, Gunson believes, was not imperialism as the Europeans understood it.

131 The Tu'i Ha'atakalaua and the ancient constitution of Tonga.
I. C. Campbell. *The Journal of Pacific History,* vol. 17, no. 4 (1982),
p. 178-94.

It has been generally held that Tonga's political development before the 19th century was a comparatively smooth and continuous process of evolution. The political order depended on the three major titles of the Tu'i Tonga, Tu'i Ha'atakalaua and Tu'i Kanokupolu. After conversion to Christianity the Tu'i Kanokupolu emerged as king, and the other two titles were absorbed by strategic marriages. In a specialized and detailed paper Campbell suggests that the system was not working and that the political history of Tonga at that time was not as has been represented, but was a game of power politics in which pragmatism and opportunism were seldom absent.

Post-1900

132   **Chief Justices of Tonga 1905-40.**
Elizabeth Wood Ellem.   *The Journal of Pacific History*, vol. 24, no. 1
(1989), p. 21-37.
Wood Ellem describes the Chief Justices appointed to Tonga during the period, their
institutional roles and personal relationships with the monarch and with the representatives of the British government. Theirs was often a lonely role, without the political
or social status that their title suggested. Some were capable and conscientious and
filled the role well, but others found their post difficult and their rulings an unwelcome
challenge to the monarch: in such cases, all confidence in the Chief Justice was
sometimes lost. Furthermore, some Tongans resented the presence of a European in
such a high position. After 1940 a new appointee, Secretary to Government, became
the government's legal adviser, while a chief justice from Fiji would visit Tonga when
required. Since full independence in 1970 the position of Chief Justice has been
allowed to remain unclear. An expatriate serves as judge of the supreme court. Queen
Sālote decided that her eldest son, the present king, should study law in Australia, and
under him the Privy Council, Wood Ellem suggests, acts very much as the traditional
council of an all-powerful chief, as Queen Sālote always felt that it should.

133   **The fire has jumped: eyewitness accounts of the eruption and
evacuation of Niuafo'ou, Tonga.**
Edited by Garth Rogers.   Suva: Institute of Pacific Studies, University
of the South Pacific, 1986. 127p. 4 maps.
The far northern island of Niuafo'ou was devastated by a massive volcanic eruption in
1946. Though no one was killed, the capital village of Angahā was obliterated and the
government decided to evacuate the whole population, first to Tongatapu and then to
'Eua. Not all the islanders complied with this decision, and in 1958 nearly half of
them returned. The story ends with the distribution of 426 tax allotments in 1981. In
this book, eyewitnesses, both Tongans and foreign residents, tell their stories of the
eruption; their accounts are accompanied by some vivid photographs of the eruption
and the damage caused.

134   **The king of Tonga: King Taufa'ahau Tupou IV.**
Nelson Eustis.   Adelaide, Australia: Hobby Investments, 1997. 294p.
3 maps. bibliog.
Despite his title, Eustis begins his book with a sketch of the history of Tonga up to the
accession of the present king in 1966. The chapters on his reign essentially consist of
a chronicle of events: a succession of newspaper reports, with little description of their
context or analysis of their significance. Eustis' theme is the complete commitment
and enormous energy of the king in working for the benefit of the people of Tonga,
and the book is a record of much that he has done.

135 Mālō Tupou: an oral history.
Tupou Posesi Fanua, as told to Lois Wimberg Webster.   Auckland,
New Zealand: Pasifika Press, 1996. 175p. 18 maps. bibliog.

Between 1992 and 1994 Lois Webster tape recorded Tupou Posesi Fanua telling of her
eventful life in Tonga from her birth in 1913 until her wedding in 1934. She was a
self-willed child, whose mother died in the great influenza epidemic of 1918, her
description of which is one of the most vivid sections of the book. She tells of her
childhood, education and young adult life in a Tonga which is now in many ways very
different and yet which is still strongly based on family and on traditions as she
describes them. The book is significant inasmuch as few other Tongans have written
of their own early lives. *Mālō* means thank you: the title was Lois Webster's in thanks
for a personal account of life in Tonga which brings the period described to life.

136 Queen Sālote of Tonga: the story of an era, 1900-1965.
Elizabeth Wood-Ellem.   Auckland, New Zealand: Auckland
University Press, 1999. 376p. 3 maps. bibliog.

Dorothy Crozier provided an immediate evaluation of Queen Sālote in her obituary in
The Journal of the Polynesian Society, vol. 75, no. 4 (1966), p. 401-03. Other evaluations
can be found in general histories of Tonga, written since her death, including the chapter
by Dr Wood-Ellem and her father A. H. Wood in *Friendly Islands: a history of Tonga*
(item no. 92). Now Dr Wood-Ellem has produced what must become the definitive
account of her life and a considered evaluation of her reign, based on twenty years'
research and her own knowledge of Tonga and Tongan society. The richness of detail
will ensure that the book will be, to use her own words, 'a springboard for later work'
both by Tongans and by others who seek to understand the significant achievements of
the Queen's reign. Wood-Ellem draws out in particular Queen Sālote's singular ability
to develop what was distinctive in Tongan culture while establishing the respect with
which Tonga was held in the world. This reflects Crozier's conclusion that her wisdom
as a ruler lay in her critical but generous appreciation of both Tongan and Western
cultures and what each had to contribute to the welfare of her people.

137 Queen Sālote Tupou of Tonga as Tuʻi Fefine.
Elizabeth Wood Ellem.   *The Journal of Pacific History*, vol. 22,
no. 3-4 (1987), p. 209-27.

Queen Sālote's blood rank derived from a chief's descent from the Tuʻi Tonga Fefine,
sister of the male sacred ruler, the Tuʻi Tonga. But in terms of political power, blood
rank is only one qualification for leadership. As Queen Sālote herself said, age, rank,
supporters and ability were the essential qualifications for rulers in Tonga. Her own
relatively low blood rank did not overrule everything, nor did the young age of
eighteen at which she succeeded to her titles. She had ability and supporters and
gained recognition of both chiefs and people that she had the highest moral authority
and presence (*mana*) of any chief and was, in the view of both the people and the
chiefs, the greatest political leader in Tonga's history. Wood Ellem traces her descent
and that of her husband Tungī Mailefihi. Their marriage needed to be strong to hold
the kingdom together and preserve its independence. The only model to follow was
that of the traditional dual leadership of a male chief and his 'eldest sister'. It was thus
appropriate that she should assume the authority that belonged to a sister while he
looked after the land and assumed the lesser political powers of the male chief: though
of senior blood rank, descended from a senior title, he never aspired to her position or
to be her equal. Wood Ellem describes the complexities of her relationships with her

half-brothers and half-sisters in order to minimize any dissent or claim to authority, arranging marriages favourable to the royal house. By the end of her reign, having united all Tonga in one *kāinga* (extended family), she was in effect the 'eldest sister' of all the chiefs, the new Tu'i Fefine upon whose authority the welfare of the entire kingdom depended.

138 Sālote of Tonga and the problem of national unity.
Elizabeth Wood Ellem. *The Journal of Pacific History*, vol. 18, no. 3 (1983), p. 163-82.

Wood Ellem suggests that the attempt by Queen Sālote Tupou III and her consort Tungī to reunite the factions of the Wesleyan Church (item no. 171) was concerned with temporal power rather than church unity, and that the dispute was about whether she and her consort could rule Tonga or might be deposed. In the face of opposition from some prominent chiefs in parliament in 1919 and 1920, they needed to prove that they could unite Tonga under their rule. Although the attempt at reunification of the church factions did not succeed, Queen Sālote emerged from the affair with much credit, and with her position enhanced in the eyes both of the Tongans and the British. Any threat of annexation was now removed and Tonga became increasingly self-governing. Her devoted activity on behalf of the Free Wesleyan Church brought her into close contact with every village in Tonga through its church. By the end of her life it could be said that unlike any other Tongan, she had ruled over a united and peaceful Tonga.

139 Savage Island: an account of a sojourn in Niue and Tonga.
Basil Thomson. London: John Murray, 1902. 234p. map.

Ten years after his time in Tonga recorded in his work *The diversions of a Prime Minister* (item no. 122), Basil Thomson returned in 1900 to negotiate its change in status to a British Protectorate and to obtain the agreement of King George Tupou II. The deal was perhaps one-sided, and Thomson's attitude to the 'little people' of Tonga, though typical of his time, was somewhat condescending; but he was fond of Tonga and wished what he saw as the best for it. His account of the negotiations, and of Tonga at the time, gives a personal insight into an important episode in Tongan history. An appendix on Tongan music is fully utilized by Moyle (item no. 411).

140 'South Seas reminiscences': Mrs. Emma Schober in the Kingdom of Tonga 1902-1921.
Emma Schober. Nuku'alofa: Lupelahi Foundation, 1997. 69p.

There are few first-hand accounts of the early days of the sizeable German community in Tonga, which consisted mainly of traders who arrived in the latter part of the 19th century, many of whose descendants live in Tonga today. There are also few accounts of early Tonga by women. Emma Blase sailed from Germany in 1902 to marry Ludwig Schober. They first lived in Vava'u, where they were married in 1903, and moved to Nuku'alofa in 1905. In both places she describes the domestic and social life of the German community and, even though she came to love Tonga, she seems to observe Tongans, and even other Europeans, from a distance. During the First World War all German businesses were closed and Schober and her husband were deprived of all news from Germany. In 1921 they returned to Germany, regretfully but for the sake of their children's education. She died in 1959 and her youngest son passed the manuscript journal to a German now living in Tonga, Kurt Düring, to translate and publish. Born and raised in imperial Germany, Schober absorbed its values and prejudices, but her journal illuminates the everyday life of the Germans in Tonga and also notes major events in Tonga at that time, such as the marriage and then the death of King George II and the accession of Queen Sālote. It is illustrated with many evocative period photographs.

141 Tonga ma'a Tonga kautaha: a proto-co-operative in Tonga.

Noel Rutherford. *The Journal of Pacific History*, vol. 16, no. 1 (1981), p. 20-41.

'The Tonga for the Tongans Trading Association' was founded in 1909 by a Scots trader in Tonga to prevent the commercial exploitation of Tongan copra growers by European middle men who controlled the market, though his motives were as much to make his fortune as to increase income for Tongans. Its rapid growth incurred the opposition of the traders who took him to court over alleged irregularities in its finances. On appeal the instigator of the scheme was cleared, but in the process the incident became more important for its political than its economic significance. The declaration of the British protectorate in 1900, and the supplementary agreement of 1905, gave the British consul important rights over the king and his government, which were resented by many Tongans. The insensitive and arrogant consul at this time attempted to force his will upon King George Tupou II, but the king stood firm, and the British High Commissioner in Fiji had to admit at the end that the consul had the right only to advise, not to coerce, and that the Tongan Constitution took precedence over the British treaty. 'In one stroke a decade of British encroachment on Tongan independence was cancelled', concludes Rutherford. It was a small but significant moment in Tongan history.

142 The *Tonga ma'a Tonga kautaha*: a watershed in British-Tongan relations.

Penny Lavaka. *Pacific Studies*, vol. 4, no. 2 (1981), p. 142-63.

Lavaka tells much the same story of this crucial event in Tongan history as does Rutherford in his paper published in the same year (item no. 141). She draws the same conclusion: that the king was judged to have the right to rule in his own kingdom, and that the British Agent should be consulted on important issues, but his advice need not be followed; his authority was hereafter carefully circumscribed.

143 The United States occupation of Tonga, 1942-1945: the social and economic impact.

Charles J. Weeks. *Pacific Historical Review*, vol. LVI, no. 3 (1987), p. 399-426.

When US forces entered Tonga in 1942 many residents were worried about their social and cultural impact. By the time they left in 1945 Tonga's social heritage remained relatively intact, but Tongans had been suddenly exposed to the goods and values of an industrialized society, and the episode proved a turning point in the history of Tonga as a nation. 7,800 soldiers and 862 sailors formed the first contingent, and during the first phase, to March 1943, when there was a real threat of Japanese invasion, the discipline and morale of the American troops remained high. Weeks describes the initial relationship of mutual respect with Queen Sālote: the troops built and improved roads, instituted public health measures and built a large field hospital, all to the benefit of Tongans. Subsequently, when Tonga became, militarily, an isolated backwater, relations became quite strained. But the influx of large sums of money increased prices and wages, and memories of plenty remained afterwards. For the first time large quantities of beer and cigarettes became available, but prostitution and venereal disease were also introduced, and there seemed to be a general decline in honesty. Tongan laws were flagrantly ignored by Americans trying to recover stolen goods. The occupation, Weeks concludes, did not have a fatal impact on Tongan society, but it did plant the seeds for political and economic change. Tonga abruptly became aware of the world outside, and could no longer remain isolated.

Language

144 Bibliography of Oceanic linguistics.
H. R. Kleineberger.   London; New York; Toronto: Oxford University
Press, 1957. 143p. (London Oriental Bibliographies, volume I).

The earliest list of Tongan words was compiled by Le Maire on his visit to
Niuatoputapu and Tafahi in 1616 (see item no. 157). A briefer list was published in
the account of Cook's third voyage (1776-80) (item no. 50). Neither of these is listed
by Kleineberger. The earliest of the twenty items on Tongan cited in his bibliography
dates from 1802 (written by Labillardière, not La Billardière as he cites it, and the date
for Labillardière's first edition should be 1800). Kleineberger includes language
descriptions in the accounts of explorers and early settlers, and language materials
produced by missionaries. Apart from the earliest omissions noted above, the listing is
comprehensive up to the date of writing in 1955.

**145 Intensive course in Tongan: with numerous supplementary
materials, grammatical notes and glossary.**
Eric B. Shumway.   Honolulu, Hawai'i: University of Hawai'i Press,
1971. 723p. (PALI Language Texts: Polynesia).

Based on material prepared for Peace Corps volunteers in Tonga, this comprehensive
course consists of 130 lessons, conversational materials, Tongan proverbs and songs,
specialized word lists and a glossary. These provide a systematic oral-aural approach
to the study of the grammar and phonology of the language, to enable the student to
speak and understand Tongan as it is currently spoken. Each lesson provides brief and
realistic dialogues, explanatory grammatical notes and intensive drills.

146 An introduction to the Tongan language.
Edgar Tu'inukuafe.   Auckland, New Zealand: Pacific Islanders'
Educational Resource Centre, 1979. 68p. map.

This brief introductory course is arranged by theme and function, presenting those
aspects of the language which a learner will find of practical value and later be able to

Language

develop. The sixteen chapters begin with greetings and also cover home activities; seasons and time; the weather; prices; travel; and interviewing. They also provide an introduction to grammar.

147 **The linguistic position of Niuafoʻou.**
T. S. Dye. *The Journal of the Polynesian Society*, vol. 89, no. 3 (1980), p. 349-57.

Earlier scholars disagreed over how far the language of Niuafoʻou was Tongan. Through a detailed analysis of the phonology and morphology Dye concludes that it is related to languages of the Samoan outlier group, overlaid with extensive recent Tongan borrowings, and that Tongan will soon replace it.

148 **On the origin of the Tongan definitive accent.**
Ross Clark. *The Journal of the Polynesian Society*, vol. 83, no. 1 (1974), p. 103-08.

In a short note Clark examines the stress shift in the definitive accent in Tongan, and suggests an explanation of its historical origins, from a Proto-Polynesian demonstrative system, through assimilation which led to a consequent shifting of stress.

149 **Pacific languages: an introduction.**
John Lynch. Honolulu, Hawaiʻi: University of Hawaiʻi Press, 1998. 359p. 16 maps. bibliog.

The author says that he wrote this book in response to many people who asked him to recommend 'a good general book on the languages of the Pacific' aimed at those who have not studied linguistics in depth. He tries to steer a course between being too simplistic and too technical, in covering the interrelationship and connections between over 1,400 languages, their history and current status, and the relationship between language, culture and social organization. He describes their geographical distribution and history, their phonological and grammatical structure and their social and cultural context. The book is a useful and up-to-date introduction to the groups of languages which include Tongan, and relates some of its features to those of its neighbours.

150 **Simple sentences in Tongan.**
Claude Tchekhoff. Canberra: Department of Linguistics, Research School of Pacific Studies, The Australian National University, 1981. 95p. bibliog. (Pacific Linguistics, series B, no. 81).

Tchekhoff is concerned with basic and near-basic sentence structure in the language of the ordinary people of Tonga (as opposed to royalty or nobility). She classifies two types of morphemes and examines the way in which lexical units are made up, and how they depend on function markers for the part they play in the sentence. Her description is set out in the terminology of academic linguistics: this is not a language-teaching manual but a technical analysis.

151 A simplified dictionary of modern Tongan.
Edgar Tu'inukuafe.   Auckland, New Zealand: Polynesian Press, 1992.
278p.

Tu'inukuafe's dictionary is far shorter than Churchward's (item no. 154), comprising about 10,000 entries in each language, and giving single-word equivalents, but it is an accessible introductory listing and the first to be compiled by a Tongan. It includes guides to pronunciation and grammar. Tu'inukuafe points out how much the language has changed since Churchward wrote his grammar (item no. 155) and how its analysis needs to be liberated from European grammatical constructions. It is up to date on modern technical vocabulary, even though Tongan often simply uses the English word in its Tongan form: 'komipiuta' for computer, 'ovani maikoloueivi' for microwave oven.

152 Supplementary Tongan vocabulary.
E. E. V. Collocott.   *The Journal of the Polynesian Society*, vol. 34 (1925), no. 134, p. 146-69; no. 135, p. 193-213.

Collocott prints a list of some 900 Tongan words to supplement Baker's dictionary of 1897, based on that of Rabone in 1845. These were words which Collocott encountered in conversation and in reading Tongan poems and tales. Much of the material was originally collected by Dr Moulton, his predecessor as teacher and missionary. The general list is followed by words for measuring and counting tapa cloth, fish and yams, some proverbial expressions (to supplement item no. 379) and words for phases of the moon (to supplement item no. 371). What Collocott calls 'the highly desirable task of compiling a satisfactory and adequate dictionary of the Tongan language' had to wait a further thirty-five years, for the publication of Churchward's dictionary (item no. 154).

153 Tongan definitive accent.
Iovanna D. Condax.   *The Journal of the Polynesian Society*, vol. 98, no. 4 (1989), p. 425-50.

Definitive accent in Tonga is a stress pattern found in nouns with definite references, that is nouns preceded by a definitive article or other such marker. Syllables affected by the definitive accent are unusual and phonetically unlike other syllables. Condax takes further the work by Clark (item no. 148) and other writers on Tongan, though she is more concerned with describing present-day phenomena than with seeking historical origins. She provides detailed phonetic measurements of vowel duration which add detail to and support earlier writers' findings, through a technical analysis of recordings of native speakers. An appendix provides the Tongan text recorded, with English translation. Nine figures illustrate the phonetic analysis.

154 Tongan dictionary (Tongan-English and English-Tongan).
C. Maxwell Churchward.   London: Oxford University Press, 1959.
836p.

Churchward was appointed by the Government of Tonga in 1946 to prepare a grammar and dictionary of the Tongan language. Although he used earlier vocabularies established by Shirley Baker and others, his was an entirely new dictionary. The meaning and usage of many of the over 20,000 words in the Tongan-English section are illustrated with examples. The English-Tongan section serves as an index to it. Like his *Tongan grammar* (see item no. 155), this remains the definitive work, though it has to be supplemented for modern technical vocabulary.

155　Tongan grammar.

C. Maxwell Churchward.　London; New York; Toronto: Oxford University Press, 1953. 305p.

This grammar sets out to describe the structure of the Tongan language for the English reader: parts of speech; articles; tenses and verbs; nouns and pronouns; adjectives and adverbs; and the language appropriate for the social level of the person addressed. The first comprehensive grammar of Tongan using formal Western terminology, it remains unsurpassed although written nearly fifty years ago.

156　Tongan speech levels: practice and talk about practice in the cultural construction of social hierarchy.

Susan U. Philips.　In: *Currents in Pacific linguistics: papers on Austronesian languages and ethnolinguistics in honour of George W. Grace.*　Edited by Robert Blust.　Canberra: Department of Linguistics, Research School of Pacific Studies, The Australian National University, 1991, p. 369-82. (Pacific Linguistics, series C, no. 117).

Tongans use three different terms to refer to the same actions of commoners, nobles and the king, though in practice words for both kingly and noble actions are extended to other high-status social categories. Philips sets out examples from other writers on Tongan and notes that Tongans learn these different terms from government textbooks in high school. She sets out the standard view of the three levels, and their evolution as Tonga developed into a Western-style nation state in the 19th century. However, she finds from transcripts of spoken Tongan that in actual practice the use of the three levels suggests a far less clear-cut and more complex construction of social hierarchy. She provides examples from newspapers, prayers in church, village meetings and the law courts and suggests that the use of noble terms is very fluid, though royal terms are restricted.

157　The vocabularies of Jacob le Maire.

R. A. Kern.　*Acta Orientalia*, vol. XX, part 3-4 (1948), p. 216-37.

The crew of the Dutch ship *Eendracht*, in the course of a voyage to attempt to find Terra Australis, discovered Niuatoputapu and Tafahi and stayed there for three days, 11-13 May 1616. The ship's commander le Maire compiled a vocabulary of 118 words which Kern reprints in full with original Dutch and modern English translation. Kern relates the language to Samoan rather than to Tongan. Be that as it may, this is the earliest vocabulary of any language spoken in the present Kingdom of Tonga.

Religion

158 Additional wooden images from Tonga.
Te Rangi Hiroa. *The Journal of the Polynesian Society*, vol. 46, no. 182 (1937), p. 74-82.

As a supplement to his earlier paper (item no. 165), Hiroa describes and illustrates three wooden and one ivory image from a private collection, three standing and one sitting. He relates them to similar figures in other collections. Two of them, according to their labels, seem to have been god images cut down by Taufa'ahau (later King George Tupou I) on embracing Christianity in 1830.

159 After the missionaries came: denominational diversity in the Tonga islands.
Shulamit R. Decktor Korn. In: *Mission, church and sect in Oceania.* Edited by James A. Boutilier, Daniel T. Hughes, Sharon W. Tiffany. Ann Arbor, Michigan: The University of Michigan Press, 1978, p. 395-422. (Association for Social Anthropology in Oceania Monograph, no. 6).

Korn is concerned to examine the place of religion in contemporary Tongan society, the multiplicity of denominations, and the implications for the country. Nineteen denominations were recorded in the 1966 census, although only seven were significant, and only the Free Wesleyan Church has members throughout all the island groups. She sets out the affiliation figures for her survey village in Tongatapu, where the Free Wesleyans dominate (45.7 per cent), followed by the Mormons (18.6 per cent). Everyone nominally belongs to some denomination and most attend church at least once a week. Status in a community depends on standing in a congregation. Free Wesleyans may become lay preachers and act as hosts at congregational feasts – both activities enhance status. Members of different denominations largely accept but do not interact with each other; doctrinal differences are seldom discussed and are considered unimportant. Members of one family or kin group may belong to different denominations and thus attend each other's activities without compromising their affiliation. People change denominations quite readily and marry across denominational lines. Korn concludes that there are so many denominations because there are few pre-scriptions and prohibitions in Tongan society. In most matters Tongans have a range of alternatives and can make free choices. Tongans are attracted to new denominations because they make new stratagems possible. 'Missionization' is a dynamic process in which local people are agents and manipulators.

160 **The emergence of the Maamafo'ou movement from the Free Wesleyan Church of Tonga.**
Makisi Finau. In: *Island churches: challenge and change.* Edited by Charles W. Forman. Suva: Institute of Pacific Studies of the University of the South Pacific, 1992, p. 141-205. 9 maps. bibliog.

The most recent of the separations from the original Wesleyan church of Tonga led to the formation of the body which came to be known as the Tokaikolo ('Christ shall be honoured in our midst') Christian Fellowship, and it was the first, Finau suggests, which took place for devotional and spiritual rather than political reasons. The founder, the Rev. Senituli Koloi, was a Free Wesleyan minister who in the 1970s came to believe that personal holiness was more important than the institutional church, and that undue honour was given to ministers, to Tongan tradition and to the king. In 1978 he led a breakaway from the Free Wesleyan Church which soon gathered 3,000 members, including over 100 lay preachers in Tongatapu alone. Originally known as the Maamafo'ou Fellowship, they adopted the name Tokaikolo Fellowship in 1979. In 1980 he died, but the fellowship continues. By 1985 the Free Wesleyan Church was admitting that the reason why people were leaving was spiritual hunger. Finau tells the story largely from personal interviews with many of the people involved. He concludes that the Free Wesleyan Church should re-read the history of John Wesley and encourage class meetings and personal devotion. His story reveals something of both the strengths and weaknesses of the churches of Tonga.

161 *Fakakakato*: **symbols in a Pacific context.**
Winston Halapua. *The Pacific Journal of Theology*, series II, no. 20 (1998), p. 21-32.

Halapua asks to what extent the dominant presentation of theology from a Western context shows a lack of appreciation of the values which define people in the Pacific islands. Does the study of theology in the islands entail dehumanization of the islands' people? He surveys earlier work on the contextualization of theology in the way of life of people in the Pacific, and examines the Tongan word *fakakakato*, a completion of an obligation, as a holistic way of understanding symbols in the Pacific. It cements and completes all activities, as expressed in the Pacific communal life, for instance in the kava ceremony, which he relates in its totality to the Eucharist. He also considers the Tongan concept of *ifonga*, reconciliation. He sees this as unveiling a major weakness in the dualist approach which dominates Western theology, and sees even the sharing of remittances as an expression of the Pacific system of reciprocity.

162 **Introducing women's theology in a theological education curriculum: a Tongan and Methodist context.**
Lynette Mo'unga Fuka. *The Pacific Journal of Theology*, series II, no. 20 (1998), p. 55-62.

The author, a probationary minister in the Free Wesleyan Church in Tonga, examines the inclusion of women's perspectives in theology, with reference to political-economic, socio-cultural, educational and theological issues. She outlines the position of women in Tonga, equal with men in law but not always in practice, though with authority over their own kin. She describes the way in which the experience of Tongan women is being incorporated into the curriculum of the Sia'atoutai Theological College, which is the first establishment in the Pacific to do this.

163 **Inventing the Mormon Tongan family.**
Tamar Gordon. In: *Christianity in Oceania: ethnographic perspectives.* Edited by John Barker. Lanham, Maryland; New York; London: University Press of America, 1990, p. 197-219. (ASAO Monograph, no. 12).

Gordon sees Tongan Mormonism not as a wholesale adaptation of an imposed model, but as a religious idiom through which Westernization takes place, but using Tongan logic, on Tongan terms. It embodies Tongans' negotiation of their own religious identity. Opportunities for enhanced social status and economic advancement in Mormon circles depend on embracing certain idealized family structures and practices. The Mormon model of family life, with husband and wife forming an exclusive couple and decision-making unit for the nuclear family, stands in opposition to the mainstream Tongan Christian model which emphasizes bonds of obligation and resource-sharing among extended kindred and respect for hierarchical authority. Gordon examines how Tongan Mormons reconcile their differences within 'the Tongan way'. She outlines the history of the Mormons in Tonga, their organization, their role as one of the largest employers in Tonga, and the opportunities offered in employment overseas and in creating a self-sufficient class system in Tonga. She sets out the very different Mormon model of the family, particularly in the brother-sister relationship and in their concept of 'freedom to choose', and gives examples from her own surveys of how compromise and acculturation work in practice. She finds that Tongan Mormons are able to maintain the two systems as separate frames of reference, and to view one system as the ideal expression of the other, and that Tongan culture continues to be selectively permeable to the adoption of Western ideas. They see their church as hastening the inevitable advancement of Tonga as a whole, with themselves in the vanguard.

164 **The island churches of the South Pacific: emergence in the twentieth century.**
Charles W. Forman. Maryknoll, New York: Orbis Books, 1982. 285p. map. bibliog. (American Society of Missiology Series, no. 5).

This is a broad general survey of the history and present state of the churches of the South Pacific. The story of their origins is seen as one of the great missionary successes of the time. Forman takes their early history country by country, from initial dependence to subsequent independence, in which Tonga was the pioneer. For more recent times he follows themes: the role of the churches in education and medicine; the impact of emigration and tourism; urbanization; work with young people and women; and the churches' role in national and economic development. In all of these, Tonga features prominently. At the time of writing, Forman believed that the Pacific islands were in all probability the most solidly Christian part of the world. Since then, the pluralism and secularization which he observed have become stronger and the influence and centrality of the mainstream churches are probably not what they were.

165 Material representations of Tongan and Samoan gods.

Te Rangi Hiroa. *The Journal of the Polynesian Society*, vol. 44, no. 173 (1935), p. 48-53; vol. 44, no. 174 (1935), p. 85-96; vol. 44, no. 175 (1935), p. 153-62.

The author sets out in a three-part paper the fundamentals of Tongan and Samoan religion, in which the gods were localized and intangible; the office of priest was usually hereditary, the priest being a medium through whom the god could make known his commands. Places where religious observances were carried out were of three types: stone structures, wooden structures and undefined spaces. Gods, though immaterial, were associated with certain visible material forms, whose movements conveyed the god's message. As a further development, the god was regarded as actually present in the living representative. Thus some species were taboo: Hiroa lists thirty-one animate forms – mammals, birds, fish and reptiles – of which this was true. He then lists seventeen inanimate representations, both natural (such as stones, shells and teeth) and manufactured (such as mats and weapons). In addition, there were figurative representations, many of which were destroyed at the time of conversion. Hiroa describes and illustrates five surviving examples from museums and collections, in wood and ivory. The third part of the paper is mostly concerned with images from elsewhere in the Pacific. He concludes that carving was less diversified in Tonga and Samoa than in eastern Polynesia.

166 Notes on Tongan religion.

E. E. V. Collocott. *The Journal of the Polynesian Society*, vol. 30, no. 119 (1921), p. 152-63; vol. 30, no. 120 (1921), p. 227-40.

The Tongans had an elaborate theogony, narrating the birth of the great gods of sky, earth, sea and underworld who were in their turn responsible for the creation of Tonga and the adjacent islands which formed the known world. Collocott tells the stories of their exploits and describes the ways in which they were worshipped and their powers sought. Few Tongans, by the 1920s, were able to provide much reliable information, but Collocott sets out such data as he was able to obtain on individual gods, their manifestations, locations and powers. The strength of the links with the religion of Fiji is noted.

167 The outrigger of the canoe: Tongan women missionaries to Melanesia.

Fangailupe Tu'ineau. *The Pacific Journal of Theology*, series II, no. 20 (1998), p. 12-20.

The wives of missionaries were rarely mentioned in letters and reports. In this paper, a summary of an MTh thesis, the author notes the comment of the wife of one missionary, 'I am the outrigger of the canoe; where the canoe goes I go'. The Tongan church preferred to send married couples rather than single men, but many of the wives felt their own strong sense of calling. Tu'ineau describes their preparation and departure, their work with their husbands, the risks they faced, and some of their successes and failures. An appendix lists those who went to Papua New Guinea and the Solomon Islands from 1891 to 1986.

168 Seeds of the Word: Tongan culture and Christian faith.

Cliff Wright. Vila: Pacific Churches Research Centre, 1979. 43p.

This brief booklet, the report of a workshop, represents a thoughtful attempt by Christians of all denominations to relate the continuing power of traditional beliefs and practices to their Christian faith. Participants examined some of the fundamental elements of Tongan myths and culture, such as kava, and concluded that God was at work before the arrival of the missionaries, and that in a profound sense Christ is the fulfiller of the culture. Both the approach and the conclusion would have shocked the early Protestant missionaries who saw traditional culture as the antithesis of the Christian gospel. The participants may at times have over-stretched themselves in seeking to identify traditional beliefs with Christianity, but the approach is illuminating.

169 They loved her too much: interpreting spirit possession in Tonga.

Tamar Gordon. In: *Spirits in culture, history and mind.* Edited by Jeannette Marie Mageo, Alan Howard. New York; London: Routledge, 1996, p. 55-74.

'Possession by spirits is a commonplace reality among modern-day Tongans, many of whom can expect, at one or more times in their lives, to be catapulted into this "other" state', writes Gordon. In her own two years in Tonga she heard much talk about spirit possession and witnessed cases of it. Tongans say that the dead are even more outraged than the living by social transgressions, and people are often possessed by spirits who 'love them too much'. She considers this phenomenon in the context of data from elsewhere and the records of pre-European Tonga noted by Mariner as well as in its present-day social context. In modern Christian Tonga spirit possession persists as a parallel though not contradictory belief system. Tongans can keep them separate and can assert that neither prayer nor Western medicine can address the true status of an attack. Gordon notes the stresses undergone particularly by women (who suffer attacks more than men) due to the obligatory relations of respect and reciprocity governed by the unequal rules and statuses from father's and mother's side; she also emphasizes the power of anger as well as of love. She narrates and analyses three possessions, in one of which she was personally involved, and finds that possession is of a piece with the conflicts and changes of social life. The phenomenon itself is not, and presumably cannot be, explained.

170 Tongan evangelism: a Wesleyan mode of evangelism from the South Pacific.

Tevita Maliepo Siuhengalu. *The Pacific Journal of Theology*, series II, no. 20 (1998), p. 74-84.

The author outlines the work of the early Wesleyan missionaries to Tonga, noting that they had little training in theology and none in anthropology but that they were proud of the English heritage and expression of Christianity, believing it to be the model to follow. Tonga was swept into Christianity in little more than five years and the old religion collapsed almost completely. But consolidation did not always follow conversion, and evangelism came for many to be a low priority. Siuhengalu reflects on the implications of this for the church in Tonga today and notes that many new converts in recent years have been attracted to the Pentecostal Churches. He sees many signs of new life in the Wesleyan Church in Tonga, but also new challenges, and the need to seek a mode of evangelization that embraces the evolving culture of Tonga.

171 **Tonga's tortured venture in church unity.**
     Charles W. Forman. *The Journal of Pacific History*, vol. 13, no. 1 (1978), p. 3-21.

The church history of Tonga is the most turbulent of all the Pacific islands, as the enormous variety of churches there today bears witness. Only in Tonga did church disputes lead to warfare and deportation. This paper explains something of the background to the present situation. The moves by King George Tupou I and his Prime Minister, Shirley Baker, to give the Wesleyan Church in Tonga its independence led to two churches, the Free and the Wesleyan, both Methodist in background and, in 1924, still with Europeans as presidents. Forman tells how, in that year, the young Queen Sālote, who belonged to the Free Church but whose husband was a Wesleyan, attempted to bring the leaders of the two churches together, with some initial success. But harmony did not last in the face of vested interests and a strong sense of independence. The Queen had to depose the Free Church president from office, and court cases and appeals followed. A third church even emerged, the Church of Tonga. Isolation was seen by some as a matter of principle, based on a fear of foreign control. Only in 1973, after the era of foreign church presidents was over and when all the things that the 1924 rebels had objected to had disappeared, was the Tonga Council of Churches formed; at that point the churches began to work together in matters such as theological education. Yet the churches still remain separate, different in style and in ethos if not in basic doctrine. Forman believes that it was political factors and nationalist feelings which were responsible for the failure of the 1924 scheme, and such factors' legacy still determines the church scene in Tonga today.

172 **Winds of change: rapidly growing religious groups in the Pacific islands.**
     Manfred Ernst.   Suva: Pacific Conference of Churches, 1994. 357p.
     8 maps. bibliog.

Membership in Tonga of what Ernst defines as historic mainline churches declined from 90.1 per cent in 1966 to 68.1 per cent in 1992, while that of new religious groups (principally Assemblies of God, Mormons, Seventh-Day Adventists, Jehovah's Witnesses and Baha'i) increased from 9.7 per cent to 29.5 per cent in the same period. The decline in the first group and the rise in the second is sharper than in any other country in the region. Ernst's comprehensive survey of the invasion of new religious movements in the Pacific is based both on written records and his own extensive surveys. In Part I he gives facts and figures on the more than forty new religious groups and evangelical-fundamentalist para-church organizations, with numbers of ministers, adherents and churches. Part II contains six detailed case-studies, of which Tonga is one. In Part III Ernst assesses the growth and impact of the new religious groups and reflects on the reasons for their success. He relates this both to broader socio-economic and political factors such as urbanization, and to specifically ecclesiastical factors such as patterns of ministry, style of worship, financial resources, better schools, and a different approach to the relationship between individual faith and the world. The book contains a wealth of information, with many tables and graphs.

Society

173 **Alternative social structures and the limits of hierarchy in the modern kingdom of Tonga.**
George E. Marcus. *Bijdragen tot de Taal-, Land- en Volkenkunde*, vol. 131, no. 1 (1975), p. 34-66.

In the light of classical distinctions concerning social differentiation between class, status and power, this paper is primarily concerned with stratification by status, specified in cultural ideologies of rank. Marcus examines the extent to which routine everyday interpersonal relations within a low status group or class in a highly stratified society are in fact permeated by the same concerns with status differentiation or rank determination that characterize social relations between status groups and classes. At the village level researchers have not found a predominantly hierarchical quality in the everyday interactions among commoners, and Marcus's own research confirms this. Principles of rank and status differentiation are important in some situations but not in others, and he identifies two alternative structural domains, the village community and the dispersed bilateral kin set. Marcus discusses the major changes that have occurred in Tongan society, the structure of the family estate and the village in which he lived, and the integration of these alternative social structures in terms of an individual's strategies for managing his varying social situations.

174 **The atomization of Tongan society.**
Keith L. Morton. *Pacific Studies*, vol. 10, no. 2 (1987), p. 47-72.

Morton observes profound changes in the structure of Tongan society in the last few decades. He examines writings on Tongan society since the 1940s and notes weakening social relations and the growth of the nuclear family as the major structural unit, defined as 'atomization'. He suggests that the primary cause of this is the change in the social relations of production, specifically the adoption of individualized land tenure, which has established the economic conditions necessary for independent nuclear-family households by replacing traditional social relations in the production process. He sets out the history of the change, against the background of traditional Tongan society, and provides a case-study of a village, analysing households and production, in which kinship has a limited and peripheral role. He finds that most economic transactions occurred in the course of normal daily life, and only very few during ceremonial events. He concludes that Tongan local organization today is not a chaotic mixture of traditional and Western culture but is a result of the way in which Tonga has responded to its peripheral status in broader political and economic systems.

175   Becoming Tongan: an ethnography of childhood.

Helen Morton.   Honolulu, Hawai'i: University of Hawai'i Press, 1996. 343p. 2 maps. bibliog.

Helen Morton, an Australian anthropologist, married a Tongan; she later returned to Tonga with their young son, and had a daughter there. She lived in a village on Tongatapu and learnt to speak Tongan fluently. She was thus ideally qualified to write about the process of becoming Tongan, and the social processes whereby the Tongan child acquires what are seen as the ideal characteristics as it grows to adulthood, moving from being *vale* (ignorant, socially incompetent) to being *poto* (clever, socially competent, understanding hierarchical relations and values such as obedience, respect and submission to authority). Her study spans the period from before birth to late adolescence, situating children within the wider social context in which they live. She describes attitudes to reproduction, pregnancy and childbirth; the major events of childhood; Tongan notions of personhood and its associated cultural values; and the ways in which children absorb these values in the home, at school and at play. She is particularly concerned with, and troubled by, physical punishment, which sometimes seems violent and cruel and yet which is claimed to be given with love and for the child's benefit. She considers how children learn to manage their emotions, particularly anger and humour. She links all of this to current debates about political reform and what many perceive as a loss of culture among children today. She concludes by wondering how future generations will construct a Tongan identity, how they will become Tongan.

176   Blood and garland: duality in Tongan history.

Aletta Biersack.   In: *Tongan culture and history.*   Edited by Phyllis Herda, Jennifer Terrell, Niel Gunson.   Canberra: The Journal of Pacific History, 1990, p. 46-58.

Biersack observes the difficulty in discovering well-defined structures in the Tongan ranking system. The title system is said to be immutable, yet Tongans acknowledge that social and political dynamics are as crucial as structural statics. Thus she explores the distinction between the rank of a title or 'garland' and the rank of a person or 'blood'. Others who have studied Tongan social structures have noted the distinction between a form of ranking that operates within kinship networks and one that pertains to groups of political titles, the distinction between rank and authority. Ranking principles operate in different contexts and at different levels. Biersack notes the factors determining personal rank, the mother's blood carrying more weight than the father's, and titles which are associated with men. She examines duality in the Tu'i Tonga origin myths and relates this to the kava ceremony, a complex symbol. She discusses the place of marriage in conferring status and in developing political capital, the most spectacular example being Taufa'āhau, founder of the current dynasty as King George Tupou I. She concludes that the structure has no prescriptive rules: 'What actors take up is not the system as such but the possibilities the system opens up'.

177 **Brother/sister and gender relations in ancient and modern Tonga.**
Futa Helu. *Journal de la Société des Océanistes*, nos. 100-01 (1995),
p. 191-200.

Helu presents, as a philosopher rather than as an anthropologist, an argument concerning
the brother/sister opposition, which he believes has been misunderstood because of
inadequate translations and the lack of a word for the nuclear family before European
contact. European writers have failed to bring out the prime fact of Tongan society,
that social customs are all based on group interests and must be seen through the eyes
of socio-political advantage. All Tongan kinship terms are of this kind and the
brother/sister rules must be grounded in this rather than in sexual or biological interests.
He contests those anthropologists who have seen the power of the sister as mystical;
this, he argues, is an effect of her role rather than a cause of it. He examines the division
of labour in Tongan history, the role of women in producing articles of traditional
wealth while men produced utilitarian objects, and the way in which Tongan society
developed, noting women who exemplify how sisters become a principal ladder on
which their tribes ascended in society. He sees Christian influence and the forces of
modernization as attenuating the brother/sister relationship and women as moving out
of their traditional roles, with Queen Sālote epitomizing the abolition of the functional
segregation of men and women. The phenomenon of the working couple is strengthening
the emerging middle class.

178 **Change in rank and status in the Polynesian kingdom of Tonga.**
Charles F. Urbanowicz. In: *Political anthropology: the state of the
art.* Edited by S. Lee Seaton, Henri J. M. Claessen. The Hague,
Paris; New York: Mouton, 1979, p. 225-42.

Neither research nor memory may give an accurate picture of pre-contact Tonga.
Urbanowicz notes this as he outlines the four major titles of traditional Tonga, the
three Tu'i titles and the Tamaha, their respective roles, and the changes resulting from
European contact. He examines the development of the concept of *'eiki* (chief),
signifying noble birth but not always power, and the importance of consensus and
flexibility through which power is held. Rank was possessed through birth: status
could be achieved through marriage or skill in leadership or war. Urbanowicz shows
the confusion of European observers who expected to find a coherent system
and could not make sense of the complexity which they found. He sees the early
missionaries as setting Tongan against Tongan to achieve their ends, and destroying
aboriginal Tongan culture in the process. In a following comment Claessen suggests
that Urbanowicz may place too much reliance on 19th-century missionaries as
trustworthy informants.

179 **Changing roles for Tonga's women.**
Meleseini Faletau. *Pacific Perspective*, vol. 11, no. 2 (1983),
p. 45-55.

The author surveyed the role and work of women in nineteen villages in Tongatapu,
Ha'apai and Vava'u. She sets out the roles of unmarried daughters, wives and mothers,
grandmothers and sisters in household activities, the production of handicrafts and
agriculture. She found that most women accepted and enjoyed their work and that 88
per cent of husbands help their wives in household activities, but when men do not
help or are overseas, then women often assume the role of both wife and head of family.
67 per cent of women claim to organize family affairs and keep the family income.
The problems which they face include poor housing and, particularly, a poor water

supply. Many male heads do not earn an adequate income and 72 per cent of women help to generate income, mostly through handicrafts. Faletau concludes that their main needs are opportunities for employment, informal education and improved water supplies. The results of the survey are set out in eleven tables.

180 **Clothes in tradition: the *ta'ovala* and *kiekie* as social text and aesthetic markers of custom and identity in comtemporary Tongan society.**
Jehanne Teilhet-Fisk. *Pacific Arts*, Part I, no. 5 (1992), p. 44-52; Part II, no. 6 (1992), p. 40-65.
Distinctive to Tonga is the wearing of a waist garment as an institutionalized form of clothing over an individualized dress. These garments are of many types. Teilhet-Fisk asks why Tongans continue to wear this form of clothing, which serves no practical purpose. By examining the motives that govern their manufacture, the materials that they are made of, when they are worn and their social context, she concludes that they are worn in an emblematic fashion that broadcasts messages which denote respect for societal rank, social status and national identity. She notes the pressure on Tongans in the 19th century to dress in the European way, the decline in the wearing of waist mats by the chiefly class until the 1950s, when Queen Sālote encouraged the wearing of traditional garments as inspiring a collective sense of allegiance to and pride in Tonga. Teilhet-Fisk describes the weaving of mats and their use to form a *ta'ovala*, and the more recent development of the *kiekie*, the value set on mats and the occasions on which they must be worn. She considers this revival of traditional dress in relation to movements towards democracy, and concludes by noting that Tongans perceive the wearing of the *ta'ovala* as a way of binding their country round them.

181 **Dealing with the dark side in the ethnography of childhood: child punishment in Tonga.**
Helen Kavapalu. *Oceania*, vol. 63, no. 4 (1993), p. 313-29.
In this paper Kavapalu (later Morton) sets out her first ideas about the harsh child punishment which she observed in Tonga, and which later developed into her book *Becoming Tongan* (item no. 175). She records her own observations, discusses the concepts and goals of socialization in Tonga, and notes the association of punishment and love. She sees ambivalence towards punishment as part of a broader ambivalence towards hierarchical relationships, and a change in attitudes to physical punishment.

182 **The development of marriage in Tonga.**
Sela Fonua. *The Pacific Journal of Theology*, series II, no. 20 (1998), p. 85-94.
Fonua describes traditional ideas of marriage in Tongan society, the polygamous life of the chiefs, and marriage ceremonies for chiefs and for commoners. Marriage was a form of social contract, an effective social control between families. She then considers the changes in Tongan society brought by the missionaries and their enforcement of monogamous marriage. They may have swept away ideas of ownership and domination in marriage, but many of the helpful aspects of traditional Tongan ideas about marriage are retained, particularly the sense of community joy and participation. 'The tradition has been redeemed, the culture has been sanctified', she concludes.

183 **Developments in Polynesian ethnology.**
Edited by Alan Howard, Robert Borofsky. Honolulu, Hawai'i:
University of Hawai'i Press, 1989. 373p. bibliog.

Experienced researchers assess the state of Polynesian ethnology in the light of the large amount of work published in the 1970s and 1980s. This increasingly showed the diversity and flexibility of Polynesian social systems and in some areas, particularly the field of Polynesian origins, produced a completely new picture. Each contributor summarizes the research of the period, considers its significance and suggests new research themes for the future. The themes examined are: prehistory (Patrick Kirch); social organization (Alan Howard and Judith Kirkpatrick); socialization and character development (James Ritchie and Jane Ritchie); *mana* and *tapu* (Bradd Shore); chieftainship (G. E. Marcus); art and aesthetics (Adrienne Kaeppler); the early contact period (Borofsky and Howard); and looking ahead (Borofsky and Howard). Tonga features throughout, particularly in the chapters written by specialists on Tonga (Kirch, Marcus and Kaeppler). The bibliography provides a comprehensive listing of the work of the period.

184 **Effeminate males and changes in the construction of gender in Tonga.**
Kerry E. James. *Pacific Studies*, vol. 17, no. 2 (1994), p. 39-69.

Male effeminacy and transvestism are well known in Polynesia through the accounts of early travellers, though less so in Tonga. James updates the record. She examines the discontinuities between the *tangata fakafefine* (a man behaving like a woman) of former times, primarily having a preference for women's work and company, and the modern *fakaleitī* (from the English 'lady') which refers to a much wider range of behaviour, Western-style transvestism and drag queen beauty contests and cabarets. She looks at the difficulties of constructing a viable identity as a Tongan male today, in contrast to the continuities of Tongan womanhood, and describes the playing out of sexual politics between men and women. She describes the *fakaleitī* of modern Tonga from her own observations and from what they have told her, and outlines the way they are brought up, live and behave. She notes that the annual drag queen contest (entitled, since this paper was written, Miss Galaxy) now attracts a larger audience than the Miss Heilala pageant, a beauty contest for women. She considers reasons for the recent increase in numbers of *fakaleitī*, which some in Tonga have suggested may be related to the emigration of so many males, the lack of employment for many young males in Tonga, and employment in offices rather than on the land. For a subsequent treatment of this topic see Besnier (item no. 214).

185 **'The father's sister is black': a consideration of female rank and power in Tonga.**
Garth Rogers. *The Journal of the Polynesian Society*, vol. 86, no. 2 (1977), p. 157-82.

Rogers examines the principle of ancient Tongan society, based on brother and sister who occupy distinct realms, the male line organizing power and utilitarian functions, and the female controlling more abstract honours. Cook observed the superior rank of the sister of the late king and Mariner observed that rank descended from the mother's side. Rogers describes his paper as an exercise in speculative reconstruction, using fragmentary folk beliefs and observed contemporary customs to present a hypothesis about the status of women in Tongan society. He examines the relationship between fathers and mothers and their sons and daughters; between brothers and sisters; the authority of the father's eldest sister in childbirth, marriages and funerals; and lineages and their representation in ceremonies. He sees Tongan kinship as a series of patrilines bisected by matrilines to demonstrate the power of the father's sister who can, if crossed, be 'black'. Melenaite Taumofolau refutes some of Rogers' arguments in an article of 1991 (item no. 191).

186 The female presence in heavenly places: myth and sovereignty in Tonga.
K. E. James. *Oceania*, vol. 61, no. 4 (1991), p. 287-308.

James writes to counter the view that male rivalries are at the heart of Tongan culture and polity and that the myths of the origin of kingship and kava reveal oedipal and cannibalistic themes. She believes that this obscures the centrality of the brother-sister relationship. She sees the female principle in the Tu'i Tonga title as identified with the goddess Hikule'o, whose myth relates directly to the kava ceremony. Further, the fundamental relationship in the Tongan polity is not expressly father/son but chief/subject, and the key to that is the relationship between sister and brother.

187 Gender relations in Tonga: a paradigm shift.
K. E. James. In: *Tongan culture and history.* Edited by Phyllis Herda, Jennifer Terrell, Niel Gunson. Canberra: The Journal of Pacific History, 1990, p. 93-100.

James uses existing data, focusing specifically on gender relations, to question some previous formulations of the place of gender in the traditional Tongan socio-political order; conceptualizations of the kin group as both a corporate local group and as a synonym for a cognatic kinship system; the basically Eurocentric notion of the 'domestic' sphere as opposed to the 'political' sphere; and a degree of over-formalization of Tongan systems in general. She examines the ways in which other scholars have seen the relationship between gender, rank and authority within the kin group, the different approaches to its definition, and the way in which it operated in Tongan history. Succession was not always patrilineal, while women produced the durable valuables – mats, oil and bark cloth – which were associated with their mystical powers.

188 Identity and change in Tongan society since European contact.
Futa Helu. *Journal de la Société des Océanistes*, no. 97 (1993), p. 187-94.

In this brief sketch of a complex topic, Helu considers the impact of external forces on social change in Tonga, first as exemplified in the kava ceremony. He describes the various types of kava ceremony. The formal kava ceremony is still strong, but he notes the development of informal kava clubs where an admission fee is charged, while other types of informal kava drinking have declined. This, he maintains, is a symptom of the monetarization of Tongan culture. He also sees the entry of libertarian-humanist values and bourgeois morality as outcomes of the rise of an intellectual elite and a middle class, alongside the increasing role of women in politics and business life. Forms of social organization, Helu claims, are also changing, consistent with the weakening of the subsistence economy and accelerating market sector development.

189   **Ideology and social inequality in the Tongan kinship system.**
Paul van der Grijp. *Bijdragen tot de Taal-, Land- en Volkenkunde*,
vol. 144, no. 4 (1988), p. 445-63.

The author describes the various terms used by Tongans for kinship groupings, the relationships between members of a group living in one household, and the principles of social inequality. He examines the way in which kinship relations work through the generations, listing the Tongan terms for different relationships and setting out the appropriate behaviour between them. He considers the distinction between status and rank as exemplified in the ancestry of Queen Sālote, and concludes that rank is a projection of the remote past to the present, while kinship status only goes back a few generations. Kinship status may apply in one situation, for instance a funeral, but not in another, and individuals may move flexibly between groups. But all Tongans, he believes, accept the distinction between commoners and chiefs as self-evident and necessary for the survival of Tongan society as a whole.

190   **In search of a home.**
Edited by Leonard Mason, Pat Hereniko.   Suva: Institute of Pacific
Studies of the University of the South Pacific, 1987. 260p. 10 maps.

Throughout the Pacific, islanders are on the move, both within and between countries, usually in search of better education for their children, land to grow crops for their own needs or for sale, and employment. This collection of case-studies is particularly concerned with the land rights of migrants within the Pacific. Four concentrate on Tonga; land rights and lack of secure tenure are a problem in each case. Pesi Fonua examines a group of Fijians and Solomon Islanders living near Nuku'alofa for over fifty years, some of whom have in turn emigrated to Australia and New Zealand and since returned. Though now largely intermarried with Tongans, they are still insecure. Lopeti Takau and Luiaki Fungalei describe a group settled in swampy land at Sopu which was devastated by a hurricane in 1982, and the government's problems in attempting to resettle them on better land. Kisione Lua describes the effect that migration from the outer islands has had on Haveluloto, once a small and quiet village near Nuku'alofa and now overcrowded, noisy and even increasingly affected by crime. Paulaki Langi examines some of the same problems in Ha'ateiho, also near Nuku'alofa, and suggests some ways to encourage people to stay in the outer islands, specifically: establishing secondary schools and industry in those islands; the forfeiture of unused land for redistribution; and the granting of unregistered land to people willing to farm it.

191   **Is the father's sister really 'black'?**
Melenaite Taumofolau.   *The Journal of the Polynesian Society*,
vol. 100, no. 1 (1991), p. 91-98.

In this short, technical paper the author shows that Rogers' translation of the Tongan saying 'The father's sister is black', upon which Rogers bases his paper (item no. 185) is incorrect and that, given the correct translation, the interpretation of 'blackness' as referring to mystical powers or to the power to curse can be eliminated. This power is not contained in the word but may be inferred from the implied greatness of the father's sister. The paper demonstrates something of the syntactic and semantic structure of the saying.

192   Islanders of the south: production, kinship and ideology in the
       Polynesian kingdom of Tonga.
       Paul van der Grijp.   Leiden, the Netherlands: KITLV Press, 1993.
       264p. map. bibliog. (Verhandelingen van het Koninklijk Instituut voor
       taal-, land- en volkenkunde, no. 154).

The author is concerned with the way in which social labour is employed in the use of
tools, skills, organization and knowledge in order to 'transform nature into products'
to meet material and social needs, relating this to wider anthropological theory. He
describes contemporary Tongan society (his fieldwork was done between 1982 and
1991) and the main means of subsistence: agriculture, fishing and manufacturing. He
analyses the kinship system with its economic, political and ideological dimensions,
and describes Tongan attitudes to life, death, marriage and divorce, social rights and
obligations, migration and remittances. He examines land ownership and gifts, and the
effects on Tonga of modern capitalism, and sees an ambivalence in the view of this
as progress, since much that seems to be modern and capitalist relates to traditional
concepts and practices.

193   The kingly-populist divergence in Tongan and Western Samoan
       chiefly systems.
       Robert W. Franco.   In: *Chiefs today: traditional Pacific leadership
       and the postcolonial state.*   Edited by Geoffrey M. White, Lamont
       Lindstrom.   Stanford, California: Stanford University Press, 1997,
       p. 71-83. (East-West Center Series on Contemporary Issues in Asia
       and the Pacific).

Franco describes the sorts of chiefly systems of Western Samoa and Tonga, seen in
local and regional terms, before European contact, the state of these systems at
independence, and the global factors that influence them today. He then examines
the impact of the kingly-populist divergence on Tongan and Samoan overseas
communities. Samoan migrants, he indicates, tend to send back money to support the
noble system, while Tongan migrants keep their remittances distinct from the kingly-
noble system which they have left. However, they continue to derive cultural and
national identity from the person and position of the king.

194   Kinship organisation and behaviour in a contemporary Tongan
       village.
       Machiko Aoyagi.   *The Journal of the Polynesian Society*, vol. 75,
       no. 2 (1966), p. 141-76.

After a period in 1962-63 spent living in a Tongan village, Aoyagi sets out to examine
within what sort of kinship network people live in rural Tonga, and how they behave
in such a network. She describes the inhabitants of the village, their age structure, land
holding and occupations in agriculture and fishing. She maps and analyses thirty-five
households, the number of people in each and support for the elderly and for children.
She places them within the context of their family and kinship organization and their
church affiliation. She observes the norms of kinship behaviour between parents and
children, brothers and sisters and others, and how this operates in, for instance, the
giving of names and in behaviour at weddings and funerals. Her aim is to provide a
description rather than a theoretical analysis, but she concludes by reviewing some of
the literature on ranking and lineage, and relating it to what she has observed.

195 **Kinship to kingship: gender hierarchy and state formation in the Tongan islands.**
Christine Ward Gailey. Austin, Texas: University of Texas Press, 1987. 326p. 2 maps. bibliog. (Texas Press Sourcebooks in Anthropology, no. 14).

Gailey believes it to be generally the case that women's authority and status necessarily decline with class and state formation. She sees a conflict between producers, working for subsistence, and civil authority, protecting the classes that siphon off goods and labour. This is the background for her analysis of the history of women in Tonga, once the only creators of wealth through the valuable objects which they produced – mats, tapa cloth and baskets. She examines in great detail gender and kinship relations in pre-contact Tonga, the activities of missionaries and traders, the development of the unified state under King George Tupou I, and the effect of all these factors in subordinating women. Her study is based on fieldwork among women's groups in Tonga as well as on documentary sources. Her appendix on 'sources and methods' offers a valuable summary of oral and written materials for the history of Tonga generally.

196 **Land tenure and social organisation in Tonga.**
R. R. Nayacakalou. *The Journal of the Polynesian Society*, vol. 68, no. 2 (1959), p. 93-114.

Nayacakalou points out the individualistic as well as the communalistic aspects of land tenure in Tonga, examining the role of lineage organization through which land-lords grant lands to their subjects as individual tenants, with no communal ownership in the generally accepted sense. He sets out the statutory framework as it existed at the time he was writing, surveys a sample village and its lands, explains how an '*api* (homestead) is acquired and village lands distributed, land use and the way in which labour may be called upon, and examines the relationship of kinship and land use. He finds that, in the village surveyed, kinship is supplanted by other ties, including economic and religious. His conclusion is that at that stage of economic development the land tenure system had certain social advantages which outweighed its economic weaknesses.

197 **The long way home: dilemmas of everyday life in a Tongan village.**
Arne Alekset Perminow. Oslo: Scandinavian University Press, 1993. 166p. 3 maps. bibliog.

Perminow's study of an island in the Ha'apai group focuses on the process by which an individual is made into and kept a member of society, and remains part of or becomes alienated from a particular culture. He examines particularly the situation of young people struggling to learn and decide who and what to be; they, he believes, are no longer children living in a controlled world of limited access to alternatives. He introduces the community through a day in the life of a child, examines the attraction of migration to Nuku'alofa for older members of the family, and tells the story of three young men who left the island to train as evangelists and teach the dangers of alcohol and of the impure life of the city generally. This is contrasted with the Tongan way of drinking kava, and all that it symbolizes about the nature of Tongan life, society and relationships generally. There are many vivid accounts of directly-observed behaviour.

198 Marriage in Tonga.
E. E. V. Collocott. *The Journal of the Polynesian Society*, vol. 32, no. 128 (1923), p. 221-28.

Collocott describes the traditional Tongan marriage ceremony, following the service in church: the anointing of the bride and bridegroom with scented oil and the dressing in fine mats and cloth; the bringing of the bride to the bridegroom's home; the changing of clothes; the preparation and drinking of kava; and the distribution of food and other gifts. Traditional marriages in Tonga today still retain many of these elements. He also surveys the records of other older marriage customs.

199 *Me'a faka'eiki*: Tongan funerals in a changing society.
Adrienne L. Kaeppler. In: *The changing Pacific: essays in honour of H. E. Maude*. Edited by Niel Gunson. Melbourne, Australia; Oxford; Wellington; New York: Oxford University Press, 1978, p. 174-202.

'A man becomes a chief when he dies', is the English translation of the Tongan proverb in the title. At a funeral a public record is made of how the deceased was related to others, his dignity, rank and how much and by whom he was loved. Kaeppler shows the importance of funerals in the perpetuation and evolution of Tongan social and cultural traditions, and describes and analyses in detail the funeral of Queen Sālote Tupou III in 1965, demonstrating how the ranking of mourners relative to her affected their role, their behaviour and even their dress. Kaeppler further outlines the difficulty in reconciling the retention of Polynesian values with Western ideas of a money-based economy, personal achievement and the nuclear family, shown in changing funeral practices, and warns of the danger of adapting Western values while conjuring up a spurious form of tradition for tourists. She shows how much the funeral reveals of the real Tonga.

200 The middle classes in Tonga.
Georges Benguigui. *The Journal of the Polynesian Society*, vol. 98, no. 4 (1989), p. 451-63.

Benguigui examines the implications for the class structure of Tonga of what he calls the 'development-and-overseas oriented policy' instituted by the present king after the death of Queen Sālote. These policies included: the encouragement of migration as a response to demographic pressure; the development of tourism; the establishment of light industries; the institution of large infrastructure projects financed by overseas aid; and the improvement of education so that many positions formerly held by foreigners could be held by Tongans. He describes social stratification in Tonga, the development of middle class and professional behaviour, and its implications in the political and cultural areas. He concludes that the state, which is closely involved in much economic activity, plays a key role in the generation of middle classes, in Tonga as elsewhere.

201 Neither black nor white: the father's sister in Tonga.
Françoise Douaire-Marsaudon. *The Journal of the Polynesian Society*, vol. 105, no. 2 (1996), p. 139-64.

The place and role of the father's sister in Western Polynesia has long aroused the interest of anthropologists (see item nos. 185 and 191) and is probably among the most original features of the area. She is seen as having a negative 'black' power to curse, to compensate for her exclusion from the transmission of title and land. The author examines the core brother-sister relationship, showing its role in the socio-cosmological order as a whole, taking examples from her own fieldwork and demonstrating the singular continuity between past and present on this topic in Tonga, despite many changes.

202 **The nobility and the chiefly tradition in the modern Kingdom of Tonga.**
George E. Marcus. Wellington: The Polynesian Society, 1980. 170p. bibliog. (Memoir, no. 42).

Tonga, Marcus observes, is the only contemporary Polynesian society to have retained a traditional king and group of titled nobles. Under the Constitution nobles exist within both Western-style institutions and surviving elements of pre-contact culture. Marcus' study of chiefly culture focuses on the ideology and place of the nobility in modern Tongan social organization. He describes the concept of the chief in pre-contact Tonga, how status was acquired, and how it is still maintained and exhibited. The holders of the thirty-three noble titles established under the 1875 Constitution acquired functions in government to complement their traditional roles. Marcus depicts their role in the transmission of chiefly traditions in modern Tonga, their legal position, their life in its present social context and their relation to church and state, education and family. He provides three vivid case-studies of what he calls 'gentry nobles', living a more traditional life on their estates in contrast to elite town-dwelling nobles, each of these having different views on how honour is demonstrated within the chiefly tradition. He concludes that chiefly culture persists, that the fate of the nobility is linked ever more closely with the monarchy through strategic marriages, and that flexibility will be necessary for the system's survival.

203 **'Ofa! the treasure of Tonga.**
S. Langi Kavaliku. *Pacific Perspective*, vol. 6, no. 2 (1977), p. 47-67.

Kavaliku, then at the time of writing and still today the Minister of Education in Tonga, examines the concept of 'ofa within its setting in Tongan society. 'Ofa is broadly defined as 'love' and Tongans see it as the main characteristic feature of their society, the supreme justification for their behaviour. It is a concept experienced rather than analysed. Kavaliku looks at examples of feelings of warmth, pity, respect and admiration as aspects of 'ofa. In it are elements of sadness, kindness, concern, hope, practical care and help, sexual love and sharing. All these he illustrates from literature and from his personal experience. He believes that 'ofa not only includes all these qualities but also indicates the relationship between people using the term, and that it is used to explain anything whose end result is positive. He quotes a Tongan saying, 'The life of Tonga is 'ofa', and concludes that any study of Tongan society needs an understanding of 'ofa.

204 **On female presences and absences in heavenly places.**
Valerio Valeri. *Oceania*, vol. 65, no. 1 (1994), p. 75-92.

This is a technical contribution, in part in psychological terms, to a complex debate about the role of male and female in Tongan society, particularly as exemplified in the kava ceremony, which is sacrificially representative of how 'Aho'eitu became the first

Tu'i Tonga. His myth displays at times oedipal symbolism as it represents conflict between father and son. Valeri emphasizes the predominantly male relationships in the titular system and asserts that, even if the father is absent in the early development of the child, the relationship is still important. The basis of authority in ancient Tonga, the titular system, was wholly framed in a paternal idiom with the Tu'i Tonga as the sacred father of the whole nation. Valeri is unconvinced by arguments against the presence of oedipal themes in some of the myths. He sees the myths as using universals of human experience, found in Tonga as elsewhere, for particular purposes, and the challenge of the kava bowl lies in the intertwining of tensions between male-dominated title and female-dominated rank. In a 'Reply' which immediately follows (p. 92-93), Kerry James, whose views Valeri has been disputing, states that Valeri's use of sources is not always correct, and that he has not addressed the crucial question of the implications of his view that the symbolism of the kava bowl enabled men to 'make' kings without the intervention of women.

205 **Pangai – village in Tonga.**
Ernest Beaglehole, Pearl Beaglehole.   Wellington: The Polynesian Society, 1941. 145p. 2 maps. (Memoirs of the Polynesian Society, vol. 18).

The Beagleholes spent seven weeks in Pangai, Vava'u, in 1938-39 and produced the first, and still often-quoted, detailed study of a Tongan village from the inside. They did not claim their study was exhaustive, nor did they draw any general conclusions; however, they give in their book a vivid description of the day-to-day life of a Tongan village, now sixty years ago, covering its largely subsistence economy. They describe the village's land system; the organization of labour; agriculture; food preparation and consumption; social life within the household and relations between kin; the life cycle from pregnancy and birth to death; medicine; kava; crime; and religion. They see their village as a well-integrated blend of the old and the new and ponder questions of cross-cultural contact and influence.

206 **A Polynesian village: the process of change in the village of Hoi, Tonga.**
Penisimani Tupouniua.   Suva: South Pacific Social Science Association, 1977. 70p. 2 maps. bibliog.

Tupouniua examines the life of Hoi, a small village in Tongatapu, continuing the tradition of village studies begun by the Beagleholes in Vava'u in 1941 (item no. 205). This is a briefer sketch than theirs. He describes the setting of the village and its population; socio-economic change through the changing role of the household and the rise of the cash economy; economic changes in production and distribution; and the role of church and school. He finds that the people of Hoi are conservative over custom and tradition, selective and often resistant to change, but that they realize that they can no longer stay isolated: they hope that they can absorb change without disruption.

207 **Power and personhood in Tonga.**
Helen Kavapalu.   *Social Analysis*, no. 37 (1995), p. 15-28.

Kavapalu examines the notion of person and self in Tonga from the perspective of childhood socialization, and notions of ideal personhood in relation to the strongly hierarchical nature of Tongan society. She discusses Tongan theories of childhood development and the conflicting messages that Tongans receive about ideals of personhood, and briefly considers family and political changes taking place in modern Tonga. She finds that Tongans learn from childhood to alter their presentation of self according to context. Child socialization is inherently political and children learn to shift between high and low status behaviour, although the fundamental dichotomy between chief and commoner is nowadays being weakened and the hierarchical nature of Tongan society called into question. As with her paper on child punishment (item no. 181), Kavapalu develops material from this paper more fully, writing as Helen Morton, in her book *Becoming Tongan* (item no. 175).

208 **Power and rank in the Kingdom of Tonga.**
Elizabeth Bott. *The Journal of the Polynesian Society*, vol. 90, no. 1 (1981), p. 7-81.

Bott discusses the interplay of rank and power in the traditional political and social systems of Tonga and their partial transformation, under modern political and economic conditions, into a system of socio-economic classes similar to those of Western society, with a ruling elite of aristocratic nobles, a set of nobles of much lower rank, a variegated middle class and a peasantry. She considers that class is emerging and the traditional system of stratification weakening under the pressures of land shortage, overseas employment and a desire for Western goods. Education too has played its part. Yet fifteen years later class has by no means replaced rank. Her claim that political, economic, educational and religious developments in the last 150 years have changed the Tongan system of stratification so that it now resembles a system of social class may be overstated at this stage. Rank still seems to matter in Tonga. Like Bott's other work (item no. 221), this was greatly assisted by discussions with Queen Sālote Tupou, alongside Bott's close observation of Tongan society at both the domestic and the political level.

209 **Power on the extreme periphery: the perspective of Tongan elites in the modern world system.**
George E. Marcus. *Pacific Viewpoint*, vol. 22, no. 1 (1981), p. 48-64.

In world system terms, Polynesia is on the extreme periphery. Marcus examines the degree to which Tongan elites can be seen in relation to European concepts. He notes that long-term migration with large overseas Tongan communities may give even a home-based elite a view of a set of international possibilities. He believes that Tongan elite formation has depended on the development of international family networks. Elite Tongans are able to convert this into position and personal power, accentuated by the small scale of Tongan society. Marcus describes recent developments in overseas networks, and the roles of an old and a new elite, both in Tonga and overseas, through particular families, in the context of the king's desire to attract foreign capital for investment.

210 **Putting down sisters and wives: Tongan women and colonization.**
Christine Ward Gailey. In: *Women and colonization: anthropological perspectives*. Edited by Mona Etienne, Eleanor Leacock. New York: Praeger, 1980, p. 294-322.

Gailey contends that before there was any significant European presence in Tonga, Tongan chiefly women had means of support independent of their husbands. There was no fixed gender hierarchy; both chiefly and non-chiefly women had sources of authority and relative autonomy not dependent on personal attributes; and Tongan chiefly women were chiefly first. Gailey examines processes of production and the role of wives and mothers in the structure of society, noting particularly the relationship of men's and women's labour and products. She then considers changes during the European experience, arguing that Tongan women have lost important sources of structural authority and autonomy through a combination of missionary zeal; the institution of production for exchange; the introduction of cloth and other European commodities; the revision and codifying of customary inheritance and land use arrangements; and the creation of a civil sphere especially associated with chiefly men. These processes have restricted women's authority as sisters and redefined their role as wives in such a way as to bring them into structural and economic dependency. This is an early version of a view of the role of women in Tongan society which Gailey developed in subsequent writings (item nos. 195 and 316).

211 **Rank and leadership in Tonga.**
Kerry James. In: *Chiefs today: traditional Pacific leadership and the postcolonial state.* Edited by Geoffrey M. White, Lamont Lindstrom. Stanford, California: Stanford University Press, 1997, p. 49-70. (East-West Center Series on Contemporary Issues in Asia and the Pacific).

All cabinet ministers in Tonga are regarded as chiefs, whether of noble birth or not, but not all chiefs are regarded as effective leaders by the people, especially if they neither sit in parliament nor take an active interest in their people. Both civic and household order is strongly hierarchical. James considers the notion of chiefliness in Tonga, which most people still wish to retain. She describes the old chiefly system and the creation of the new nobility by the 1875 Constitution. She notes that the children of nobles are increasingly obtaining good educational qualifications, and examines the role of nobles today, some resident on their estates and some absentee. She considers alternate role models and relates the legitimization of their authority to the new pro-democracy movement. Unless the chiefs carve out niches for themselves in the private sector, they may well find that their functions become merely ritual and ceremonial. She concludes that the new entrepreneurs and reformers do not want to replace their unique system, but want to be able to trust and respect it.

212 **Rank in Tonga.**
Adrienne L. Kaeppler. *Ethnology*, vol. X, no. 2 (1971), p. 174-93.

In this classic and much-cited paper, based more on her own fieldwork than on published sources, Kaeppler examines the major forms of kinship groupings in Tonga. She sets out and defines the different categories of societal ranking and the behaviour expected between each grouping, their origins in myth and history, and their working out in the ancestry of the present king. She sees Tonga as characterized by having multi-dimensional ranking, and the dimensions do not all fit into one pattern. Rank must be distinguished from status. She sees signs of change at the time of her field-work, with highly educated commoners not satisfied to take a rear seat to those of high birth whom they feel to be intellectually inferior. Yet she doubts that Tonga will cease to be a rank-oriented society, though the principle of rank may shift to a greater emphasis on achievement, and she believes it likely 'not too far in the future' that real political power will be in the hands of non-traditional leaders operating new principles of rank. Over thirty years later this has not in fact happened to anything like the extent that she foresaw.

213 **Role distance in conversations between Tongan nobles and their 'people'.**
George E. Marcus. *The Journal of the Polynesian Society*, vol. 89, no. 4 (1980), p. 435-53.

Though Tonga is a highly stratified society, Marcus found instances of nobles holding their nobility apart and engaging casually in ordinary conversation with commoners, usually in the context of informal kava drinking sessions. He sees nobles as having to bear a burden of role playing and these instances as occasions when the relative discrepancy between a noble's chiefly person and office is mutually established for himself and his people. Only a few nobles embody unambiguous substance as chiefs: others are common men without chiefly substance who hold noble titles, or are formally separated from the commoner population by their titles and offices, but are of ambiguous chiefly substance. Some live in their estates, but many live in Nuku'alofa and only visit them. Marcus describes their behaviour and that of their people in various situations to show the different degrees to which nobles can interact socially with their people, and reflects on its significance for the role of the nobles generally in modern Tonga. A slightly revised version of this paper was published in *Dangerous words: language and politics in the Pacific*, edited by Donald Lawrence Brenneis and Fred R. Myers (London; New York: New York University Press, 1984, p. 243-65).

214 **Sluts and superwomen: the politics of gender liminality in urban Tonga.**
Niko Besnier. *Ethnos*, vol. 52, nos. 1-2 (1997), p. 5-31.

In Tonga some men identify themselves and are identified by others as taking on some attributes of womanhood on a regular basis. Many are associated with domestic social spheres and do work normally associated with women. They occupy various places in the socio-economic structure and moral order. Some are highly productive in the market economy: others are principally concerned with casual sex relations and are branded as unproductive consumers; this is the more frequent stereotype. Besnier analyses the ethnographic diversity of transgendered relationships, the way in which symbolic and material forces relate in defining these identities, and the power of stereotyping in the lives of those on whom these forces play. He describes the very different life-styles and achievements of two such men, occupying opposite poles in the range of possible identities. Some similar and related ground is covered by James (item no. 184).

215 **State formation, development and social change in Tonga.**
Christine Ward Gailey. In: *Social change in the Pacific islands.*
Edited by Albert B. Robillard. London; New York: Kegan Paul International, 1982, p. 322-45.

Gailey presents a view of Tongan social and political dynamics before and since European contact, focusing on changes in the content and form of social strata, land tenure, gender roles and the relations of production and societal reproduction. The papers in this volume are written from a neo-Marxist viewpoint and Gailey, in a complex thesis for specialists in political economy, contrasts her approach to class and state formation with a conventional national agenda among the elite. The crystallization of class and a kingdom in the 19th century, she argues, had profound effects on the structure of Tongan society in all its aspects. Changes in gender roles, the development of a cash economy and the role of migration are seen as particularly important.

Classes, she observes, are still forming and the state is in flux. Her earlier work *Kinship to kingship: gender hierarchy and state formation in the Tongan islands* (item no. 195) provides a fuller treatment of this theme.

216 **Succession disputes and the position of the nobility in modern Tonga.**
George E. Marcus. *Oceania*, vol. 47, no. 3 (1977), p. 220-45; vol. 47, no. 4 (1977), p. 284-99.

The nobles of Tonga, created by King George Tupou I from the old chiefly establishment in the 1875 Constitution, have been seen as anachronistic and conservative. But, although fixed and rigid in principle, the nobility has been characterized by a degree of fluidity and has shown flexibility and accommodation in response to modernizing and liberating changes. Marcus examines the public litigation of modern succession disputes and discusses what these indicate about the position of the nobility in modern Tongan society. He analyses in detail some cases which raise issues relating to the traditional legitimacy not only of the nobility but also of the present dynasty itself, in the light of some irregular appointments made by King George Tupou I and King George Tupou II, and demonstrates the historical ambiguity concerning the nobility. He sees these cases as raising important issues relating to the relationship of the monarch to law and legal process, relationships between noble kin groups, and the overall status of the nobility in contemporary society. These various considerations demonstrate that the privileged sector of society, the nobility, has been thoroughly infiltrated by socially levelling and individualizing forces, within what Marcus calls 'the westernising trends of the post-1875 compromise culture in Tonga'.

217 **Tongan adoption.**
Keith L. Morton. In: *Transactions in kinship: adoption and fostering in Oceania.* Edited by Ivan Brady. Honolulu, Hawai'i: The University Press of Hawai'i, 1976, p. 64-80. (ASAO Monograph, no. 4).

Morton defines adoption in Tonga as a specific formal process within the kinship system that both creates new kin relationships and redefines kinship networks: it is goal-directed kinship behaviour. His data came from a survey of almost all households in one village in Tongatapu, where the dominant form is the nuclear family joined into kinship groups. Nearly all Tongans have had some experience of adoption, either directly or indirectly, but few adoptions are formally sanctioned through the courts. There are two types: 'the adoption of non-kinsmen' and 'the adoption of consanguines', the latter being much more frequent. Morton describes the procedures for adoption, usually initiated by adopters rather than parents, and usually closely connected with achieving adult status. Most parents are willing to assist kinsmen who wish to adopt. Morton explains the respective roles of mother's and father's kinsmen and notes that grandparent-grandchild adoption is quite common, but only after the natural parents have agreed to relinquish their rights. Generally speaking, adoptees benefit from adoption because it enlarges the network of their close kin and gives the advantage of reckoning kinship status either from natural or adoptive parents: this expands and reinforces their access to strategic resources.

218   **Tongan kin groups: the noble and the common view.**
Shulamit R. Decktor Korn.   *The Journal of the Polynesian Society*,
vol. 83, no. 1 (1974), p. 5-13.

Korn notes that most Polynesian specialists focus on the upper classes of society and on political leaders. She brings together kinship in its rank aspect and kinship operating at the local level. Her concern is to describe the more important types of kin groups and to differentiate their scope of operation. She examines the *ha'a*, which is a network based on groupings of chiefly titles, membership of which is a claim to high rank. She relates this to smaller household and family groups, and compares their nature and function. She concludes that a noble view is a faulty basis for generalizing about an entire society.

219   **Tongan rank revisited: religious hierarchy, social stratification, and gender in ancient Tongan polity.**
Kerry James.   *Social Analysis*, no. 31 (July 1992), p. 79-102.

James takes as her text a statement by Queen Sālote, 'Rank overrules everything'. She puts forward the view that rank is best conceptualized in terms of an underlying cosmic hierarchy, which bears only a problematic relationship to the principles underlying external forms of social stratification. She believes that the underlying structure of social differentiation in Tonga has long eluded observers. Tonga is one of the most stratified societies in Polynesia, yet has systems of rank and power that are contradictory. Rank ascribed by birth, power achieved in performance and authority vested in titles overlap. But, if seen in terms of religious hierarchy, rank can be conceptualized as the primary value that encompasses all others. James examines this, and the way in which it has been understood by modern scholars, in considerable detail. She sees *mana*, the mysterious power derived from the gods, to be clearly associated with high rank, and as distinct from *pule*, political power. She considers how this hierarchy was worked out in Tongan myth and history, particularly in the last century with the coming of Christianity. It is remarkable, she notes, that so many ideas and practices, having their roots in the old religious hierarchy, still have such salience in Tonga.

220   **Tongan society.**
Edward Winslow Gifford.   Honolulu, Hawai'i: Bernice P. Bishop
Museum, 1929. 366p. map. bibliog. (Bernice P. Bishop Museum
Bulletin, no. 61).

Gifford refers back to Mariner (item no. 46), over a century earlier, as providing the most extensive and accurate account of Tongan society until his time, and advises his readers to consult Mariner's account for further information. He notes a surprising similarity between his account and Mariner's. Nevertheless, his work, based on a visit to Tonga in 1920-21, marks the first attempt to provide a scholarly and systematic study. His range is wide, covering population; the family; the lineages of the royal and chiefly lines; social structure and organization; kava; land tenure; law; the major events of life (birth, marriage and death); warfare; entertainment; names; religion; and much else. In many respects scholars since have developed or questioned his account, and doubt has been cast on the accuracy of some of his information, but, seventy years on, the work remains the classic introduction to the subject, the point from which further work must begin.

221 **Tongan society at the time of Captain Cook's visits: discussions with Her Majesty Queen Sālote Tupou.**
Elizabeth Bott with the assistance of Tavi. Wellington: The Polynesian Society, 1982. 187p. bibliog. (Memoir, no. 44).

Elizabeth Bott's study of the historical basis of Tongan society, although undertaken and originally written in the late 1950s, remains the foundation of much work since. Her aim was to describe the social and political organization of Tonga as visited by Cook in the 1770s. In this she had the unique assistance of Queen Sālote Tupou. Bott describes Cook's experience of Tonga, before giving a generalized account of Tongan political and social organization based on her own observations in Tonga as well as information from Tongans. Finally she describes the events – largely as expressed in myths, legends, traditions and genealogies – that are thought by Tongans to have led to the form of Tongan society that Cook observed. In all this, Queen Sālote Tupou was able to add much interpretation and explanation, passed down through her own family and developed through her long reign, though Bott admits that the picture as visualized by the Queen is somewhat idealized. The work was originally written as a private report to the Queen and the Government of Tonga, and was published many years later after a further visit to Tonga to review and check the paper.

222 **Under the *toa* tree: the genealogy of the Tongan chiefs.**
Aletta Biersack. In: *Culture and history in the Pacific.* Edited by Jukka Siikala. Helsinki: The Finnish Anthropological Society, 1990, p. 80-106. (Transactions, no. 27).

Biersack examines the dualistic foundations of Tongan kingship by way of exploring the historicity of the Tongan polity. While paramounts descended 'from the sky' they were also kinsmen of the villagers and people living under them, and the terms of sovereignty needed to be negotiated. She aims to interpret the 19th-century revolution when Taufa'āhau, a secondary chief, suppressed the Tu'i Tonga title of his superior and created a superordinate one, and examines the strategies of Queen Sālote for defending and celebrating the conquests and reforms of the 19th century. Biersack sets out the founding legends of the Tu'i Tonga, both divine and human, his role in Tongan society, and the history of the title. She relates this to Queen Sālote's definition of what constitutes a 'good chief', concerned to look after the land and the people. Chiefly power is as much populist as kingly, and Biersack believes that, despite the union of the three Tu'i titles through the marriage of Queen Sālote to Tungī Mailefihi, the Tongan polity remains restless, mobile and self-transforming.

Kava

223 Drinking in the Polynesian kingdom of Tonga.
Charles F. Urbanowicz. *Ethnohistory*, vol. 22, no. 1 (1975), p. 33-50.
Urbanowicz seeks to explain not the ceremonial of kava but why drinking kava rather
than any other beverage continues to function as an integrating force in Tongan life.
He finds that kava drinking has been the way in which Tongans have maintained their
identity. He sets out the different types of kava drinking, everyday and ceremonial, the
same structural features which apply to all, and the role of rank. He describes the attitude
of the early missionaries to kava, of which they disapproved. In the 19th century kava
drinking sessions were a way of discussing current affairs and maintaining Tongan
unity in the face of missionary influence. He outlines kava's role as a 'seal on all
occasions' whether formal or informal, and the way in which it was observed by the
first Europeans and its role today, particularly the royal kava ceremony. He concludes,
'A kava drinking session is a model of Tongan society'.

224 Informal kava drinking in Tonga.
Henry Feldman. *The Journal of the Polynesian Society*, vol. 89, no. 1
(1980), p. 101-03.
In this brief note Feldman describes the drinking of kava not as a formal ceremony
symbolic of social stratification but as an informal social event. He describes the
procedures followed both in private kava drinking and in public kava clubs where a
fee may be charged and funds raised for churches and schools.

225 The interpretation of ritual: essays in honour of A. I. Richards.
Edited by J. S. La Fontaine. London: Tavistock Publications, 1972.
298p. bibliog.
This book contains three papers which contribute to the debate on the nature and
meaning of the Tongan kava ceremony. In 'Psychoanalysis and ceremony' (p. 203-37)
Elizabeth Bott considers it from the two viewpoints of an anthropologist and a psycho-
analyst. Both from her observations of the ceremony and from her reading of the
myths underlying its origin, she sees the kava ceremony as clarifying social principles

and social roles, where rank is separated from political power; as a conserving and conservative tradition; and as expressing a fundamental contradiction, bringing together people who in other contexts might be opposed. It resolves problems of dependence, envy and rivalry, and transmits messages on many different levels. In 'The structure of symbolism' (p. 239-75) Edmund Leach takes issue with her psycho-analytical approach to the myths, and offers a structuralist reading with leads him to different and suggestive conclusions. In a brief 'Rejoinder to Edmund Leach' (p. 277-82) Bott acknowledges the value of some of Leach's views but professes herself dissatisfied with the structuralist approach, feeling that her own interpretation that the kava ceremony and myths are statements about emotional and social as well as logical and cognitive problems remains valid. The debate is complex and the terminology technical.

226 **Kava, alcohol and tobacco consumption among Tongans with urbanization.**
Sitaleki A. Finau, John M. Stanhope, Ian A. M. Prior. *Social Science and Medicine*, vol. 16, no. 1 (1982), p. 35-41.
This is a report of a study in Nuku'alofa and the island of Foa in 1973. It found that kava was consumed by 48 per cent of men but almost no women; alcohol consumption was almost exclusively urban and predominantly male; and tobacco consumption was higher among men and in the urban population. Kava seems to have lost ground to alcohol as urban Tongans adopt a more cosmopolitan life style, and kava might be promoted as a less unhealthy alternative to alcohol and tobacco. Results are set out in tables and graphs. The report notes that alcohol is a socially unacceptable but prestigious agent, which temporarily releases the young from social responsibilities in a confining feudal system, while kava is an agent of Tongan cultural identity.

227 **Kava ceremonial in Tonga.**
E. E. V. Collocott. *The Journal of the Polynesian Society*, vol. 36, no. 141 (1927), p. 21-47.
Much has been written in more recent times by scholars such as Bott and Leach (item no. 225) on the meaning of the kava ceremony, but this paper provides factual information gathered by the author from observing several kava ceremonies of the Tu'i Kanokupolu, when Queen Sālote drank kava with her chiefs. He illustrates the structure of the kava ring, setting out the relationships which determine the order of seating. He describes the order of the ceremony, the presenting of the gifts of food and kava and their counting, the preparing of the kava root, the mixing and straining, the distribution, by rank, of the food and of the kava. He suggests how the kava ceremony of the Tu'i Tonga might have differed.

228 **The kava ceremony in Tonga.**
W. H. Newell. *The Journal of the Polynesian Society*, vol. 56, no. 4 (1947), p. 364-417.
Newell describes Tongan social structure and suggests that the material tools used in the kava ceremony are determined by and related to this structure. He suggests that kava was introduced from Micronesia and the eastern islands. He shows how the modern kava ceremony has a ritual and symbolic character, and discusses the relationship between that of the Tu'i Tonga and that of the Tu'i Kanokupolu. He considers the role of the kava ceremony at times of war and marriage, and describes the differing

forms of kava bowl found in Fiji, Tonga and Samoa. His description of the ceremony itself is based largely on Collocott (item no. 227), but he examines further the concepts of *tapu* and ritual status, and shows how the kava ceremony reinforces the functioning of the ranking system. He lists the occasions – social and ceremonial – on which kava ceremonies are held.

229 **Kava, the Pacific elixir: the definitive guide to its ethnobotany, history and chemistry.**
Vincent Lebot, Mark Merlin, Lamont Lindstrom.   Rochester,
Vermont: Healing Arts Press, 1997. 255p. 4 maps. bibliog.

This comprehensive guide summarizes the literature and research on kava, consumed throughout the region as a relaxing beverage for social interaction. The authors believe it to be superior to alcohol, nicotine, tranquillizers and other substances used to reduce stress and improve mood. The book surveys kava from the point of view of the horticulturalist, the ethnobotanist and the pharmacologist. The authors examine the morphology, biogeography and origin of the species which produces kava, its chemical composition, its cultivation and preparation, its place in traditional medicine, its cultural significance and social use and its economics as a cash crop, both domestic and export. They note that some Western drugs contain kava extract and suggest that it might become a world drug. While the emphasis of the book is more on Melanesia, Tonga is included in the coverage, though for kava as a crop rather than for the kava ceremony.

230 **Kava'onau and the Tongan chiefs.**
Aletta Biersack.   *The Journal of the Polynesian Society*, vol. 100,
no. 3 (1991), p. 231-68.

As is widely agreed, the Tongan kava ceremony is central to any understanding of the Tongan polity. Biersack examines the myths of the origin of kava and of 'Aho'eitu, the first Tu'i Tonga, and the interpretation of them by modern scholars. She describes the status systems which govern people within kinship networks, and the system of titles, and how this is reflected in the order of seating at the royal kava ceremony and in the way it is conducted, with taboos governing what is done. The myths and the ceremony link the obligation to serve a superior with the reciprocal responsibilities of chiefly paternalism, a pact of mutual sacrifice between the leader and the led. The analysis is complex and detailed. Biersack concludes: 'The kava ceremony is more than a reflection of an existing order. Each performance is a structure-making event'.

Health and Welfare

231 **Blood groups of the Tongan islands.**
Olga Kooptzoff, R. J. Walsh. *Oceania*, vol. 27, no. 3 (1957),
p. 214-19.

The authors report the results of their analysis of 102 blood samples from Tonga. The
results are tabulated and gene frequencies are compared with those of related populations.
The authors conclude that Polynesians are not homogeneous throughout Polynesia and
that there has been considerable intermixing of Polynesians and Melanesians.

232 **Developments in the role of the Tongan healer.**
Claire D. F. Parsons. *The Journal of the Polynesian Society*, vol. 92,
no. 1 (1983), p. 31-50.

Parsons first reviews historical comments on the origins of the healer role in Tonga.
She then shows that, contrary to what might be expected, traditional healing practices
have not declined since the days of European contact. Rather, they have developed
alongside, and in spite of, Western medical practice. She draws out an association
between the early priestly role and the secular role of the traditional healers and their
practice. She describes the contemporary role of healers, differentiating between their
skill and their power to heal. Finally, she refers to notions of payment and of gift-
exchange for healing services, which involve the social-moral value of the healer role
in the community.

233 **Eclectic elements in Tongan folk belief and healing practice.**
Wendy E. Cowling. In: *Tongan culture and history*. Edited by
Phyllis Herda, Jennifer Terrell, Niel Gunson. Canberra: The Journal
of Pacific History, 1990, p. 72-92.

Present-day folk beliefs in Tonga regarding the causes of some illnesses appear to be a
synthesis of pre-contact religious ideas and of Christian-derived beliefs. These,
together with ideas on the functioning of the dead in the after-life, appear to be in a
constant state of modification and development. In recent years there seems to have

been an increase in a form of culturally specific illness which appears to be a form of depression, for which traditional healers are consulted. Cowling lists the five types of this traditional illness known as *'avanga*, with folk explanation, physical symptoms and precipitating factors. Cowling examines the role of traditional healers, the nature of the treatments they offer – some symbolic and some therapeutic – and the role of the family and community in healing. The increase in the numbers of people consulting traditional healers for 'spirit-caused sickness' is mostly among women, and she suggests that this may be the result of rapid social change and economic development, and thus likely to continue to increase. An appendix lists some of the leaves and barks used in traditional treatments.

234 **Epidemiologic, clinical and virologic observations on dengue in the Kingdom of Tonga.**
Duane J. Gubler, Dwayne Reed, Leon Rosen, James C. Hitchcock.
American Journal of Tropical Medicine and Hygiene, vol. 27 (1978), p. 581-89.
The authors examine a relatively mild outbreak of dengue fever in Tonga in 1974 and a more severe one in 1975. They describe the types of mosquito prevalent in Tonga, the courses of the two outbreaks and their symptoms, and suggest some reasons for the difference in severity.

235 **Epidemiology and the Tongan health care system.**
Sitaleki A. Finau. *Fiji Medical Journal*, vol. 7, no. 7 (1979), p. 192-94.
Finau examines the position of epidemics in Tonga, which is difficult to determine because of the lack of data. He considers the position of tuberculosis and diabetes and believes that many cases must remain unknown. He calls for a health education programme on chronic and degenerative diseases, and for more data in order to plan for the best way to meet needs.

236 **Ethnomedicine in Tonga.**
M. A. Weiner. *Economic Botany*, vol. 25, no. 4 (1971), p. 423-50.
Weiner reviews the practice of traditional medicine in Tonga from its first recording by Mariner. He lists plant families with their Latin and Tongan names, identifying where the same Tongan name is given to different species. He describes his interviews in Tonga with traditional practitioners, recording ninety-one remedies using fifty-nine different species of plants. These were identified using Yuncker (item no. 65) and are set out with botanical descriptions, the complaints for which they are applied and the method of use.

237 **Folk medicine in Tonga: a study on the use of herbal medicines for obstetrics and gynaecological conditions and disorders.**
Yadhu N. Singh, Talita Ikahihifo, Monalisa Panove, Claire Slatter.
Journal of Ethnopharmacology, vol. 12, no. 3 (1984), p. 305-29.
The authors studied the use of traditional medicinal practices in two communities in Tonga, one rural and one urban, with particular emphasis on obstetrics and gynae-cological complaints. They collected data on the nature and frequency of complaints, patterns of consultation and preferences for Western and traditional practitioners, and

examined the expertise of traditional practitioners. The survey suggests that reliance on traditional medicine is rapidly declining in favour of Western medicine, but that self-administration of herbal remedies was still common, especially in rural areas, and might even be on the increase. Sixty plant specimens used in treating complaints were collected and identified, and are listed with Latin and Tongan name; therapeutic indications and plant part; and form of remedy.

238   The incidence of twins in the Kingdom of Tonga and maternal and perinatal implications.
Mario Felszer.   *Fiji Medical Journal*, vol. 7, no. 6 (1979), p. 156-62.
From his analysis of the birth of twins in Tonga from 1975 to 1978, Felszer finds that the incidence of twins is higher than in many of the countries of Europe and Asia. He charts them by age of mother, lists some of the possible implications, and concludes that pre-natal diagnosis is a high priority.

239   Marketing and primary health care: an approach to planning in a Tongan village.
Sitaleki A. Finau.   *Social Science and Medicine*, vol. 17, no. 8 (1983), p. 511-16.
Finau uses a village in Tonga as an example of the marketing approach to the planning of health care facilities and to determining priorities at the village level in the light of the wishes of the villagers. They sought a local service, in a Tongan environment, to deal largely with immediate first aid, and this was to be provided by a trained village health worker with a suitably equipped motor vehicle, to be financed by a low-interest loan. Finau tells how the matter was discussed in the village and decisions reached.

240   Mental health, ethnopsychiatry and traditional medicine in the Kingdom of Tonga.
Wolfgang G. Jilek.   *Curarae*, vol. 11, no. 3 (1988), p. 161-76.
Tonga has been seen as having very little psychiatric disorder, but this is based on Western perceptions and excludes most of the many cases interpreted as due to possession by spirits of the dead. Jilek examines the symptoms of such cases, the reaction of patients to the application of plant extracts, and the visions and dreams of the patient, which are validated by elders and traditional healers. Traditional healing involves plant remedies and massage, supported by collective and individual suggestion and by active family involvement. In most cases there is complete remission or significant improvement. Jilek analyses the different types of spirit-caused condition, illustrated by case-studies. He suggests that, whatever the benefit of plant remedies, the efficacy of Tongan healing will always depend upon the skilful use of cultural symbols and of collective suggestion by the individual healer.

241   The 1986 national nutrition survey of the Kingdom of Tonga.
Elizabeth Maclean, François Bach, Jacqui Badcock.   Noumea: South Pacific Commission, 1992. 77p. map. bibliog. (Technical Paper, no. 200).
This report, based on an eight per cent random sample of the population of Tonga, sets out information on dietary habits, infant feeding patterns, maternal and child health care practices, nutrition knowledge and anthropometric indicators. The main findings

of the survey were generally encouraging; however, there was a high prevalence of obesity in adults, which is a primary causal factor in diabetes, hypertension and heart disease. Those in urban areas eat more imported food than those in rural areas. The report provides much information on dietary patterns in Tonga, detailed statistics, and discussions of their implications. It recommends to the government measures to improve nutritional status.

242 Sickness, ghosts and medicine in Tonga.
E. E. V. Collocott. *The Journal of the Polynesian Society*, vol. 32, no. 127 (1923), p. 136-42.

Collocott describes the attitude of Tongans to illness and pain, their lack of a concept of diagnosis of illness and its causes, and the part played by ghosts of the dead in the illnesses of the living. Traditional medicines may cause the illnesses they should cure if not treated properly, and healers guard their knowledge jealously. Massage is very effective in many cases, and Tongans are constantly attentive to the sick.

243 Small island health needs: follow-up approaches in Tonga.
Sitaleki A. Finau, et al. *Pacific Perspective*, vol. 13, no. 2 (1983), p. 91-95.

Finau and colleagues review the work of village health workers, introduced in an attempt to improve health care throughout Tonga. They surveyed six islands in Ha'apai, each of which selected one female worker, trained over twelve weeks in basic health care and given a limited stock of medicines. The survey, after three months, analysed the illnesses reported and dealt with, and considered the relationship with traditional healers. It was obvious that the health workers were meeting a real need. Fever and wounds were by far the two largest categories of illnesses dealt with.

244 Tongan healing practices.
Claire D. F. Parsons. In: *Healing practices in the South Pacific*. Edited by Claire D. F. Parsons. Honolulu, Hawai'i: University of Hawai'i Press for the Institute of Polynesian Studies, 1985, p. 87-107.

Parsons conducted fieldwork in Tonga in 1979, to understand how Tongans talk about sickness, what they know and believe about it, and what they do when they are sick. She found the public and government officials at variance over the effectiveness of indigenous healing practices, proscribed by Western-trained doctors yet still widely used. In her article, she defines the Tongan concept of the healthy life as the maintenance of harmony in relationships, lists the Tongan terms for various aspects of illness, and describes the differences between what are seen as Western and Tongan illnesses in which supernatural spirit influences are at work. Some are seen as controllable by Western medicine and some by Tongan. For some Tongans all illness is caused by spirits, and she describes Tongan ways of dealing with it, including massage and traditional medicines. Treating Tongans, she concludes, is not simply a matter of providing medicine or surgery but involves dealing with an extensive range of meanings reflecting a fundamentally different worldview.

245 **Tongan herbal medicine.**

W. Arthur Whistler.   Honolulu, Hawai'i: University of Hawai'i Press, 1992. 122p. 2 maps. bibliog.

Tongans traditionally saw illnesses as of two types, those of natural origin or whose origins could be seen, such as wounds and broken bones, and ailments such as internal illnesses and tumours whose origins were thought to be caused by the actions of supernatural beings. Even today Tongans still often turn first to Tongan medicine and consult healers. Whistler reviews the medical problems of Tongans, the role and practice of traditional healers as revealed in the literature and as he finds it today, and in particular the role of herbal medicine, its preparation and prescription. He then lists seventy-seven Tongan medicinal plants with Tongan, Latin and English name, habitat, botanical description and discussion of medical use. He concludes with a glossary of Tongan medical terms. The book is illustrated with many of his own photographs.

246 **Traditional medicine in Pacific health services.**

Sitaleki A. Finau.   *Pacific Perspective*, vol. 9, no. 2 (1980), p. 92-98.

Finau asserts that a marriage of old Pacific knowledge and new Pacific scientific medicine must take place, without sacrificing one to the other. He describes the concepts underlying traditional Tongan medicine and its coexistence with new scientific medicine. To ghosts, spirits and taboo have been added the Bible and God. The death rate in hospital is high because many people try traditional medicines first. He believes that a proportional and integrated approach to modern medicine is required: some psychiatric illnesses are more responsive to traditional healers than to scientific medicine. He further suggests that kava should perhaps be served at official functions rather than alcohol. He concludes that there should be more research on the traditional life styles that are conducive to health: it is time to model health systems in the Pacific way.

247 **Traditional medicine in Tonga: a preamble to a Pacific model.**

Sitaleki A. Finau.   *Fiji Medical Journal*, vol. 9, nos. 6 and 7 (1981), p. 93-99.

As in his earlier article (item no. 246), Finau stresses the need for a marriage of traditional and scientific medicine. Tongans are still dying of pre-contact illnesses such as dengue fever, as well as suffering from one of the world's highest rates of diabetes and high blood pressure. Traditional medicine must enhance new concepts. Tongans believed that heredity and the breaching of taboos were major predisposing factors to illness. Finau describes the way in which illnesses were dealt with and treated, and suggests how government policies may encourage the best of the traditional and the new. He concludes that more indigenous health research is needed.

Politics and
Government

248   Democracy bug bites Tonga.

'I. Futa Helu.   In: *Culture and democracy in the South Pacific.*
Edited by Ron Crocombe, et al.   Suva: Institute of Pacific Studies,
University of the South Pacific, 1992, p. 139-51.

Futa Helu and his Atenisi Institute have been the intellectual base of the movement
for greater democracy in Tonga. He sees Tonga as progressing from aristocracy to
kingship rather than, as in classical Greece, from kingship to democracy. But, even if
Tonga would never become a liberal society through natural evolution, he sees
overseas travel, migration and education as now moving it in that direction. However,
a party political system, which he anticipated, has not yet developed. There is no
common ideology uniting pro-democracy People's Representatives in the Legislative
Assembly other than the call for greater democracy itself.

249   The doctrine of accountability and the unchanging locus of power in Tonga.

I. C. Campbell.   *The Journal of Pacific History*, vol. 29, no. 1 (1994),
p. 81-94.

Campbell traces ideas on power and accountability in Tonga through the three
elections of 1987, 1990 and 1993, when discussion began to focus on the role of
elected representatives and their relationship with a hereditary head of state who is
also head of government. The 1987 election was the first to be based on issues, and
newly-elected People's Representatives were determined to scrutinize government,
which they believed should be accountable to them. But he observes that the king's
authority derives from tradition, conquest and inheritance, and not from the Constitution,
which itself depends on the authority of the king. The idea that power derives from the
people and not from the king is not acceptable in Tonga. The initially interlocking
issues of democracy and of sound and accountable government have become separated:
democracy has become a separate issue from alleged corruption. Campbell sees the
central issues in Tongan politics through these years as concerning content and structure
rather than policy; alternative constitutional possibilities were not under consideration.

A considerable degree of consensus persisted concerning the state, its identity, functions and so on, and there was no threat to its stability. Questions about the accountability of government threaten neither lives nor livelihoods.

250   The emergence of parliamentary politics in Tonga.
I. C. Campbell.   *Pacific Studies*, vol. 15, no. 1 (1992), p. 77-97.

During the late 1980s the people of Tonga became more aware of the process of politics and more open to suggestions of constitutional change. But it would be wrong to assume that the challenge to authority and demand for change were without precedent. Only in the latter part of Queen Sālote's reign was the image of stability, peace and unity made a reality. She marginalized parliament by dealing directly with the people and dispensing patronage in traditional ways and through the church. The present king inherited the legacy of stability, but his dedication to modernization has implied a preference for social, and thus political, change. Campbell outlines signs of popular discontent through parliament from the 1970s, over land ownership and other issues. He considers the role of the churches and of education; the development of a wealthy middle class independent of the old aristocracy; the role of 'Akilisi Pohiva and his pro-democracy movement; the significant general election of 1987; and the contentious parliamentary session that followed, culminating in a walkout and the bitter election of 1990 which produced a vote for change, yet of a very conservative sort. Campbell saw change at that time as necessary, though a few minor reforms could persuade people of the honour and integrity of their hereditary leaders.

251   The 1990 election in Tonga.
Rodney C. Hills.   *The Contemporary Pacific*, vol. 3, no. 2 (1991), p. 357-78.

The 1990 election in Tonga took place against a background of unprecedented concern over the accountability of ministers with regard to expense allowances, passport sales, land deals and financial management generally. Many Tongans, who travelled or had families overseas, were learning of other patterns of parliamentary democracy. The unofficial press was increasingly outspoken, and traditional loyalties and behaviour patterns were breaking down. While political parties did not emerge then, and have not subsequently, a group of candidates standing broadly on a platform of constitutional reform and ministerial accountability to parliament rather than to the monarch was elected with large majorities. Hills, Australian High Commissioner to Tonga at the time, was able to observe this remarkable election at first hand. He describes the parliamentary system under the present Constitution, the conduct of the campaign, the candidates and the issues, and considers the election's significance for the government of the day, and for Tonga's national interest.

252   Predicaments in Polynesia: culture and constitutions in Western Samoa and Tonga.
Rodney C. Hills.   *Pacific Studies*, vol. 16, no. 4 (1993), p. 115-29.

Hills sees both similarities and differences in the constitutional development of Tonga and of Western Samoa. They began in the 19th century with similar social and political conditions. Each tried to adapt representative government to its own traditions, and each has found that the compromise with chiefly authority has worked only partially. Tonga adopted the features of the modern state earlier, with the Constitution of 1875, but the centralized and relatively authoritarian government, while laying the foundation of a century of stability, was a distortion of Polynesian traditions that Tongans themselves now seem unwilling to accept. Hills feels that Western Samoa has tackled the challenges more successfully than Tonga, where the system lost its flexibility with the introduction of hereditary titles. Tonga now needs to allow the expression and adoption of dissenting views. It must be added that the years since the paper was written have demonstrated just how much freedom there is to express dissenting views, both in parliament and in the kingdom generally, even if the system of government has not yet changed.

253 Report of the Minister of Lands, Survey and Natural Resources.
Nuku'alofa: Government of Tonga. annual.
The report records the activities of the Ministry in offering services directly relating to the three basic needs of any development process: land, energy and capital. The Ministry facilitates the development of land rights and the geological search for indigenous natural resources. Statistics on the registration of land holdings during the year, on survey activities and on energy planning and imports are provided.

254 Report of the Prime Minister.
Nuku'alofa: Government of Tonga. annual.
The Prime Minister's annual report sets out the principal activities of his office for the year, and of related activities including production of *The Tonga Chronicle* and the activities of the Tonga Traditions Committee, the Printing Department and the Governors' offices in the island groups other than Tongatapu.

255 Thy kingdom come: the democratization of aristocratic Tonga.
Epeli Hau'ofa. *The Contemporary Pacific*, vol. 6, no. 2 (Fall 1994), p. 414-28.
Hau'ofa sees the present movement for democratization in Tonga, perhaps paradoxi-cally, as the consequence of the Constitution of 1875, which abolished the real power of the nobles but which ultimately exposed a centralizing but now vulnerable monarchy directly to the ordinary people of Tonga, often better educated and with more economic power than the nobles. He sees the nobles as still having a role to perform as a focus of culture and of identity, but he believes that they have been 'transformed from knight-hood into pawnhood' as the powers of the monarchy have increased. He does not note that the interests of the monarchy and the nobility have become increasingly identified through intermarriage, strengthening the role of the nobility in one respect at least.

256 Tonga.
Ropate Qalo. In: *Decentralisation in the South Pacific: local, provincial and state government in twenty countries.* Edited by Peter Larmour, Ropate Qalo. Suva: University of the South Pacific, 1985, p. 238-42.
In this brief note Qalo sets out what little there is to be said on local government within Tonga. The major units of government are the three island groups of Tongatapu, Ha'apai and Vava'u. Each is divided into districts containing a number of villages. Each village has a town officer whose role is to mediate between village and government and to deal mainly with public health, cleaning, weeding, etc. Each reports to a district officer. On Tongatapu town officers report directly to the Prime Minister's office. Ha'apai and Vava'u both have a governor, to whom their district officers report. Both town and district officers are elected for three years. The law also

provides for several levels of public meeting (*fono*) called by senior government officials, a noble or a village.

257 Tonga: the last Pacific kingdom.
Emiliana Afeaki. In: *Politics in Polynesia*. Edited by Ron Crocombe, Ahmed Ali. Suva: Institute of Pacific Studies of the University of the South Pacific, 1983, p. 55-78.

Afeaki describes the political system in Tonga as it operates under the terms of the 1875 Constitution, a unique transplant of the English model of government to a Polynesian kingdom with traditional roles and relationships between ranks. The King exercises power through a Privy Council and a Cabinet, whose members he appoints. Its members, together with an equal number of Nobles' and People's Representatives, constitute the Legislative Assembly. Afeaki predicts some of the economic and political pressures which have become clearer since she wrote, with tentative, though as yet largely unsuccessful, moves towards party politics.

258 Tonga since the 1990 election: things change but stay the same.
I. C. Campbell. *The Journal of Pacific History*, vol. 27, no. 3 (1992), p. 61-65.

Campbell provides a general overview of Tonga after the 1990 election, which saw an overwhelming vote for critics of the government and an apparent unity of interest among the People's Representatives. Two years later there was little sign of the dramatic developments anticipated by some observers, despite popular dissatisfaction over the government's handling of passport sales to non-residents and other matters. However, the People's Representatives have obliged ministers to examine their own behaviour more critically. The economy saw the value of remittances fall, and the growth of pumpkin exports which has brought riches to some. The questions remained how far the government would foster economic development and social change without either conceding a larger share of political power to the new interests or resorting to repression. Campbell saw the people at that stage as expectantly waiting for change rather than pressing for it.

259 Tradition versus democracy in the South Pacific: Fiji, Tonga and Western Samoa.
Stephanie Lawson. Cambridge, England: Cambridge University Press, 1996. 228p. 4 maps. bibliog.

Lawson sees the political elite in Tonga as using a largely invented tradition to defend its power and privilege against demands for accountability and participation. She traces the political history of Tonga from the Constitution of 1875 to the pro-democracy movement of the late 1990s as an attempt by chiefly elites to use invented tradition to sanctify their own dominance. She quotes the Tongan writer Epeli Hau'ofa: 'It is the privileged who can afford to tell the poor to preserve their traditions'. There is truth in this, but there are many still who value tradition with its ancient origins, when freed of abuse, and who see the nobles created by the 1875 Constitution as but the ancient chiefdoms continued. Lawson quotes the Hon. Fusitu'a, Speaker of Tonga's Legislative Assembly at the time, as saying that a country that decides *for itself* how to run a democracy *is* a democracy. This observation, in the Tongan context, not judged by the standards of Western liberal democracy, may be more valid in Tonga even today than Lawson might admit.

Constitution and Legal System

260 **After the vanilla harvest: stains in the Tongan land tenure system.**
Paul van der Grijp. *The Journal of the Polynesian Society*, vol. 102, no. 3 (1993), p. 233-53.
This is a detailed case-study of the inheritance of land within a kin group, at a stage of transition from shifting cultivation to intensive agriculture, from self-sufficient production and gift exchange to commercial agricultural production, from a society in which everyone has a place of their own to one which engages extensively in wage labour. The author sets out the historical background to land tenure in Tonga, and then examines a village in Vava'u in which vanilla has become the main cash crop; the way in which capital is invested and the cash returns are spent; and the effect of cash on patterns of inheritance of land. The cost of gifts to nobles for the right to land has greatly increased and traditional concepts of access to land are changing.

261 **The constitution and the traditional political system of Tonga.**
Laki M. Niu. *Pacific Perspective*, vol. 13, no. 1 (1985), p. 67-70.
From a brief review of the process that led to the Constitution of 1875, Niu concludes that a sharing similar to the one made then between king, chiefs and people must now be made again.

262 **The early accommodation of traditional and English law in Tonga.**
Guy Powles. In: *Tongan culture and history*. Edited by Phyllis Herda, Jennifer Terrell, Niel Gunson. Canberra: The Journal of Pacific History, 1990, p. 145-69.
The introduction of British concepts of law to Tonga was accompanied by some controversy and conflict, but the architects of the new state of Tonga selected elements from each legal culture and arrived at an early accommodation with Tongan legal culture. In this way, Powles claims, Tonga was able to lead Pacific island societies in establishing stable central government. This paper examines the establishment of that accommodation and how it was enforced during the period 1875 to 1930. It presents data and analysis in the form of three studies – the essentials of the 1875 Constitution

in their early context; constitutional and statutory changes in the law from 1875 to 1903; and the implementation of laws by central government to 1930. A useful appendix lists all the codes, early treaties, laws and revisions from 1836 to 1988.

263 **The impact of the British on the Tongan traditional concept of justice and law.**
Sione Lātūkefu. In: *European impact and Pacific influence: British and German colonial policy in the Pacific Islands and the indigenous response.* Edited by Hermann J. Hiery, John M. MacKenzie. London; New York: I. B. Tauris in association with the German Historical Institute, 1997, p. 177-88.

Lātūkefu notes that before European impact Tongan society, being non-literate, lacked codified laws and relied on the oral transmission of knowledge of traditions and customs from one generation to the next. In its stratified society chiefs ruled and developed traditions and customs to perpetuate, protect and legitimize their status. These were based on concepts of *mana* (sacredness) and *tapu* (prohibition). The system at its best relied on reciprocity when not abused, but there was no concept of personal liberty, social equality or justice for commoners. These concepts have been considerably modified through British influence, although that influence remained indirect in accordance with British colonial policy for small countries like Tonga. Lātūkefu describes how King George Tupou I saw that the missionaries could help him to rule his people in the British way, riding the wave of European impact rather than going against it. He outlines the law codes which the King promulgated with the missionaries' help, from the Vava'u Code of 1839 to the Constitution of 1875. But he notes, with personal reminiscences of the behaviour of chiefs when he was young, that the tension between introduced laws of equality and social justice and traditional Tongan culture has not been completely resolved even in the present day.

264 **Laws of Tonga: comprising all laws, acts, ordinances and subsidiary legislation in force on the 31st day of December 1988.**
1988 revised edition prepared under the authority of the Laws Consolidation Act, 1988 by Neil James Adsett. Nuku'alofa: The Government of Tonga, 1989.

The most recent edition of *Laws of Tonga* is published in five volumes, with each act paginated but no continuous pagination. Volume 1 contains a general preface setting out the changes since the previous edition in 1967, consequent upon independence in 1970, a complete Table of Acts and an index to the laws. Acts are set out under the following titles: A – Interpretation (chapter 1); B – Government (chapters 2-8); C – Administration of justice (chapters 9-24); D – Civil law (chapters 25-34); E – Police, prisons, public order (chapters 35-40); F – General administration (chapters 41-54); G – Defence (chapters 55-58); H – Nationality and immigration (chapters 59-63); I – Revenue (chapters 64-73); J – Health and medical (chapters 74-85); K – Education and national heritage (chapters 86-91); L – Government services (chapters 92-101); M – Finance and banking (chapters 102-12); N – Commerce (chapters 113-21); O – Fish and plants (chapters 122-31); P – Land and minerals (chapters 132-35); Q – Marine (chapters 136-45); R – Animals (chapters 146-50); S – Aircraft (chapters 151-54); T – Road and traffic (chapters 155-57); U – Diplomatic and international relations (chapters 158-64); V – Entertainment (chapters 165-69). The five volumes contain the following chapters: Volume 1 – chapters 1-38; Volume 2 – chapters 39-73;

Volume 3 – chapters 74-101; Volume 4 – chapters 102-35; Volume 5 – chapters 136-69. Volume 5 also has a chronological table and general index by topic. An annual volume of new and amended legislation is prepared and issued by the Ministry of Justice. A new complete, consolidated edition of the *Laws of Tonga* is planned.

265 **Litigation, interpersonal conflict and noble succession disputes in the Friendly Islands.**
George E. Marcus. In: *Access to justice, Vol. IV, the anthropological perspective, patterns of conflict management: essays in the ethnography of law.* Edited by Klaus-Friedrich Koch. Alphen aan der Rijn, the Netherlands: Sijthoff & Nordhoff; Milan, Italy: Dott. A. Giuffré Editore, 1979, p. 69-104.

Marcus observes that the traditional means of expressing and managing disputes among Tongans are in principle contradictory to the procedures of a European-style legal system based on an adversary relationship between disputing parties. Tongans are avidly litigious, yet bitter disputes in court are followed by smooth social relations. Marcus considers the significance of litigation in the broader context of interpersonal conflict, concentrating on litigation involving land and titles. He describes informal traditional methods of dispute resolution as governed by traditional Tongan behaviour, knowing how and when to get angry, how to ask forgiveness and how to express residual resentment; he also considers the role of gossip and public opinion. He describes the court system and legal profession, and the nature of litigation over nobles' titles and estates. He examines and analyses three title disputes in detail. His conclusion is that litigation offers possession or compensation in a way that traditional resolution does not, and that the use of lawyers avoids direct confrontation between adversaries, allowing for the ideal pattern of smooth social relations. The best long-term interests of litigants often appear to be served by mutually rejecting the disruptive role of past litigation in their continuing public relations.

266 **Pacific courts and legal systems.**
Edited by Guy Powles, Mere Pulea. Suva: Institute of Pacific Studies, University of the South Pacific, in association with the Faculty of Law, Monash University, 1988. 376p. map.

This book consists of fifty-five short papers by people engaged in courts and legal work. Most combine personal reflection with systematic description. There are three papers on Tonga. Hingano Helu ('Independence of adjudicators and judicial decision making in Tonga') makes clear the effect on the adjudicator's work of Tongan traditions of gift making and of obligation to relatives and friends. 'Alisi Afeaki Taumoepeau ('The Land Court in Tonga') raises the growing problem of the legal status of the tax allotments of Tongans who have left to live overseas. Taniela Manu ('Lawyers in Tonga: a personal view') observers that, of thirty lawyers licensed to work in Tonga, only eight have law degrees and some of them live overseas. Most have been trained and gained experience locally. For them more training is needed, but he believes that there will always be a place for lay lawyers in Tonga alongside law graduates, providing a service within reach of the common people.

267 **Pacific law bibliography.**
Jacqueline D. Elliott.   Hobart, Australia: Pacific Law Press, 1990.
2nd ed. 659p.
The 'countries' section of this bibliography lists forty-eight items for Tonga, including
the Constitution, statutes, law reports and articles in books and journals, classified by
topic and published to May 1990. All items are also printed in a general subject
sequence.

268 **The report of the Attorney General and Minister of Justice for the
year 1996.**
Nuku'alofa: Government of Tonga, 1996. 142p.
The annual report (in both English and Tongan) sets out the work of the Ministry of
Justice, provides statistics from the Chief Justice and Registrar General on criminal
and civil cases by type of offence and in total, and on births, marriages and deaths by
island group. It also records the activities of the Crown Law department in legislation
and in court work, with summaries of some of the most significant criminal, civil, land
and family cases.

269 **Right and privilege in Tongan land tenure.**
Kerry James.   In: *Land, custom and practice in the South Pacific*.
Edited by R. Gerard Ward, Elizabeth Kingdon.   Cambridge, England:
Cambridge University Press, 1995, p. 157-97.
James begins by pointing out that the Constitution of 1875 set Tonga on a course
quite different from that of its neighbours. There was no distinction between freehold
and customary title. All land became the property of the crown and was divided into
royal, government and noble estates. The history of land tenure is thus concerned with
changes in social strata and in the nature of the value of land. James identifies and
develops four major themes: commoners exercising their rights by applying for allotments; the increase in population which makes it now impossible for many Tongans to
acquire land; the government's resistance to change in the original land measures; and
the appearance of an informal land market with extra-legal payments for the lease or
use of land, which has grown rapidly since the 1970s, fuelled by the impact of
remittances. James describes the pre-European system of land holding and the reforms
of the 19th century and subsequent developments. She exemplifies customary practice
from a detailed survey of the pattern of landholding on an island in Vava'u, with case-
studies of patterns of transmission of land. In the late 1970s the government amended
the Land Act so that farmers could acquire holdings larger than their statutory
allotment and could use land as security to obtain bank loans. Subsistence farmers are
becoming commercial growers and can pay considerable sums to lease land, as can
those needing urban land for housing. James concludes that land practice has never
been in step with the legal code and that the illusion that the present is not really
different from the past has become more difficult to preserve as commercial activity
leads to a greater assertion of individual land rights.

270 **Tonga.**
H. H. Marshall. In: *International encyclopedia of comparative law,
vol. 1: national reports T.* Edited by Viktor Knapp. Tübingen,
Germany: J. C. B. Mohr (Paul Siebeck); Paris, The Hague: Mouton,
no date (c. 1973), p. T25-26.
This two-page entry briefly summarizes the constitutional system of Tonga (nationality,
territorial division, state organs and the judiciary) and sources of law and present law
(the Constitution and the basic law).

271 **Tonga.**
C. Guy Powles. In: *South Pacific islands legal systems.* Edited by
Michael A. Ntumy. Honolulu, Hawai'i: University of Hawai'i Press,
1993, p. 315-41.
The sources of Tongan law are the Constitution, statutes and subsidiary legislation of
Tonga, English common law and some statute law. Powles outlines these sources, the
constitutional system and form of government, and the law in its particular respects:
international; financial; criminal; land and titles; family; wills and successions;
contract; and commercial. He also describes judicial procedures and legal education.
The book treats the law of all the South Pacific countries, following the same scheme
of headings. The law and legal system of Tonga can thus be compared usefully with
those of its neighbours.

272 **Tonga: equality overtaking privilege.**
Alaric Maude, Feleti Sevele. In: *Land tenure in the Pacific.* Edited
by Ron Crocombe. Suva: University of the South Pacific, 1987,
3rd ed., p. 114-42. 2 maps. bibliog.
Maude alone wrote the chapter on Tonga for the first edition of this book in 1971; for
the third edition his contribution has been updated by Sevele. They describe the
pre-contact landholding system as far as the evidence allows, the claim by King
George Tupou I to all land in 1850, the consolidation of this process through the 19th
century, and the important 1976 amendments to the Land Act whereby land could be
mortgaged to secure bank loans and landlords can lease out their allotments. They
describe the present system, with statistics on ownership and distribution, and discuss
the problems of rising population and uneven distribution of land, with migration from
the outer islands and the villages both to the towns and overseas. They suggest some
of the problems over allocation and tenure which will have to be faced in the future
but which have largely not been resolved in the years since they wrote.

273 **Tonga law reports: Volume I, cases decided in the Supreme Court of Tonga, 1908-1959.**
Edited by D. B. Hunter.   Nuku'alofa: Government Printer, 1961. 220p.
Tonga law reports: Volume II, reports on Land Court cases, 1923-1962, Privy Council decisions, 1924-1961.
Edited by D. B. Hunter.   Nuku'alofa: Government Printer, 1963. 220p.
Tonga law reports: Volume III, Land Court cases and Privy Council decisions, 1962-1973.
Edited by H. Steed Roberts.   Nuku'alofa: Government Printer, 1974. 52p.
Tonga law reports, 1974-1980.
Edited by D. Paterson, N. Hampton.   Nuku'alofa: Ministry of Justice, 1995. 109p.
Tonga law reports, 1981-1988.
Edited by D. Paterson, N. Hampton.   Nuku'alofa: Ministry of Justice, 1995. 144p.
Tonga law reports, 1989.
Edited by D. Paterson, N. Hampton.   Nuku'alofa: Ministry of Justice, 1995. 110p.
Tonga law reports, 1990.
Edited by G. W. Martin, D. Paterson.   Nuku'alofa: Ministry of Justice, 1994. 208p.
Tonga law reports, 1991.
Edited by N. Hampton.   Nuku'alofa: Ministry of Justice, 1997. 71p.
Tonga law reports, 1992.
Edited by N. Hampton.   Nuku'alofa: Ministry of Justice, 1997. 84p.
Tonga law reports, 1993.
Edited by N. Hampton.   Nuku'alofa: Ministry of Justice, 1997. 42p.
All these volumes report on the most significant cases concerning criminal, civil, land and family law. At the time of writing, the volume for 1994 is in the press and those for 1995 and 1996 are being prepared.

274 **Tonga: legal constraints and social potentials.**
Mosikaka Moengangongo. In: *Land rights of Pacific women.*   Suva: Institute of Pacific Studies of the University of the South Pacific, 1986, p. 87-102.
The author believes that, in spite of the limits of legislation in Tonga in giving land rights to women, their 'silent rights' are still significant, but now inadequate. She describes the system of ranking in Tongan society and how it impinges on land rights. Traditional land tenure was predominantly the domain of men. Under the present system brought in by the Land Act of 1862, land is acquired largely by inheritance, the male being preferred to the female because the land belongs to the male-headed extended family. A widow is entitled to a life estate in her husband's property but this

automatically terminates if she remarries. It is possible for a daughter to inherit if there is no male heir. However, only two per cent of tax allotments were then held by women, and under terms which can be restrictive. Women are increasingly involved in income-generating activities; uncertainty of tenure is a major constraint to long-term capital investment, and land laws need to be revised.

275 **The Tongan Constitution: a brief history to celebrate its centenary.**
Sione Lātūkefu. Nuku'alofa: Tonga Traditions Committee, 1975.
152p. map. bibliog.

That Tonga remained the only independent nation in the Pacific by 1900 was largely due to the Constitution of 1875. Completed by King George I from material prepared by Shirley Baker, and building on the earlier codes of 1839, 1850 and 1862, it established the fundamental freedom of all Tongans, limited the power of the chiefs, made land inalienable and defined a constitutional monarchy of an appropriately Tongan style. Lātūkefu describes the development of the Constitution and its place in the history of Tonga in the following century. He concludes that, for all its short-comings, it has served Tonga well. Appendixes give the complete texts of the Constitution of 1875 and that of 1975, which is updated but still essentially the same.

Foreign Relations

276 The Annual Report of the Minister for Foreign Affairs and Defence.
Nuku'alofa: Government of Tonga. annual.
The annual report summarizes the work of the Ministry during the year, together with bilateral, regional and international negotiations, within the context of Tonga's foreign policy, which it defines as 'to maintain friendly relations with all countries'. As of 1996 Tonga maintained diplomatic relations with forty-three countries, with five missions resident in Nuku'alofa (Australia, New Zealand, the Republic of China, the United Kingdom and the Commission of the European Union) and six honorary consuls. Overseas representation is largely covered through the Tongan High Commission in London, where the High Commissioner is also accredited to eleven other countries. There are also seven honorary Tongan consuls. The report also records Tonga's membership of regional and international organizations, royal, ministerial and official visits, and projects funded by overseas aid, and provides a general review of regional affairs. The section on defence in the most recent report (1996) notes the patrolling of Tongan waters to ensure legal fishing, the acquisition of an aircraft to supplement three patrol boats, and other bilateral defence arrangements and exercises.

277 Kingdom, People's Republic formalize diplomatic relations.
The Tonga Chronicle, 5 November 1998, p. 1, 3.
In a surprising and dramatic development in October 1998 Tonga established diplomatic relations with the People's Republic of China, ending twenty-six years of warm and close relations with Taiwan. Taiwan had provided much aid in infrastructure projects and such public works as the Queen Sālote Memorial Hall and the 'Atele Stadium, and as recently as July 1998 had sent a large, high-level delegation to Tonga for the King's eightieth birthday celebrations. It had recently built a large new embassy. The report in *The Tonga Chronicle* says that China will build a new embassy and provide financial assistance and an interest-free loan to assist economic development. The Vice-Foreign Minister, Yang Jiechi, in Tonga for the announcement on 2 November, said that there was no conflict of fundamental interest between the two countries. 'The Chinese people stand ready to join hands with the people of Tonga to build an even better world', he said. According to the report the decision was made when the King visited China in July 1997.

278　Microstates and nuclear issues: regional cooperation in the Pacific.
Yoko S. Ogashiwa.　Suva: Institute of Pacific Studies, University of
the South Pacific, 1991. 92p. map. bibliog.

Few issues have more united the independent states of the South Pacific than nuclear
testing and the dumping of nuclear waste. Testing started with the Americans in 1946,
followed by the British and then, from 1966, by the French. Protests from the island
states, including Tonga, began in 1970, and the book records their progress to the
signing of the South Pacific Nuclear Free Zone Treaty in 1985 by eight countries.
Tonga, however, did not sign, believing that its security depended on the American
military presence, supported by a nuclear-armed force. For a while it was the only
independent Pacific state to accept US warships in its ports. The book quotes Tonga's
Foreign Minister, Crown Prince Tupoutu'a, as saying that the ban was an emotional
reaction and that Tonga's approach was more strategic. The book brings out the
independence of Tonga's policy, maintained despite its status as part of the South
Pacific community of states.

279　The Pacific island states: security and sovereignty in the post-Cold
War world.
Stephen Henningham.　London: Macmillan Press; New York:
St. Martin's Press, 1995. 174p. 7 maps. bibliog.

This is a study of security and defence issues and trends in the Pacific, and of the
challenges which the Pacific island states face to their security and sovereignty. From
the 1960s fourteen small independent states emerged, including Tonga. Initially they
maintained close connections with the Western nations. The 1980s were less stable,
with the USA, France, Japan, the former USSR (which approached Tonga in 1976 for
port access in return for aid) and even Libya paying increased attention to the region.
With the end of superpower rivalry in the 1990s, the island states faced new
challenges, with less interest from the wider world. Writing for both an academic and
a general audience, Henningham pays particular attention to three topics: French
nuclear testing and related issues; the role of Australia and New Zealand in the region;
and military and paramilitary intervention such as the coups in Fiji. He identifies
Tonga as the most conservative state in Polynesia in its foreign policy, giving only
cautious support to regional positions on French nuclear testing, and having a more
positive attitude than other states to French presence and policies generally. He also
notes that Tonga is one of only three Pacific states to have armed forces, Fiji and
Papua New Guinea being the others. He concludes that the region as a whole and its
links with the wider world have become more complex and to some extent more
volatile. All of them, including Tonga, face economic and environmental problems
and a lessening of interest and of aid from the major powers. Henningham sees an
uncertain future.

280　Restructuring foreign and defence policy: the Pacific islands.
Richard Herr.　In: Asia-Pacific in the new world order.　Edited by
Anthony McGrew, Christopher Brook.　London; New York:
Routledge, 1998, p. 209-28.

Herr identifies environmentalism as a substantial part of the contemporary South
Pacific's regional approach to foreign policy, though he does not note that this is
probably less the case for Tonga than for some of the other island states. He follows
the theme of 'unity in diversity' and the challenge of adapting to a post-Cold War

order. He identifies the limitations in the tiny and vulnerable states of the South Pacific – diverse in size, geography and political background – in exercising sovereignty through the management of their external affairs, and the development of regionalism as an appropriate response. He sees that the range of foreign policy options available to them has probably declined since the end of the Cold War. He records how the establishment of non-resident diplomatic relations between Tonga and the Soviet Union in 1976 startled the Western states into agreeing that Soviet involvement in the South Pacific should be opposed. He describes the importance of the 200-mile economic zones established in the early 1980s, the changing relations with major Western powers and with Australia and New Zealand, and the possible roles of Japan, China and Taiwan. Finally Herr looks at the domestic dimension, with political changes, population pressures and environmental concerns all of significance. He concludes that, small as they are, the island states have been and can continue to be effective. All this is in general terms: Tonga's concerns and constraints are not always those of the other islands, but most of the general factors identified which affect them, affect Tonga too.

281 **The South Pacific foreign affairs handbook.**
Steve Hoadley.   Sydney: Allen & Unwin, in association with the New Zealand Institute of International Affairs, 1992. 258p. 3 maps. bibliog.

'Tonga has been perceived as slightly eccentric in foreign policy', writes Hoadley, citing such events as the talks with the Soviet Union in 1976 over facilities for fishing in return for upgrading the airport, its diplomatic relations with Taiwan, and its friendship with France despite nuclear testing. Hoadley sees the policy as part of a movement to widen room for manoeuvre and broaden the resource base of a small island state. The general introductory chapters describe Tonga's place in the international and regional structures of the South Pacific. The chapter devoted to Tonga describes how the Government of Tonga works out its stated aim of 'harmonious relations and mutual cooperation . . . with all nations and international organizations'. In his thorough summary Hoadley's only major omission is perhaps the importance of the particularly close relations with Fiji, resulting from historical and dynastic factors and shown in Tonga's expression of some support for the military coups there.

282 **Strategic cooperation and competition in the Pacific islands.**
Edited by F. A. Mediansky.   Sydney: University of New South Wales, Centre for South Pacific Studies; [Philadelphia]: Pennsylvania State University, Australia-New Zealand Study Center, 1995. 390p.

This general survey of strategic and security issues provides two general overviews, four papers on economic, political, security and regional cooperation perspectives, and papers on the major external powers: Australia; France; Japan; New Zealand; the United States; the (former) Soviet Union; China; and others. Tonga surfaces briefly when appropriate. Given the considerable Taiwanese presence in Tonga at the time of writing, with an embassy and an aid programme, more might have been said of Taiwanese intentions and the relationship of the island countries with China. The King, on a recent and perhaps unprecedented visit, was warmly received in both countries, although diplomatic relations with Taiwan have since ended in the wake of formalized relations with China (see item no. 277). The island states cannot isolate themselves from the political and strategic concerns of the world's major powers, and this book records the main issues and relationships, which affect Tonga as much as the other states.

Economy, Trade and Labour

283 Between the forest and the big lagoon: the microeconomy of Kotu island in the kingdom of Tonga.
Arne Aleksej Perminow. *Pacific Viewpoint*, vol. 34, no. 2 (1993), p. 179-92.

Perminow sets out to understand the character of the everyday economics of a peripheral local community in Tonga, a small island in the Ha'apai group which is farmed mostly for subsistence crops, though the islanders grow kava as a cash crop on the neighbouring island of Tofua. The large lagoon provides a major source of sea food, which has also become significant in the cash economy. Perminow examines patterns of cultivation, trends in population and the increasing role of the cash economy, finding that enhanced social recognition and respectability are more important than cash in itself. Examples are given of the careers of the church president and a business entrepreneur. The analysis of the island's economy and of the central role of the church indicates that the economic activities of the islanders resonate strongly with the past while at the same time encouraging acumen and business entrepreneurship.

284 The birth and growth of a Polynesian women's exchange network.
Cathy A. Small. *Oceania*, vol. 65, no. 3 (1995), p. 234-56.

Small describes the birth and growth of a commoner women's exchange network in Tonga, within what has been called 'the compromise culture'. It developed in the first two decades of this century, beginning with the inter-island exchange of women's prestige wealth. It expanded to incorporate groups in Fiji and Samoa, to cover Western commodities and cash, and to include Tongan migrants resident overseas. The story demonstrates the deeply conservative nature of seemingly radical change in Tonga, and the profound changes in Tongan life now under way.

285   **Corned beef and tapioca: a report on the food distribution systems in Tonga.**
Epeli Hau'ofa.   Canberra: The Australian National University, 1979. 180p. map. (Development Studies Centre Monograph, no. 19).

There are now two or three supermarkets in Nuku'alofa as well as some sizeable shops, and smaller general stores in Pangai (Ha'apai) and Neiafu (Vava'u), but every village has its small store selling mostly imported tinned and processed goods, while fresh local produce is largely sold in the markets in Nuku'alofa and Neiafu. Hau'ofa describes and analyses the commercial distribution of foodstuffs in Tongatapu. He finds out that most retail stores are very small, undercapitalized and unstable; that most market vendors are semi-subsistence and semi-commercial growers; and that with the growth of urbanization there is a move towards more commercial farming. His findings are based on a wealth of detailed statistical tables.

286   **Country Profile: Pacific Islands – Fiji, New Caledonia, Samoa, Solomon Islands, Tonga, Vanuatu.**
London: Economist Intelligence Unit. annual.

To supplement its quarterly reports, which provide briefings on the political and economic state of each country and analyse current trends, the Economist Intelligence Unit produces annual reports providing background information. The most recent notes, for Tonga, the development of the pro-democracy movement, current economic performance and the state of the infrastructure, manufacturing and foreign trade. Key economic statistics are tabulated from data provided by the Bank of Tonga, the Asian Development Bank, the IMF, the World Bank, etc. over a five-year period. The 1997-98 edition shows, for example, external debt increasing and rising as a proportion of GDP.

287   **Economic development in seven Pacific island countries.**
Christopher Browne with Douglas A. Scott.   Washington, DC: International Monetary Fund, 1989. 219p. 8 maps.

The main value of this book lies in the twelve tables provided for each of the seven countries surveyed, including Tonga. These provide detailed information and analysis for the five fiscal years 1982/83 to 1987/88 on: GDP by sector; consumer price index; central government budget, revenue and expenditure; the monetary position; interest rate structure; balance of payments; exports and imports by commodity; external debt; and international reserves. Each country chapter also describes geographic and demographic features, outlines the economic structure and institutions and traces the evolution of the economy and the economic strategy to generate growth while retaining the traditional structure of society. The authors conclude that cautious domestic financial management remains crucial, given the particular difficulties of such small and isolated countries dependent largely on a few agricultural products for exports, supplemented by remittances and by income from tourism. The IMF sees the 1980s as largely a success story, with accelerating growth and improved living standards, with the traditional way of life preserved amid the development of modern institutions. A comparative table of the seven countries shows Tonga mid-range in GDP, with the highest population density but lowest but one of the countries in population growth, and with the highest calorific intake. There are annexes on multilateral and bilateral economic assistance programmes in the Pacific and on IMF relations with Pacific island countries, showing the type of support given to each.

288 **The economic impact of tourism in Tonga.**
Simon Milne. *Pacific Viewpoint*, vol. 31, no. 1 (1990), p. 24-43.
Tourism is supposed to bring great economic benefits, but it also incurs costs. Milne examines the role of tourism in Tonga's development plans, in the context of its overall trading position and of its concern to minimize negative cultural impacts. He analyses visitor statistics, estimates of what visitors spend, and the need to import to meet their needs. He suggests that in 1987, estimated tourist expenditure of T$8 million led to the generation of T$3.34 million in local income and government revenue of T$1.9 million. Finally, Milne suggests that locally run small hotels and guest houses generate more than larger hotels, and that the government should devote more resources to the development of tourism.

289 **Entrepreneurship and business venture development in the Kingdom of Tonga.**
S. Deacon Ritterbush. Honolulu, Hawai'i: Pacific Islands Development Program, East-West Center, 1986. 200p. 2 maps. bibliog.
The purpose of this exploratory research was to determine the factors that assist or obstruct entrepreneurial attempts at business development in Tonga; it does not claim to be exhaustive. A number of recent indicators have shown Tonga to rank high in economic self-sufficiency, largely because of its lack of mineral wealth and its geographical isolation. But new challenges mean that the private sector must be encouraged, in order to produce a more balanced business sector. Ritterbush researched 185 local entrepreneurs and concluded that the prognosis for business development in Tonga appeared to be favourable, especially for small- and medium-sized businesses and commercial fishing ventures, but that much structural and attitudinal work needed to be done if Tonga was to continue to develop and expand. Local entrepreneurs must be given the opportunity to master the basics of business and financial management. The survey findings are fully tabulated.

290 **Entrepreneurship in an ascribed status society: the Kingdom of Tonga.**
S. Deacon Ritterbush. In: *Island entrepreneurs: problems and performances in the Pacific.* Edited by Te'o I. J. Fairbairn. Honolulu, Hawai'i: Pacific Islands Development Program, East-West Center, 1988, p. 137-63.
Some theorists have suggested that traditional ascribed-status societies such as Tonga are not culturally pre-adapted to entrepreneurship. Status is recognized through kinship affiliation rather than through individual economic achievement. This may be too simplistic, and in this paper, Ritterbush attempts a comprehensive analysis of the complex and varied factors that have affected and now affect indigenous entrepreneurship and private sector growth. In the early years of European contact Tongans were largely outside the cash economy. In the mid-1970s, a public campaign encouraged citizens to save, invest, and reinvest income. By 1980, many, particularly commoners, had responded with enthusiasm, though the failure rate was still quite high. Ritterbush conducted interviews in 1983. She found that many had started with inadequate information or advice but that traditional communal obligations were often a motivating force, although they also created problems. The more successful entrepreneurs, better educated and travelled, were more able to manipulate the environment to suit their own needs, and make communalism work to their favour. Emblems of status are

slowly changing and increasing numbers of women, unable to progress in traditional sectors, are establishing their own businesses.

291   **A historical perspective on aid and dependency: the example of Tonga.**
I. C. Campbell. *Pacific Studies*, vol. 15, no. 3 (1992), p. 59-75.
Campbell notes the heavy dependency of many Pacific island nations on aid, often linked to the donor's political interests; dependency also operates in the sense that much of their commercial sector is owned by foreign interests. Aid and trade often seem closely related. Campbell traces Tonga's pattern of trade from the 1880s, and shows that Tonga's quasi-colonial status made no difference to its economic development before 1970. He considers how foreign aid might have compounded Tonga's economic dependence since. Until 1965, during the reign of Queen Sālote, Tonga was economically independent, receiving no budgetary or commercial subsidies. From 1965, aid was intended as an interim arrangement to accelerate the coming of economic independence when island economies would 'take off' and become self-sustaining. The first two five-year development plans were intended to be largely self-financed, but from the third in 1975, large amounts of foreign aid were anticipated, though economic independence remained the ultimate aim. Campbell concludes that aid dependency is not the cause of structural weakness. Growing payments deficits are largely caused by private consumer demand paid for by remittances from Tongans overseas. Export productivity has not kept pace with government spending, and the ratio of exports to government revenue has fallen from 300 per cent in 1955 to 26 per cent in 1985. The loss of remittance income would be much more serious than the ending of foreign aid.

292   **Kingdom of Tonga – annual foreign trade report 1997.**
Nuku'alofa: Department of Statistics, Government of Tonga, 1998. 153p.
This annual report covers all goods imported into and exported from Tonga, compiled from data supplied by importers and exporters. Import entries show country of consignment and of origin, description and value of each item and duty collected. Exports and re-exports show port of shipment and country of destination and description and value of each item. Classification of commodities is based broadly on the International Trade Classification Revised. All imports and exports are classified by sector – private, government and quasi-government. Graphs show total figures for the previous ten years and various breakdowns for 1997. Twenty-one tables provide detailed statistics.

293   **Labour absorption in the Kingdom of Tonga: position, problems and prospects.**
Michael Hess.   Canberra: Research School of Pacific and Asian Studies, Australian National University, 1996. 22p. bibliog.
(Economics Division Working Papers, South Pacific, no. 96/1).
The local labour market in Tonga is weak both in terms of demand and supply. Opportunities for paid employment are limited, yet in some areas there are shortages of skilled workers. Employment growth is difficult given the lack of capital investment and the small size of the domestic market. The Small Industries Centre has not been very successful, perhaps as much because of distance both from raw materials and

from markets as because of lack of labour productivity. Hess believes that agriculture is unlikely to absorb more labour and that the potential of tourism to create more jobs has not yet been realized. Many Tongans readily find work overseas, but Hess sees the only real prospects of growth in Tonga to be in public sector services, though this is dependent on budgetary constraints and requires better human resource management than at present. Education, he concludes, needs to be oriented more to job skills.

294 **Labour markets in the South Pacific: an overview of Fiji, Solomon Islands, Tonga, Vanuatu and Western Samoa.**
L. J. Perry. Canberra: National Centre for Development Studies, The Australian National University, 1986. 44p. bibliog. (Islands/Australia Working Paper, no. 86/11).
The few pages on Tonga in this brief report summarize (as at 1986) recent trends in population, employment and unemployment, wage trends and policy issues. It identifies the relatively slow population growth, largely because of migration to seek work opportunities overseas. Both unemployment and underemployment are problems in Tonga, with an imbalance between demand for labour and supply. On the other hand, the fifty-one per cent shown working in agriculture, forestry and fisheries would be largely self-employed. Tables show population and growth from 1966 to 1984 by island group and employment by industry sector, with estimated figures for mean household income by island group. The successful development of small secondary industry was seen as a success at the time of writing, but has not developed since in the way that had been hoped.

295 **A macroeconomic framework of the Tongan economy.**
Mark Sturton. Honolulu, Hawai'i: Pacific Island Development Program, East-West Center, 1991. 146p. bibliog.
This paper describes the economic model and social accounting matrix which were built to form the basis for the macroeconomic framework for Tonga's sixth development plan. The model must provide a consistent economic basis for planning and provide a set of projections, including variables, taking note of the relationship between the public and private sectors, given that Tonga is a mixed economy. The paper describes the model in detail, covering the major categories of the economy, and sets out the equations for preparing accounts on each. There are thirty pages of detailed tables.

296 **Ministry of Civil Aviation, Kingdom of Tonga, Annual Report.**
Nuku'alofa: Government of Tonga. annual.
This annual report records Tonga's civil aircraft register, airline operation statistics (domestic and international), and data on airports and on meteorological services.

297 **Mobilizing money in a communal economy: a Tongan example.**
Keith L. Morton. *Human Organization*, vol. 37, no. 1 (1978), p. 50-56.
Morton examines Tongan methods of saving, through a study of credit organizations, in an economy that was then a 'dual economy' and that was monetized but also non-commercialized. He distinguishes between the market economy working through money and the communal economy working through reciprocity. Food and many goods should traditionally be exchanged as a gift, not sold, and even money is treated

reciprocally. At that time cash income, whether from agriculture or from wage labour, was negligible outside Nuku'alofa. It was difficult for the individual household to accumulate money because of social pressures and obligations, so savings clubs and credit associations were used. Morton presents data on these, gathered in Tonga in 1970-71. He describes how they are organized and operate, and also mentions associated fund raising concerts. These organizations rely on values and methods within the communal economy to achieve their goals. Money is collected communally, not commercially, and principles of reciprocity, not of the market, determine its flow within the communal economy.

298 New Zealand aid and the development of class in Tonga.
Andrew P. Needs. Palmerston North, New Zealand: Massey University, 1986. 140p. 2 maps. bibliog.

Needs examines the redistributive effect of New Zealand aid to Tonga, principally the Banana Export Scheme, and concludes that, although large sums of money were pumped into the Tongan economy, a concern with productivity undermined the redistributive aims of the aid, which largely benefited those who already had access to land, capital and labour. In the course of doing this, Needs sets out the history of New Zealand aid to Tonga, the overall approach to that aid and the centrality of land in Tongan economics. He describes the Banana Export Scheme, the nature of the labour force (largely family-orientated) with case-studies of some participants, and considers the effects on class relations and inequality. It should be noted that the scheme is now defunct and bananas are no longer exported.

299 A note on economic development in Tonga.
M. U. Tupouniua. *The Journal of the Polynesian Society*, vol. 69, no. 4 (1960), p. 405-08.

This brief note on the economic development of Tonga is of more than historical interest. The author, who later became Deputy Prime Minister and has recently returned to Tonga to take an active role in politics as a People's Representative in parliament, sets out a broadly optimistic picture of aspirations and developments in produce marketing, commercial fishing, agriculture, shipping and other areas which might help Tonga meet the needs of the modern age. Forty years later it can be seen that there have been some successes, such as vanilla in Vava'u, which Tupouniua foresaw as likely to become a useful new industry, and the development of a banking system. Other areas, such as commercial fishing, have yet to achieve their potential.

300 The pangs of transition: kinship and economy in Tonga.
Epeli Hau'ofa. *The Australian and New Zealand Journal of Sociology*, vol. 14, no. 2 (1978), p. 160-65.

Hau'ofa sees three periods of development in the last 150 years of Tonga's history: the reign of King George Tupou I who established a new order in part on a Western model; the reigns of King George Tupou II and Queen Sālote who consolidated these achievements while shielding Tonga from undue foreign influences; and the reign of the present king who has opened the hitherto closed community to the outside world. Writing in the late 1970s, Hau'ofa looks at two issues, the nature of the kinship system and the direction of economic development. He sees the extended family as becoming burdensome and the kinship system as inadequate for a modern Tonga. He believes that there must be a clear separation between public and private affairs. In economic development he feels that Tonga is drifting, at the mercy of forces beyond its control, with contradictions in its development policy, while Tongans dream of growing rich quickly. He regrets moves to link shipping and telecommunications to foreign interests. King George Tupou I worked to ensure Tonga's independence but it now seems as if Tonga is moving in the opposite direction. Hau'ofa sees Tonga's basic problem as an authoritarian attitude which permeates all relationships in society. The media, he maintains, should be more independent; what Tonga needs is a new national consensus.

301 The performance and prospects of the Pacific islands economies in the world economy.
A. P. Thirlwall.   Honolulu, Hawai'i: East-West Center, 1991. 66p. map. (Pacific Islands Development Program, Research Report Series, no. 14).

The average per capita income in the Pacific islands in 1987 was $US 800, with Tonga at $US 720; however, their economies are small, isolated and vulnerable. Thirlwall provides an economic analysis of the Pacific islands, including Tonga, in the context of the world economy. In the 1970s the islands were reasonably successful, but they fared less well in the 1980s with the fall in commodity prices. Tonga recorded better rates of economic growth than most of its island neighbours between 1977 and 1987, though it also experienced higher rates of inflation. Thirlwall tabulates and analyses rates of growth of GDP, of investment and of export earnings, balance of payments and inflation. He sees the best hope for the 1990s in developing exports of high-value commodities, which, although he wrote too soon to observe it, is exactly what Tonga is doing with its new export trade in squash.

302 Private sector development in the Kingdom of Tonga.
Sione Ramanlal.   Honolulu, Hawai'i: Pacific Islands Development Program, East-West Centre, 1990. 137p.

Ramanlal provides an overview of the performance of the productive sectors of the Tongan economy, detailing GDP by sector, and of the role of the public sector. He examines Tonga's resources, the opportunities for private sector investment, and constraints and problems involving such investment. He sets out specific factors affecting investment climate – political, economic, legal and social – and suggests how risks might be reduced, what training and promotional programmes might be needed, what the government has done so far to promote private sector development, and what it might do in such areas as land tenure, infrastructure development and the regulatory regime. He ends by projecting prospects for export growth.

303 Report of the Minister of Finance.
Nuku'alofa: Government of Tonga. annual.

This annual report records government finances (income and expenditure), the development budget, prices and inflation, the money supply and domestic credit, overseas trade (imports, exports and invisibles, and the balance of payments), foreign reserves and investments, and government lending and public debt. There are departmental reports for each section of the ministry.

304 **Report of the Minister of Labour, Commerce and Industries.**
Nuku'alofa: Government of Tonga. annual.

This report records each year the activities of the Ministry, and includes data on imports, exports and re-exports; trade by type of goods and country; weights and measures; prices of controlled goods; companies' registration; industrial development; overseas assistance and private sector development; the Small Industries Centre; and the co-operative department.

305 **Report of the Minister of Marine.**
Nuku'alofa: Government of Tonga. annual.

This annual report records the activities of ports and of shipping, policy relating to them and their administration.

306 **South Pacific: an annotated bibliography on regional development.**
Nagoya, Japan: United Nations Centre for Regional Development, 1984. 388p.

This bibliography aims to provide an essential information base for the study of the regional development problems of the countries of the area, and for the evolution of specific policy responses. For each entry, works are listed by subject, author and title, with a bibliographic description. The thirty-one works listed for Tonga at that time are a mixture of published books and reports by the Tongan government and external aid and development bodies; some are probably of historical interest rather than of contemporary relevance.

307 **Sustaining livelihoods: promoting informal sector growth in Pacific island countries.**
Margaret Chung.   Suva: United Nations Development Programme, 1997. 82p. bibliog.

It is likely that labour force growth in Tonga and other Pacific islands will almost certainly outstrip formal sector jobs. This reinforces the need to sustain and develop the semi-subsistence or informal sector as the main source of employment in the Pacific islands in the foreseeable future. This report outlines opportunities to stimulate the informal sector and suggests how to overcome barriers such as lack of skills, lack of access to credit and poor communications. Comparative tables for the countries surveyed show Tonga as having quite a low proportion of the formally employed and the highest percentage of women classified as not economically active, together with the highest but one for men. However, it has one of the lowest figures for population and labour force growth and from 1985 to 1994 had one of the highest rates of per capita GDP growth.

308 **Tonga – a brief on Tonga and sustainable development and population: a personal view.**
Langi Kavaliku. In: *Sustainable development and population: proceedings of the fourth Pacific islands conference of leaders, June 24-26, 1993, Tahiti Nui, French Polynesia.* Edited by Sitiveni Halapua, Barbara Naudain. Honolulu, Hawai'i: Pacific Islands Development Program, East-West Center, 1995, p. 150-57.

The deputy Prime Minister of Tonga offers his own view on the related issues of population and development. He characterizes the government's approach as trying to achieve faster economic growth while deciding on sustainable development and population for the future. The mechanisms, he maintains, are in place: family planning and population education, environmental policies, conservation measures and human resource development. In the immediate future, with a young population and a relatively weak employment sector, migration remains a critical issue and remittances are crucial to economic survival. Employment creation is a longer-term issue. He sees these as matters not just of material things but of a philosophy of life, without being nostalgic for a past 'classical Pacific period'. Each country has to ask what standard of life-style it can afford. The countries of the west should not simply give aid and return home but stay to experience living in the environment of the poor, where the choice is often not between different qualities of life, but between life and death. Two themes need to be remembered: that each generation must live with the past and participate in the present as a basis for the next generation; and that one must live a good life in accordance with one's own philosophies and values and with a pride in being Tongan and not just a Pacific version of what is Western and modern.

309 **Tonga – recent economic developments.**
S. Nagai, C. H. Lim, O. Liu. Washington, DC: International Monetary Fund, 1995. 76p. (IMF Staff Country Report, no. 95/67).

The authors note the obstacles of Tonga's isolation, its heavy reliance on a state-led development strategy, its cautious economic management, its low rate of growth and its dependence on external transfers, with about one third of imports financed by remittances. It does not have a diverse productive base. They record the problems caused by drought and by declining copra prices, as well as by increased expenditure on civil servant salaries, set against the benefits of the development of squash cultivation, the scaling back of the public sector and the introduction of competition into the commercial banking system, all of which began to revive the economy, though problems remain from over-dependence on a single crop. They survey in some detail agriculture; manufacturing and construction; wages and prices; the government's finances; public sector commercial activities; banking and finance; and trade. They summarize the tax system as at March 1995. Comprehensive statistics are presented in tables from 1989/90 to 1993/94 for many sectors of the economy.

310 **The Tongan economy: setting the stage for accelerated growth.**
T. I. Fairbairn. Canberra: Australian Government Publishing Service, 1992. 53p. map. bibliog.

At the time of writing, economic growth in Tonga had been moderate, but stability was threatened by fiscal deficits, inflation, and pressure on the balance of payments through buoyant import demand. The report suggested that macroeconomic stability needed to be restored through the expansion of vanilla, squash and watermelon exports, the moderate expansion of tourism and light industry and increased receipts from personal transfers and external aid. Accelerated economic growth would be achieved by pursuing growth-oriented policies and structural reforms in key areas of the economy. The size of the public sector should be reduced and the private sector encouraged to play a more dominant role, while the environment should be protected. The report contains economic data on Tonga in tables and charts.

Population, Migration and Remittances

311 **The Asian and Pacific island peoples of Australia.**
Charles A. Price.   In: *Pacific bridges: the new immigration from Asia and the Pacific islands.* Edited by James T. Fawcett, Benjamin V. Curino.   Staten Island, New York: Center for Migration Studies, 1987, p. 175-97.

Price's analysis of migration to Australia includes within the general category of Pacific islanders data on Tongans, whose population by 1981 was 2,795. He tabulates distribution by state (sixty-eight per cent of Tongans were then in New South Wales) and by occupation (most in production or processing).

312 **Creating their own culture: diasporic Tongans.**
Helen Morton.   *The Contemporary Pacific*, vol. 10, no. 1 (1998), p. 1-30.

Following her work on the way in which children in Tonga are brought up to acquire their Tongan identity (item no. 175), Morton examines the extent to which Tongans resident in Australia regard themselves as Tongan in terms of their cultural identity. From a survey of migrants in Melbourne she finds significant variation and complexity. Some very deliberately seek to retain their Tongan identity, particularly through Tongan churches; others reject their Tongan identity at least in part or seek to maintain a balance between being Tongan and being Australian; others are ambivalent and confused. The degree to which parents try to ensure that their children speak Tongan in the home is an important factor. Morton notes how some Tongans relate to the recent resurgence of Polynesian identity generally.

313 **The determinants of remittances among Tongans in Auckland.**
Mele Fuka Vete.   *Asian and Pacific Migration Journal*, vol. 4, no. 1 (1995), p. 55-68.

Vete examines factors explaining variations in remittances-related behaviour among Tongans in Auckland. She finds that gender differences, length of stay and residence status are important. Most migrants, especially of recent status, send substantial sums, up to fifteen per cent of net income; most remittances are sent for subsistence needs, though many remitters are not concerned about use and believe that the duty of supporting kin is the critical factor.

314 **Do migrants' remittances decline over time? Evidence from Tongans and Western Samoans in Australia.**
Richard P. C. Brown. *The Contemporary Pacific*, vol. 10, no. 1 (1998), p. 107-51.

It is generally believed that the value of remittances sent home by migrants overseas declines over time. Brown's analysis of Tongan households in Sydney shows this not to be so. Migrants are motivated by many factors to send money home – sometimes for their own benefit, sometimes for that of their community. Among those surveyed, the value increases in early years and then remains steady at between $A 3,000 and $A 3,500 per year. Given that total recorded remittances to Tonga in 1992 were $T 27.2 million, representing twenty per cent of gross domestic product and ninety per cent of total exports of goods and services, these new findings, if equally valid for all Tongans overseas, will be significant for the Tongan economy.

315 **The global flea market: migration, remittances and the informal economy in Tonga.**
Richard P. C. Brown, John Connell. *Development and Change*, vol. 24, no. 4 (1993), p. 611-47.

The authors examine and question, through a study of one group of remittance recipients in the flea market of Nuku'alofa, some common assumptions about the form and use of migrants' remittances. They suggest that economic analysis and policy recommendations based on data on recorded remittances should be treated with caution. The unrecorded inflow of remittances in kind, and the associated spread of the domestic informal sector, has important implications for Tonga's economy and may be influencing other changes in the domestic economy. The flea market, with over 100 stalls at times, sells a wide range of second-hand clothes, furniture and other goods sent by Tongans overseas, usually relations of the stall holders. The authors' survey estimates the annual turnover at more than T$ 2 million, a significant amount and one which has affected the formal retail sector. Some traditional Tongan goods and craft products are sent to relatives overseas in return. The authors identify four phases of activity: goods sent for family maintenance, instead of cash to earn income; as a source of income for investment; and to produce income for reinvestment in the domestic economy and produce export goods.

316 **A good man is hard to find: overseas migration and the decentered family in the Tongan islands.**
Christine Ward Gailey. *Critique of Anthropology*, vol. 11, no. 1 (1992), p. 47-74.

Overseas migration for work has created what Gailey calls 'decentered' families, where the husband is absent overseas. The relations of men and women in the producing class in Tonga show the strain of trying to balance the promotion of the nuclear family by church and state, and the economic necessity for decentring. Gailey outlines the historical context of gender, marriage and family in Tonga, and the world context of migration and gender. She notes the general view that it is usually men alone who migrate, but finds that in fact many women migrate too. She sets out the reasons for migration: an increase in landlessness and limited availability of credit, as well as an increasing need for cash for domestic and social obligations. She examines who migrates and the situation of migrant families overseas; the effect of migration on family relationships in Tonga; and the place of remittances. Migration has had an impact on the family; certain gender and kin roles have been redefined because of it.

317 Hidden foreign exchange flows: estimating unofficial remittances to Tonga and Western Samoa.
Richard P. C. Brown. *Asian and Pacific Migration Journal*, vol. 4, no. 1 (1995), p. 35-54.

Brown shows how sample survey data from both the remitting and receiving ends can be used to derive estimates of total remittances and provide information on the way they are sent. Unrecorded remittances are found to form a highly significant part of total remittances, and estimates from official balance of payments data should be treated with caution. It was found that sixty-seven per cent of households in Tonga received remittances, amounting to thirty-six per cent of average household income.

318 The impact of remittances on rural development in Tongan villages.
Sione 'U. Faeamani. *Asian and Pacific Migration Journal*, vol. 4, no. 1 (1995), p. 139-55.

Faeamani examines the use of remittances in two villages in Tongatapu, one in Ha'apai and one in Vava'u, all primarily agricultural. In three of the villages, remittances constitute more than half of all income. In the other, waged employment was important. Faeamani finds that remittances were primarily sent for religious donations, food and housing, but that a proportion was also invested in the small business sector. Church expenditure also supports village development and remittances directly support village projects.

319 Island populations of the Pacific.
Norma McArthur. Canberra: Australian National University Press, 1967. 381p. 6 maps. bibliog.

For each of the main countries or island groups in the Pacific, including Tonga, the author provides a résumé of pre-censal estimates of population, setting them in their historical context. She then tries to assess the size of each population, and the directions and sources of change since European contact. She describes censuses and analyses the growth of population as revealed in the data, with patterns of gender distribution, mortality and fertility, noting the effects of war and epidemics. For Tonga the data begins with Cook's estimates, followed by those of other early travellers and missionaries. The first census for which data survives was in 1891, although registration of births and deaths began in 1867. Within the period surveyed the population grew from perhaps about 20,000 to 56,838 in 1956, and McArthur anticipates the effects of the future pressure of population growth on land resources. This book presents the historical background to discussions of population today.

320 **Land shortage and population pressure in Tonga.**
Alaric Maude.   In: *The Pacific in transition: geographical perspectives on adaptation and change.*   Edited by Harold Brookfield.
London: Edward Arnold, 1973, p. 163-85.

At the time of writing Tonga faced annual population growth of 3.1 per cent and potential problems of land shortage and population density as severe as any in the Pacific. Maude looks at the land resources of the different island groups; the land tenure system, agriculture being by far the most important use of land; and the perception of and response to population pressure by Tongans. He also attempts to relate the Tongan material to more general statements on the effects of population growth on man/land relationships. His work is based on the 1956 and 1966 censuses; some detailed household and village surveys; interviews with key informants in some other villages; and historical material. He sees the main response to population pressure on land resources as emigration, both internal and external, rather than a change in the traditional techniques of agriculture. In the years since this paper was written emigration has continued to mitigate the effects of population growth.

321 **Migration and remittances: a Tongan village perspective.**
K. E. James.   *Pacific Viewpoint*, vol. 32, no. 1 (1991), p. 1-23.

James believes that reciprocity and obligation between kin may be increasingly discharged by trading partnerships, overseas hospitality to migrant workers and other forms of help, rather than by direct remittances, and that remittances may stimulate rather than stifle the production of cash crops and items of traditional wealth. The children of migrants may also be fostered within the home communities. Studies in one village show that the largest and most dependable remittances take the form of savings for oneself and immediate family, rather than of gifts for a larger family group. Many Tongans overseas now send back goods rather than money. Over ninety per cent of the villagers have adult family members working overseas, and twenty-five out of thirty households reported that they received help. James believes that the fulfilment of kinship obligations is being constantly reformulated to accommodate the pulls between the increasing need for cash and the desire to honour relationships.

322 **Migration, employment and development in the South Pacific: country report no. 18, Tonga.**
John Connell.   Noumea: South Pacific Commission, 1983. 65p. map. bibliog.

Connell gives a general overview of the Tongan economy and then examines in more detail employment and incomes, population data and migration between the island groups and overseas. He considers the reasons for emigration, principally the opportunity for education, wage employment and a wider social life, and the impact of remittances on the Tongan economy, though noting the inadequacy of available data on which to base such studies. He sees migration as important to Tonga's economic and development strategy.

323   **Migration, metascience and development in island Polynesia.**
Geoffrey Hayes. *The Contemporary Pacific*, vol. 3, no. 1 (Spring 1991), p. 1-58.

Emigration from Pacific island states has increased rapidly in recent decades. Figures extracted by Hayes from official censuses, and thus probably understated, give an emigrant population of 26,664 Tongans in Australia, New Zealand and the United States in 1986, compared with 94,500 at home. The number of Tongans in New Zealand increased from 917 in 1956 to 11,691 in 1986. Two major studies in the 1980s came to different conclusions as to the effects of this migration. One saw the impact on economic development as negative, with a decline in agricultural production, a drain of the younger, better-educated and more highly skilled, and a dependence on remittances largely spent on imported foods, to the detriment of diet, and on consumer durables. The other saw a positive role in maintaining a satisfactory standard of living in the islands, with remittances benefiting community projects as much as individual needs. The main purpose of Hayes' technical and specialist paper is to attempt a theoretial synthesis of these two approaches, but in the process he offers much information on the causes and effects of migration from Tonga.

324   **Motivations for contemporary Tongan migration.**
Wendy E. Cowling.   In: *Tongan culture and history.*   Edited by Phyllis Herda, Jennifer Terrell, Niel Gunson.   Canberra: The Journal of Pacific History, 1990, p. 187-205.

Cowling offers an insight into Tongan perceptions of the factors motivating migration, based on fieldwork in Tonga and in Sydney. She identifies the underlying paradox of the difficulty in finding land suitable for subsistence agriculture while at the same time land is underutilized because of uncertainty over ownership and use rights. Many Tongans migrated first to New Zealand but problems there over status led many to see better opportunities in Australia. Yet there too, migrant labour is seen as meeting seasonal or market fluctuations. She traces the growth of migrants from 1970. By 1986 there were about 8,000 Tongans in Australia, most firmly based in church and kin networks which link them to Tonga. The reason most commonly given for migration was the desire 'to help the family' – improving its standard of living, upgrading its status and gaining more respect; yet the decision to migrate was also influenced by the other important Tongan principle of pleasing oneself. Many had no job or land in Tonga. Some resented the domination of society by nobles and the elite. Cowling describes how migration is arranged, often through family estates, and examines the attitudes of those who stay, and the effect of remittances. She observes the hardship faced by many family members who stay in Tonga, with separation of husbands and wives, and sometimes desertion. Yet many see little alternative. She concludes that sending cash as remittances is replacing the traditional Tongan values of the sharing of food and resources.

325   **The north east passage: a study of Pacific islander migration to American Samoa and the United States.**
Dennis Ahlburg, Michael J. Levin.   Canberra: National Centre for Development Studies, The Australian National University, 1990. 94p. bibliog. (Pacific Research Monograph, no. 23).

On the basis of the 1980 US census this study examines the emigration of Pacific islanders from Fiji, Tonga and Samoa to the United States. Population growth in Tonga, as elsewhere in the Pacific, has been mitigated by emigration. In 1980-81 13.9 per cent of Tonga's population was resident in Australia, New Zealand, the United States and Canada, the United States having the largest share, with 5,619 migrants and 9,661 Tongans by race or ancestry. In most categories they were the second largest group after Samoans. Tongan migration dates from the late 1960s and was facilitated by the growth of the Mormon Church in Tonga. Tongans are concentrated in California, Hawai'i and Utah. This study examines the reasons for migration; the age and sex profile of the migrants; family size; income and employment; education; and ability in English. It concludes that the motivation for emigration was primarily economic but that Tongan families were twice as likely as all US families to be below the poverty line, and were more likely to be in less skilled occupations. There is a similar separate analysis of immigration to American Samoa, for which the numbers – 788 – were relatively small. The authors note the discussion on whether emigration is, overall, good or bad for the country of origin but doubt that there is sufficient information for an assessment. However, they do conclude that emigration results in a permanent loss of young, educated, skilled labour, and they doubt that countries such as Tonga can continue to depend on aid and remittances rather than on productive export-oriented activities. Their analysis is supported by fifty tables.

326 **Pacific 2010: challenging the future.**
Edited by Rodney V. Cole.   Canberra: National Centre for Development Studies, Australian National University, 1993. 134p. bibliog.

Population growth in the South Pacific averages 2.2 per cent, well above world levels and a threat to reasonable levels of sustainability. People expect a more affluent life style, which available space and natural resources cannot support. The Pacific 2010 research project was set up to look at the effects of population growth and the outlook for resources, employment and health. Chapters on the general picture, with many tables comparing the countries of the region, are followed by chapters on each country. Kalo Funaki, writing on Tonga, notes that population growth peaked in 1966 at 3.2 per cent and has declined since, with a negative figure of −1.3 per cent between 1986 and 1989, though that figure is largely due to the high level of emigration. Infant mortality halved between 1956 and 1986, life expectancy is increasing, and emigration may taper off. Depending on assumptions of fertility, mortality and emigration, projections for 2010 vary from 141,000 to the present 90,000. Funaki's own conclusion is that, provided some emigration continues, the population is unlikely to grow significantly, but that emigration might deskill the work force and limit economic development. Tonga is the only country in the region to project a fall in the school-age population to 2010.

327 **Population changes in Tonga: an historical overview and modern commentary.**
A. C. Walsh.   *Pacific Viewpoint*, vol. 11, no. 1 (1970), p. 27-46.

Populations have always been on the move in Tonga, even beyond its present boundaries into parts of Samoa and Fiji. Walsh analyses patterns of dispersed and nucleated settlement through the Tongan islands, the role of civil wars and of the 1875 Constitution in bringing people together. He estimates population distribution from pre-contact times to the 1966 census, noting changes overall and within each island group, patterns of internal migration within Tonga, and especially the increasing urbanization of Nuku'alofa. He wonders how long internal migrants will observe traditional social obligations and observes that, in a society where initiative belongs to the chiefs, government is the only significant innovator. It alone can reduce migration to a rate where it more closely approximates to economic development. Better shipping and investment are more urgently needed than an increase in aid.

328 Reading the leaves: the role of Tongan women's traditional wealth and other 'contraflows' in the process of modern migration and remittance.

Kerry James. *Pacific Studies*, vol. 20, no. 1 (1997), p. 1-27.

For Tongans the exchange of mats and bark cloth, traditional wealth items produced by women, is pivotal to the process of remittances from Tongan migrant communities overseas. The process reinforces kinship relations that are dominant within the Tongan community. For overseas Tongan communities the increasingly numerous and abundant exchanges of these items signal the ability of migrant families to prosper, and may help to secure or improve economic class position and social status for givers. Presentation of these goods to kin overseas represents attempts to bind them in webs of personal obligation that may widen their support networks and help their financial status. In developing this thesis, James surveys the value and use of remittances in both their economic and social context within the hierarchical structure of Tongan kinship. She quotes an estimate of T\$ 2 million as the annual value of traditional goods sent overseas, and examines the uses to which they are put, with conspicuous amounts of these items presented at ceremonies overseas. She wonders, however, to what extent second-generation Tongans overseas will retain the traditional community values of their parents.

329 Remittances and their impact: a study of Tonga and Western Samoa.

Dennis A. Ahlburg. Canberra: National Centre for Development Studies, The Australian National University, 1991. 70p. bibliog. (Pacific Policy Paper, no. 7).

Developments since the 1980 figures (item no. 324) give for 1989 about 40,000 Tongans resident overseas, forty per cent of the home population, with remittances at forty-five per cent of GDP. Of 580 households in Tongatapu in the 1984 Tonga household income and expenditure survey, ninety per cent received remittances, totalling twenty-eight per cent of household income. Remittances amounted to three times the value of exports. However, they are spent largely on consumption rather than on investment, stimulating a demand for imports rather than the development of local businesses, and probably pushing up local wage costs. Ahlburg examines the social context of remittances, provides estimates of their magnitude and source, considers their impact on the local economy and the likely future level of emigration and remittances, and suggests policy options for government. He concludes that levels of emigration are likely to fall as policies in host countries change, and that remittances per emigrant are unlikely to grow as ties between them and those at home weaken.

330   Some common fallacies about migrants' remittances in the South
      Pacific: lessons from Tongan and Western Samoan research.
      Richard P. C. Brown, John Foster.   *Pacific Viewpoint*, vol. 36, no. 1
      (1995), p. 29-45.

From their collection and analysis of primary and secondary data, the authors present findings which they claim are significant in several respects. They demonstrate that conclusions drawn from national accounts data on savings and remittances should be treated with extreme caution and that previous conclusions about the negative relationship between foreign resource transfers and savings have been drawn from fallacious interpretations of national income accounting identities. Unrecorded remittances make a significant contribution to savings and investment. Remittances in kind suggest that for many of the migrant community, business investment is a stronger motivation than altruistically-motivated family support. They find little evidence to support the orthodox view that investment in Tonga is constrained by lack of savings, and suggest that the savings element of remittances could be raised by policies which encourage the accumulation of secure financial wealth in home countries.

331   **Tonga population census 1996: bulletin no. 1.**
      Nuku'alofa: Statistics Department, Government of Tonga, 1997. 12p.

This is the first publication of the results of the 1996 census. It presents preliminary counts of local population and their distribution by division, district and village, classified by sex and household, as well as population density of inhabited islands per square kilometre. Comparative figures for 1986 and 1976 are provided, so that trends over twenty years can be observed. A brief preliminary analysis shows a three per cent increase from 1986, to 97,446, with an increase in most of the larger islands, in particular in Tongatapu, and a decline in some of the districts of Ha'apai, in Niuatoputapu and Niuafo'ou. Trends are shown in three graphs; figures are presented in seven tables. Further and more detailed information and analyses are in the course of publication.

332   **Tongans in New Zealand – a brief study.**
      Edgar Tu'inukuafe.   In: *Tongan culture and history*.   Edited by
      Phyllis Herda, Jennifer Terrell, Niel Gunson.   Canberra: The Journal
      of Pacific History, 1990, p. 206-14.

The author, who has lived in Auckland for ten years and worked for the education of Pacific islanders there, provides a broad picture of the 10,000 or so Tongans living in New Zealand at that time. Most keep their own company and are in semi-skilled work. Leadership comes from church, chiefs and government. Education is the reason most commonly given for leaving Tonga, though other reasons, economic and social, may in fact be as important. Tu'inukuafe traces the development of education for Tongans in New Zealand and efforts to maintain Tongan language and culture. An appendix prints four interviews with Tongan migrants talking about the difficulties of integration and identity.

333 **A world perspective on Pacific islander migration: Australia, New Zealand and the USA.**
Edited by Grant McCall, John Connell. Kensington, Australia: Centre for Pacific Studies, The University of New South Wales, 1993. 386p. bibliog. (Pacific Studies Monograph, no. 6).

The volume outlines how migration is an integral part of Pacific islander culture and social organization, provides the contexts of these movements, and summarizes the contributions of over thirty authors to a conference on the subject. Migrations to Australia, North America and New Zealand are examined in turn, with many references specifically to Tongans; also studied are the effects of migration, both negative and positive, on the countries from which migrants came. This section concludes with a case-study on a fishing village in Vava'u by K. E. James. There is a paper on the role of the Mormon Church in migration, which is particularly important in the case of Tonga.

Industry and Commerce

334 **Comments on Tongan commerce with reference to tourism and traditional life.**
C. F. Urbanowicz. *Pacific Viewpoint*, vol. 20, no. 2 (1979), p. 179-86.

Urbanowicz considers questions raised by the paper by Bollard on dualism (item no. 335). What is the economic impact of tourism to which Bollard alludes and what connection might there be, if any, between contemporary economic dualism and traditional Tongan society? Urbanowicz sees overlapping rather than separate spheres, and notes that the tremendous impact of tourism-generated revenue is steadily increasing. He believes that Bollard's view of the separation of economic functions in traditional Tongan society is misleading: it was, he maintains, not as rigid as Bollard implies. Urbanowicz believes that the 'dual economy' is not a valid interpretation of contemporary Tongan life.

335 **Dualism in Tongan commerce.**
A. E. Bollard. *Pacific Viewpoint*, vol. 17, no. 1 (1976), p. 78-81.

In this brief research note Bollard, writing at a time when more Tongans were looking to an alternative to farming as the commercial sector was expanding, notes the wide gulf between modern and traditional spheres of activity, which he defines as dualism. He examines the different sectors at the time: for industry he contrasts the highly capitalized firms in Nuku'alofa and the tiny backyard units in small villages, and tabulates the different industries and their locations. For services he contrasts the large modern stores and small village shops, as well as the marketing of handicrafts. He relates this dualism not to the arrival of European traders, but to the traditional Tongan stratified social structure; however, he concludes that a 'new economic nobility' is developing, supporting but distinct from the old. For a critique of this paper by Urbanowicz, see item no. 334.

336   **The Tongan construction industry: infrastructure provision in a small economy.**
Gayford George Chandler.   *Pacific Economic Bulletin*, vol. 12, no. 1 (1997), p. 97-107.

The importance of the construction industry is implicit in Tonga's development plans. Chandler provides a profile of the industry in Tonga, based on his own employment there, charting its rapid growth from 1965, with a peak in 1982 through rebuilding after the hurricane of that year, and giving sector breakdowns. Information about small-scale local building work is hard to find. The figures are dominated by the Ministry of Works and a few large contractors. He notes the lack of adequate building codes and land-use regulations, resulting in some work of very low quality. Chandler ends by analysing the sources of finance for construction, the role of foreign aid and of the banks, and environmental damage.

337   **Women's work and development in Tonga.**
Sue Fleming with Monalisa Tukuafu.   Armidale, Australia: South Pacific Smallholder Project, University of New England, 1986. 92p. bibliog. (Occasional Paper, no. 10).

The discrepancies between the role women play and predominant development practice highlight the fact that essential information on rural women is not reaching policy makers and planners: census data is inadequate. Younger women in Tonga spend considerable time on work in the house: women over thirty-five spend more on crop production and on handicrafts, for sale to supplement household income, as well as for traditional purposes. Yet the 1976 census shows only 11.5 per cent of women in the labour force. In this report, despite deficiencies in the information available, women's work activities are detailed and information on women's control over income and other resources is examined. The information is presented in seventeen tables and six figures. From the figures and analysis, a picture of the varied and vital work of women emerges.

Agriculture

338 **Brown gold: official expectations and local assessment of the Tongan vanilla production.**
Paul van der Grijp.   *Journal de la Société des Océanistes*, no. 104 (1997), p. 93-103.

The author traces the history of vanilla in Tonga, from its introduction in Vava'u in the early 19th century by a French adventurer, to its reintroduction in the 1950s. He compares the official government viewpoint on vanilla and the actual impact at village level, based on case-studies of growers. He describes its cultivation and gives figures on the scale of production, prices and exports; he also compares its export with that of squash – in 1968, T$ 1.4 million for vanilla and T$ 0.4 million for squash, in 1992, T$ 2.1 million for vanilla and T$ 8.7 million for squash. He feels that government optimism over vanilla is waning. Vanilla is still important in Vava'u but it is bringing in less income and more government support will be necessary to develop its production and marketing.

339 **Co-operative yam gardens: adapting a traditional agricultural system to the needs of the developing Tongan market economy.**
R. R. Thaman.   In: *The adaptation of traditional agriculture: socioeconomic problems of urbanization.*   Edited by E. K. Fisk. Canberra: The Development Studies Centre, The Australian National University, 1978, p. 116-28. (Development Studies Centre Monograph, no. 11).

Thaman suggests that the co-operative yam garden in Tonga is an excellent example of a traditional agricultural activity which has considerable potential for adaptation to serving the needs of developing market economies, in Tonga and elsewhere. It is a system which has evolved over a long period, requires few modern imported inputs, provides an excellent supply of nutritious and socially acceptable foodstuffs, and may have good commercial potential. New cash crops may not be the answer to Tonga's own needs. Thaman describes the organization of the yam gardens, crop types planted in the first year, economic potential in the local and export market, and the crop's social benefits and importance.

340 **Cutting the ground from under them? Commercialization, cultivation and conservation in Tonga.**
Kerry James. *The Contemporary Pacific*, vol. 5, no. 2 (Fall 1993), p. 215-42.

James draws together social and environmental factors involved in the increasing commercialization of cultivation in Tonga. In theory, every adult male is entitled to a town and rural allotment, but with population pressure land is now scarce and leases often difficult and expensive to obtain, though much land held by Tongans who have emigrated remains unused. Traditional farming systems with fallow periods and inter-cropping are giving way to the monoculture of crops for export, particularly squash. Trees are cut down, wood for fuel becomes more difficult to find and soil fertility decreases, while chemicals and fertilizers are overused. James sees the land tenure system as the heart of the problem, and doubts that government monitoring can lead to the sustainable commercial production of squash, vanilla and other export crops, given pressure from those with the strongest interests in land. She believes that the most harmful practices are not likely to be recognized or remedial measures taken until it is much too late.

341 **Farmers of the Pacific islands.**
T. F. Kennedy. Wellington; Auckland, New Zealand; Sydney: A. H. & A. W. Reed, 1968. rev. ed. 48p. 6 maps.

One chapter in this brightly illustrated school textbook is on 'An "api" in Tonga' (an *'api* is a homestead), and the daily life of Sione Afu, his wife and children in his village on Tongatapu. The life of the villagers is almost totally agricultural. We read of the way the village and his farm are laid out, the crops he grows – yams and other root crops, kava, bananas and coconuts – his working and family life and his yearly routines. His is a life style less common now on Tongatapu but still to be found in some of the outer islands. Life in a Tongan village is presented as 'easy and carefree', which is only a partial view, taking no account of difficulties and pressures.

342 **Food and national development in the South Pacific.**
Edited by R. R. Thaman, W. C. Clarke. Suva: The University of the South Pacific, 1983. 144p. bibliog.

This series of lectures comprises an examination of diet and nutrition in the South Pacific (which is often of poor quality) and of obstacles to the development of healthy and nutritious food. The lectures outline some of the more important historical, social and economic factors in the situation, the nature of agricultural systems and marketing, and the nutritional factors in disease associated with the high intake of calories, sugar, salt and fat. The authors consider what governments can do to stimulate the production of nutritionally superior local foods, and suggest potential steps towards improving the production, marketing and processing of local foods. Much of this relates to Tonga, from which many examples are taken.

343 **Food crop production in Tonga: characteristics and activity budgets.**
J. C. Delforce.   Armidale, Australia: South Pacific Smallholder Project, University of New England, 1988. 116p. bibliog. (South Pacific Smallholder Project, Research Note, no. 4).

The focus of this report is on the production of five major crops on Tongan smallholdings. These are yam (early and late varieties), taro (dryland, swamp and giant), cassava, sweet potato and banana (for export and domestic use). For each crop, the species grown are listed and their economic and cultural importance indicated. The soil and climatic requirements of the crop, its susceptibility to pests and diseases and its storage potential are then discussed. Data from the project concerning the extent of production, cropping patterns, plant densities and farmer attitudes are summarized for each crop and compared with reports by previous researchers. The distribution of output between home consumption, domestic market sales and export sales is then considered. At the end of each chapter the estimation of crop activity budgets is described. The author emphasizes that all estimates are 'best guesses' rather than confirmed facts.

344 **Land tenure and rural productivity in the Pacific islands.**
Edited by Ben Acquaye, Ron Crocombe.   Rome: United Nations Food and Agriculture Organization; Suva: Institute of Pacific Studies, University of the South Pacific; Noumea: South Pacific Regional Environmental Programme, 1984. 218p. map. bibliog.

The registration of land by a government on a legal basis is a form of infrastructure for rural development. The contributors to this book examine the different forms of land registration in use in the countries of the Pacific in the early 1980s. Yet a survey of six Pacific countries where land registration was introduced showed only one where rural productivity significantly increased and several where it decreased; in Tonga it remained about the same. Tonga's system of individual farming correlates with relatively high productivity despite serious land shortage. After three general chapters surveying land registration in the region there are surveys of individual countries. That on Tonga, by T. A. Puniani, a senior officer of the Ministry of Lands, describes the law of Tonga on land tenure and registration, and how the system operates. He reports that the arrival of commercial banks in Tonga has made it possible for farmers to mortgage their land for credit, while farmers who are emigrants or absentees and are not really interested in their land can now lease it to farmers who can use it.

345 **Leaders in squash export: entrepreneurship and the introduction of a new cash crop in Tonga.**
Paul van der Grijp.   *Pacific Studies*, vol. 20, no. 1 (1997), p. 29-62.

Squash became Tonga's prime cash crop in 1991, more successful than coconuts, bananas or vanilla. The whole crop is exported to Japan. The impact of squash has been unprecedented in Tonga's economy. The emphasis of this survey is on the role of the exporters, all local Tongan entrepreneurs, whose very existence shows how far the Tongan economy has been penetrated by the capitalist system, while remaining a Polynesian society. The paper draws on interviews with exporters and reports in the Tongan press. Van der Grijp describes the progress of the crop from its introduction in 1987 and the first shipments to Japan in 1989, and the imposition of the government's quota system. He tabulates exports in quantity and value until 1995. He notes the development of entrepreneurship in the royal family and their crucial role in the development of the crop. He concludes by profiling five exporters, noting their common qualities of education, overseas experience, entrepreneurial spirit and access to land.

346 **Ministry of Agriculture and Forestry annual report.**
Nuku'alofa: Government of Tonga. annual.

The annual report provides an overview of the work of the Ministry, in its policy and planning division and in its operations in the island groups. It provides statistics on crop production; livestock; veterinary care; handicrafts; forestry; and the quarantine service and pest control. It also examines the extension division (organic farming of some crops is increasing), the livestock division and the research division with the experimental farm, and the rebuilt Talamahu market in Nuku'alofa. It is noted that eating habits are changing and that people are eating more fresh vegetables and white meat. Trends recorded in recent years include a fall in vanilla production from 1995 to 1996, an increase in kava exports, now second only to squash, and a revival of the copra industry with new buyers in Europe and higher prices.

347 **Pacific 2010: strategies for Polynesian agricultural development.**
Euan M. Fleming, J. Brian Hardaker. Canberra: National Centre for Development Studies, Australian National University, 1995. 283p. 6 maps. bibliog. (Pacific Policy Papers, no. 15).

Recent indicators suggest that the contribution of agriculture to economic development in Polynesia is weak and possibly declining. The authors explore the uncertain future and recommend how agricultural resources might best be used. A general survey examines broad macro-level strategies: of the five countries surveyed, the authors believe that only in Tonga and Western Samoa can agriculture play a leading role, provided it is released from its current economic constraints. Each country is then surveyed in detail. The section on Tonga describes the position of agriculture within the wider economy. It notes the recent success in exporting squash and vanilla, and the dangers of excessive reliance on these two crops. It analyses modes of production, physical and other resources, and the policies of the Ministry of Agriculture and Forestry, which seem to favour centralized decision-making while officially promoting private sector development. The authors see the need to redefine the proper roles of government and the private sector, and conclude that continued success depends on how long the Japanese market for squash remains open and on the success of efforts to diversify both markets and products via a partnership between government and the private sector. They summarize the strengths and weaknesses, the opportunities and threats, to give an overall view of Tongan agriculture in 1995, and its prospects.

348 **Smallholder agriculture in Tonga. Report of the South Pacific Smallholder Project in Tonga, 1984-85.**
J. B. Hardaker, J. C. Delforce, E. M. Fleming, S. Sefanaia. Armidale, Australia: South Pacific Smallholder Project, University of New England, 1987. 90p. bibliog.

Smallholder agricultural production is the main source of employment and income for the people of Tonga, but agriculture in the mid-1980s was not doing as well as it might and the ratio of imported to locally-produced foodstuffs was rising. This report of a survey of thirty households in each of four villages in Tongatapu, Ha'apai and

Vava'u presents a wealth of detailed information on the way in which households use their land, on patterns of income, production and expenditure, and on use of time and access to capital. This information is set out in seventeen tables and sixteen figures. It identifies the problem that some households are unable to obtain access to land with secure tenure because it has not been allocated, while at the same time some allocated land is unused, often because the owner has gone overseas. Furthermore, remittances from overseas form a large part of the income of many households. The report concludes with policy recommendations on better agricultural planning, allocation of resources and access to capital.

349   **Tonga.**
In: *South Pacific agriculture, choices and constraints – South Pacific agricultural survey 1979.*   Edited by R. Gerard White, Andrew Proctor.   Manila: Asian Development Bank, in association with Canberra: Australian National University Press, 1980, p. 381-94.

This report was written at a time when the Tongan economy could be described as at an early stage of development, primarily agricultural, with copra and dessicated coconut accounting for eighty per cent of exports in 1978. Tourism and remittances were seen as too unreliable to meet persistent and growing trade deficits. The authors note fertile soils and adequate rainfall in Tongatapu, though the other island groups enjoy less favourable conditions. They consider copra and coconuts likely to remain significant exports, along with fruit and vegetables. They suggest that there is little alternative to the status quo for Ha'apai but that Vava'u might do better by turning to cacao, coffee and cattle grazing, and that vanilla might have potential. Tongatapu should have a mosaic of large- and small-scale producers growing on contract for a central marketing and processing organization, and with the Ministry of Agriculture providing extension services, aiming at the New Zealand market for fruit and vegetables. In the event, central marketing did not develop in this way, the New Zealand market proved difficult to access for technical reasons, and new crops have appeared, but the report provides a background for the present position.

350   **Tonga agricultural census 1985.**
Nuku'alofa: Statistics Department, Government of Tonga, 1988. 162p. map.

The first, and to date the only, agricultural census of Tonga presents data on land tenure; land utilization; area and production of principal crops; livestock; agricultural implements and equipment; use of fertilizers and the like; and the households involved in various agricultural activities. An introduction covers the scope, methodology and processing of the census. All results are tabulated by each island group and by district within each. The results are described and analysed, and the figures are then presented in considerable detail in seventy-nine tables grouped in twenty sections; for example, area planted and harvested and other production information is given for each of eleven major crops.

351   **Tonga: development through agricultural exports.**
Mark Sturton.   Honolulu, Hawai'i: East-West Center, 1992. 48p. map. (Pacific Islands Development Program, Economic Report, no. 4).

The economy of Tonga depends on a limited range of primary commodity exports, remittances from Tongans living and working overseas, and development assistance.

Copra was for several years the main export, but its price fell by half between 1970 and 1990. The impact of this was partly offset during the late 1980s by diversification in agriculture, first into vanilla and then into squash for the Japanese market. Tourism also developed, though not perhaps as much as some had hoped. Sturton sets these developments in their broader economic context, and analyses them in the light of the level of inflation, fiscal policy and external factors. He sees hope in the success of private entrepreneurship, but problems of imbalance in the economy have continued in the years since he wrote.

352   **Tonga: rural employment and development.**
Piyasiri Wickramasekara.   New Delhi: Asian Regional Team for
Employment Promotion and International Labour Organisation, 1993.
58p. bibliog.
This report considers the prospects for rural development against the background of the land tenure system and the high level of migration to urban areas within Tonga and overseas. It sees no immediate pressing problems but there could be a longer-term problem of high unemployment and stagnation. It summarizes the performance of individual crops – rootcrops, vanilla, bananas, coconuts, watermelons and squash (then a new crop) – as well as livestock and fisheries. It considers the need for mechanization and more capital, and notes a trend from food crops to cash crops, inequalities in rural income and asset distribution, and changing food consumption habits. It considers the role of women and handicrafts in rural development and outlines the institutional machinery of government, banks and churches in rural development and reviews existing programmes. Wickramasekara concludes by making proposals for an employment-oriented rural development strategy with a clearer policy, better planning and a review of land tenure. There are twenty-five tables of detailed statistics.

353   **Tongatapu island, Tonga.**
R. R. Thaman.   In: *Agroforestry in the Pacific islands: systems of sustainability.*   Edited by W. C. Clarke, R. R. Thaman.   Tokyo; New York; Paris: United Nations University Press, 1993, p. 89-95.
In the course of a general survey of agroforestry in the region, this short section on Tongatapu describes the present bush-fallow agroforestry system; the pattern of cycles for food crops, whether subsistence or commercial; the range of species planted; the growing of plants for handicrafts and other non-food uses; and the more than twenty-five species of fruit bearing trees and more than sixty-seven non-fruit tree species with other uses, as well as the fallow and natural vegetation. Thaman notes that many species are rapidly disappearing from the majority of Tongatapu's bush allotments.

Fisheries

354 The development of fisheries in the South Pacific region with reference to Fiji, Solomon Islands, Vanuatu, Western Samoa and Tonga.
Geoffrey Waugh.   Canberra: National Centre for Development Studies, The Australian National University, 1986. 84p. bibliog.
(Islands/Australia Working Paper, no. 86/2).
Waugh examines the two classes of fisheries in the island states of the Pacific: offshore fisheries exploited primarily for export, and inshore fisheries for the domestic market. With 200 mile economic zones, fishing resources are significant: Tonga has 700,000 square miles. In Tonga, Waugh finds that offshore fishing is relatively undeveloped. The quantity landed in 1984 could be increased three-fold. Fishing for the domestic market has potential, but better marketing, storage and inter-island transport are needed. For Tonga the offshore fishery can best be exploited through foreign fleets paying licence fees.

355 Fish and fishing in Niuatoputapu.
Tom Dye. *Oceania*, vol. 53, no. 3 (1983), p. 242-71.
Dye studied fishing in Niuatoputapu in 1976-77. He describes the fishing environments off the island (reef, lagoon and open ocean), marine flora and fauna, and thirty-seven named fishing methods using rod, net, spear, traps, diving and groping. He records catch sizes and lists the names of about 210 folk fish taxa.

356 The fish of Tonga: prey or social partners?
Marie-Claire Bataille-Benguigui.   *The Journal of the Polynesian Society*, vol. 97, no. 2 (1988), p. 185-98.
The prevalence of fish in Tongan religion and myth led the author to examine possible ritual aspects that might co-exist with fishing techniques today, Tongans' relationships with their sea environment and possible privileged relationships between man and fish. She examines the relationship between the men who fish and the women who stay

at home, and the conditions necessary for successful fishing, including ceremonial sequences and rituals, and taboos governing distribution of caught fish. These she interprets in terms of the beliefs that gods were incarnate in certain fish. She finds that Christian influence is absent in fishing, in contrast to its strong hold on those who work on the land, though she admits that much of the information which she gathered from older people is no longer current practice.

357 **Fishermen of Tonga: their means of survival.**
Sitiveni Halapua. Suva: Institute of Pacific Studies, The University of the South Pacific, 1982. 100p. 3 maps. bibliog.

Halapua studies the organization and technical base of production in the small-scale commercial fisheries of Tonga (dealing in fact only with Nuku'alofa). He describes the techniques of different types of fishing, with spear, net and handline, and calculates investment and return in each. He then examines the social relationships of production and distribution, which he believes constitute a fundamental barrier to the transition from a non-capitalist to a capitalist production process. The work combines observation of the daily lives of the fishermen (with many photographs) and economic analysis of their activity.

358 **The politics of Pacific island fisheries.**
George Kent. Boulder, Colorado: Westview Press, 1980. 191p. 2 maps. bibliog.

This study is based on research initially undertaken with the support of the Food and Agriculture Organization of the UN. The author believes that fisheries should be understood and managed as a comprehensive system that includes not only production but also processing, marketing and consumption. He outlines the overall situation in the Pacific and then surveys each country. In Tonga, he sees fishing as undeveloped, with about 1,700 full- and part-time fishermen, most working on a subsistence basis, and meeting less than half of local demand. Imports of canned fish are far greater than the value of local production and export. He notes the plan, as in the late 1970s, to develop deep water longline fishing with foreign aid. Kent then describes more generally the international organizations concerned with fishing in the Pacific, and the international law of fisheries. He considers problems concerning production; conservation and information; trade; employment; and nutrition. He proceeds to outline the comparative disadvantage of the smaller Pacific countries, and notes a developing common approach among them. Tables throughout the book provide statistics to show Tonga's position in relation to its neighbours at that time.

359 **Preliminary report on a fisheries survey of Tonga.**
Hon. Vaea, W. Straatmans. *The Journal of the Polynesian Society*, vol. 63, nos. 3 and 4 (1954), p. 199-215.

The authors describe traditional methods of community fishing: enclosing the fish and trapping them on a falling tide; setting traps; netting; spearing; line fishing; and poisoning, as well as the particular techniques for catching sharks, octopus, whales and other seafood. They list fifty-four varieties of Tongan fish, tabulating their type, habitat, habits and the method of fishing for each. Most fish is consumed at once. Preservation where necessary is by salting, sun-drying or smoking. They urge an improvement in fishing methods and processing in order to improve the diet of the population.

360 **Report of the Minister for Fisheries.**

Nuku'alofa: Government of Tonga. annual.

This annual report covers the work of the Ministry in the encouragement of fisheries both for domestic consumption and for export, the development of markets and the prevention of over-fishing. The Ministry pursues this end through the study of fish stocks, training, experimentation and market development. Data is provided by type of fish and shellfish on the quality and value of catches, and of exports.

361 **Tonga fisheries bibliography: 1st revised edition.**

Robert Gillett. Suva: Pacific Islands Marine Resources Information Systems, The University of the South Pacific Library, 1994. 115p.

This bibliography lists 619 items located at the Fisheries Division and other offices in Tonga, at the University of the South Pacific and elsewhere in the region. Each item is listed in a first section by author and in a second section by one of forty subject headings, from aquaculture to whales. Some are published in books or in journals, but many are technical reports by government departments, regional organizations, aid agencies and the like.

Education

362 **'Atenisi Institute and University.**
'I. Futa Helu. In: *Pacific universities: achievements, problems,
prospects.* Edited by Ron Crocombe, Malama Meleisea. Suva:
Institute of Pacific Studies, University of the South Pacific, 1988,
p. 203-09.

Futa Helu describes the establishment of his own private 'Atenisi (Athens) University,
inspired by the Greek classical model. An original class of eleven men began in 1963
with him as the only teacher. By 1966 it had expanded into high-school education and
was recognized by the government as a private educational institution. A small pilot
university class was established in 1971 and this became 'Atenisi University in 1978,
providing core studies for more advanced work and recognized by Australian and New
Zealand universities. Despite financial difficulties, it continues and survives, the
unique embodiment of the vision of one individual, still aiming, as Futa Helu states
'to polish its image of academism, classicism and criticism, and also to struggle
against ignorance, subjectivism and interestedness in Tonga and the Pacific'.

363 **Education for economic development in the South Pacific.**
Edited by K. G. Gannicott. Canberra: National Centre for
Development Studies, The Australian National University, 1990. 120p.
bibliog.

In recent years, rates of economic growth have been low in the South Pacific island
nations. Shortages of skilled labour are an important contributor to poor economic
performance. This volume brings together a series of studies of educational development
in the region. In a general overview Gannicott examines the cost, quality and relevance
of the education provided. His own paper on the similarities and contrasts between
educational systems in Western Samoa and Tonga notes that despite near-universal
literacy in Tonga the country is short of people with technical and managerial skills.
However, in contrast to Western Samoa, whose policy is to strengthen the vocational
aspects of education, a policy which appears to be unsuccessful, Tonga is working to
strengthen the general and academic curriculum in primary and secondary schools.

This is at a time when up to forty per cent of Tongan children in some schools seem to find it difficult to keep up with the curriculum and where buildings, equipment and supplies are all inadequate. The author believes that Tonga's policy is the better. He also considers that vocational training is better done on the job, and schools should emphasize mathematics and science. He describes the fourteen post-secondary institutions in Tonga, most very small, independent of each other and uncoordinated. At the time of writing it was planned that post-secondary education should be provided through a Community Development and Training Centre. To date this has not happened. The volume concludes with a paper on Australian aid for education in the region, with ten tables setting out what it has provided. The conclusion is that Australia's aid, largely aimed at the tertiary sector, would be better directed to the lower levels of education.

364 **The nature of education in pre-European to modern Tonga.**
Kalapoli Pāongo. In: *Tongan culture and history.* Edited by Phyllis Herda, Jennifer Terrell, Niel Gunson. Canberra: The Journal of Pacific History, 1990, p. 134-44.

Pāongo, principal of a college in Vava'u, traces the nature of education in Tonga from earliest times to the present. Traditional education was concerned with establishing how one coped with one's environment and established one's identity, and was informal, flexible and based in the family. Boys and girls learnt their different skills. The years from first European contact in 1616 to 1866 Pāongo defines as 'the thawing period', with stupendous changes, the coming of literacy and the enlightening and broadening of minds. He describes the foundation of schools by missionaries, with rules and discipline to assist formal education. 1866-82 he calls 'the golden age' with the foundation of Tonga and Tupou colleges, and students 'perhaps the best in the South Pacific Islands at that time'. He sees 1882-1945 as a time of crisis and challenge, with moves to a greater independence in church and state and a lowering of standards. From 1945 he sees a renaissance, with a greater concern for education and more money spent on it. However, he notes an over-emphasis on academic education and the necessity to broaden the curriculum to include more practical subjects.

365 **Overview of vocational training in Tonga.**
Melino Kupu. In: *Vocational training and the labour market: South Pacific.* Edited by A. M. A. H. Siddiqui. Bangkok: International Labour Organisation, Asian and Pacific Skill Development Programme, 1992, p. 65-80.

Kupu outlines the legislation and government policy on vocational training in Tonga, recommending a clearer definition of policy. The government's vocational training activities are described: teacher training, a marine polytechnic institute and centres for trade testing and development and for community development. Those run by the churches, largely for agriculture, are also listed. Priorities for Tonga are set out, in the mechanical, electrical and construction trades and in agriculture and fishing. Recommendations are set out on goals, curricula development, standards and validation and for the development of apprenticeships. Kupu concludes that a training board should be set up to improve the effectiveness of training and the development of teachers.

**366 Paradise postponed: essays on research and development in the
    South Pacific.**
    Edited by Alexander Mamak, Grant McCall.   Rushcutters Bay,
    Australia: Pergamon Press, 1978. 277p.

This volume contains papers given at a conference of young Pacific islanders held at
the University of New South Wales in 1978. It contains four papers by Tongans. In
'Some preliminary remarks on the nature of research and development' (p. 13-18)
Patelisio P. Finau, then Roman Catholic Bishop of Tonga, sounds a note of caution
over the old development model: 'The rich who give do not just look with compassion.
They also work for their own self-expansion'. Development, he adds, must free people
from domination but avoid cultural romanticism. In 'Research for development in
Tonga' (p. 176-79) Penisimani Topi Tapuelulu states that unless the core problem of
economic development in faced, all research for development will be like 'collecting
shellfish in an open-bottomed basket'. More research is needed on both political and
religious structure, and more research should be undertaken by Tongans rather than by
Europeans. Research must promote development as total liberation. In 'Concluding
remarks on the nature of research and development' (p. 234-40) Sione Lātūkefu hopes
that the views expressed will help Pacific islanders to decide for themselves what is
relevant to their needs and aspirations. In a brief report, 'Session on case studies and
current research trends' (p. 245-46) Epeli Hau'ofa suggests the need for research on
emigration, the activities of multinational corporations, increasing dependence on
imported foodstuffs, foreign aid and the role of Pacific elites. Twenty years later many
of these research needs remain, and more research still needs to be done by Tongans.

367 Report of the Ministry of Education.
    Nuku'alofa: Government of Tonga. annual.

This annual report provides detailed information and statistics for primary, secondary
and tertiary education in Tonga. It describes developments in the year generally in
respect of teacher training, curriculum development, overseas aid and scholarships.

**368 Science and technology in Australasia, Antarctica and the Pacific
    islands.**
    Jarlath Ronayne, Campbell Boag.   Harlow, England: Longman, 1989.
    335p. 4 maps. (Longman Guide to World Science and Technology,
    no. 11).

This guide to the organization of science and technology, and to facilities for scientific
and technological research and education provides information regionally and by
country. There is not a great deal to report on Tonga: the experimental farm, research
division and fisheries division of the Ministry of Agriculture, Marine Fisheries and
Forests, some activities of the Ministry of Lands, Survey and Natural Resources and
the Ministry of Education, and the Rural Development Centre of the University of the
South Pacific. Covered in a general introduction to the region are the South Pacific
Forum, the University of the South Pacific and other bodies which serve all the
countries of the region including Tonga. A directory at the end gives addresses of the
institutions mentioned.

369 **Thinking in Tongan society.**
'I Futa Helu. In: *Thinking: the expanding frontier.* Edited by
William Maxwell. Philadelphia, Pennsylvania: The Franklin Institute
Press, 1983, p. 43-56.

Futa Helu begins by considering aspects of thinking, the difference between what we
think and how we think. He then relates this to the ways in which Tongans think,
under the influence of what he calls 'the powerful indoctrinating forces of church
organization, socio-economic grouping, traditional customs etc.' He does this by
considering two Tongan myths. He believes that myths are tools for maintaining a
static society and are inimical to a dynamic and liberal society. Futa Helu describes
some of his own work at 'Atenisi University (item no. 362) to determine Tongans'
concepts of their own identity, and detects a new materialist and individualist trend in
Tongan society.

370 **Tonga.**
R. Murray Thomas. In: *Schooling in the Pacific islands: colonies in
transition.* Edited by R. Murray Thomas, T. Neville Postlethwaite.
Oxford; New York; Toronto; Sydney; Paris; Frankfurt, Germany:
Pergamon Press, 1984, p. 236-61.

Thomas sketches the history of education in Tonga from the time of European contact,
noting the key role of education in achieving economic self-sufficiency and a compatible
integration of Polynesian and Western cultures. He then describes the present schooling
ladder, extending from a six-year primary school education to four years at middle or
lower secondary school to three years at upper secondary school. Primary education is
essentially provided by the government but secondary education is largely private,
provided by the churches. Among the few post-secondary education institutions are a
nursing school, a theological college and a police training school. Thomas describes
the roles of the government and the churches in the administration of education,
curricula and examinations with their emphasis on academic intelligence, and the
recruitment and training of teachers. To face the issue of the compromise culture, he
sees the need for social analysis and goal definition, and he wonders whether Tonga
has either the will or the resources to do this. In a final table he compares aspects of
schooling in 1882 and 1982.

371 **Tongan astronomy and calendar.**
E. E. V. Collocott. Honolulu, Hawai'i: Bishop Museum Press, 1922.
19p. (Occasional Papers of the Bernice Pauahi Bishop Museum of
Polynesian Ethnology and Natural History, vol. VIII, no. 4).

Collocott sets out the information which he obtained from Tongan informants on
astronomy and the recording of time. Most Tongan star lore was embodied in sailing
directions. Collocott gives the three areas or zones of the heavens, the southern, the
mid-sky and the northern, and the Tongan names for the main stars in each, identifying
them where possible with the Western names. He explains the Tongan concept of
time, with a year usually having twelve months with agricultural names. Tongans
count by nights rather than by days, and he gives names for different phases of the
moon and divisions of night and day, as well as miscellaneous terms for stars, comets
etc.

372 **Training the majority: guidelines for the rural Pacific.**
G. N. Bamford.   Suva: Institute of Pacific Studies of the University of
the South Pacific, 1986. 133p. map.

In the 1960s and 1970s increasing attention was being paid in the Pacific to the
improvement of rural living, but little information was available to compare rural
training programmes in different countries. This book arises out of a 1984 ILO/UNDP
study of some of the most effective rural training programmes. Comparative tables in
the introduction show that in the 1976 census, 77.7 per cent of Tonga's population
was rural – one of the highest figures in the Pacific – and 76.2 per cent of exports were
agricultural. After some general guidelines on rural training, Bamford provides ten
case-studies, one of which concerns the Fualu Rural Training Centre on Tongatapu,
established by the Roman Catholic Church. Its innovative and effective programmes
are designed to train young men for a farming career, introducing skills that can take
some of the drudgery out of farming. Course content combines work in both class-
room and field and involves work on the trainee's own land. Money to help with
running costs and trainees' expenses is generated from the sale of crops grown during
the course. Bamford suggests some of the common features contributing towards
effective rural training and concludes that training for rural living cannot of itself
solve the problem of urban drift and unemployment, but that it can make an important
contribution.

Literature

373 Kakala.
Konai Helu Thaman.   Suva: Mana Publications, 1993. 94p.

Konai Helu Thaman's mother is Tongan and her father American. Educated in New Zealand and California, she now works at the University of the South Pacific in Fiji. Kakala are sacred, fragrant Tongan plants used in garlands and to scent coconut oil. They are commonly referred to in Tongan legends, songs, dance and poetry as a symbol of respect and love. This collection of poems, in English with a glossary of Tongan terms, conveys in a vivid and imaginative manner something of the tensions and pressures facing Tongans and other Pacific islanders in the modern world, trying to hold together cultural conservatism and modern liberalism.

374 'Ko e fakalāngilāngi: the eulogistic function of the Tongan poet.
Eric B. Shumway.   Pacific Studies, vol. 1, no. 1 (1977), p. 25-34.

The performing arts in Tonga are more than high entertainment. Besides fulfilling a psychic need in giving emotional release to performer and spectator through musical harmony and rhythmic movement, they are a ritual reinforcement of the fundamental values that bind Tongan society together. Shumway identifies these as worshipful respect to the royal house; the maintenance of the sovereign prerogative of the nobility; the love of country and church more than self; and the insistence that Tonga is the best of all possible worlds. The function of the poet is to proclaim and restate the most urgent social and political imperatives of both past and present. He composes as a public duty, and for personal acclaim within that duty. Shumway describes, provides extracts from and analyses the work of some modern Tongan poets within this context. Though there are signs that poets may become social critics or work to the taste of foreign audiences, it is unlikely that the poet will forget his responsibility to remind Tongans of their heritage, and their duty to sustain and enrich it.

375 **Lali – a Pacific anthology.**
Edited and with an introduction by Albert Wendt. Auckland, New
Zealand: Longman Paul, 1980. 303p. map.

Writing in 1980, the Samoan author Albert Wendt looked back at colonialism's rejection
of much of traditional Pacific culture but also at the beginnings of recovery. Since the
1960s, a Pacific literature in English had emerged, arguing for the speeding up of
decolonialization and the development of identity based on Pacific ways, values and
visions, helping the people of the Pacific to understand who and where they were and
where they were going. This was the first anthology of such writing, and the pieces
from Tonga reflect the theme of the troubled relationship between the traditional and
the modern, with two short stories by Epeli Hau'ofa, one by Vili Vete, and three
poems by Konai Helu Thaman, all either richly sardonic or quietly tragic. The *lali* is a
wooden gong with a deep booming sound, 'commanding, definite, yet capable of
many subtle nuances'.

376 **Lisitala: a bibliography of Pacific writers.**
Edited by Esther Wininamaori Willams. Suva: Pacific Information
Centre in association with the 4th Festival of Pacific Arts Committee,
1984. 344p.

This bibliography sets out to list known Pacific writers with biographical details, and
to list and describe their creative and scholarly works under broad subject headings. It
is based on information compiled at the University of the South Pacific. A general
introduction dates the beginning of creative writing in English by Pacific islanders to
1960, though scholarly writing began much earlier. The section on Tonga lists about
250 works by 32 authors. The largest sections are on education (18), literature (136,
though the same piece if published more than once in different places is listed for each
appearance), and social science (52). Some of the items listed are unpublished, are
brief pieces in magazines or are ephemeral, such as course guides for the University.

377 **Nuanua – Pacific writing in English since 1980.**
Selected with an introduction by Albert Wendt. Auckland, New
Zealand: Auckland University Press, 1995. 405p.

This successor to *Lali* (item no. 375), published fifteen years earlier, contains a rich
diversity of writing from ten countries, symbolized by the book's title which means
rainbow in many Polynesian languages (though not in Tongan). In his general
introduction, Wendt states his belief that, although colonialism has changed the
Pacific radically, the cultures of the islands have survived and adapted. Western art
forms, including the novel, have been indigenized. Two of the Tongan authors are also
contributors to *Lali*, Epeli Hau'ofa with an extract from his novel *Kisses in the
Nederends* and a poem, and Konai Helu Thaman with three poems. Pesi Fonua
contributes a short story. Wendt notes in his introduction that much has changed in the
Pacific in fifteen years, but the same themes recur, still powerfully expressed.

378 **Po fananga – Folk tales of Tonga.**
Tupou Posesi Fanua. San Diego, California: Tofua Press, 1975. 96p.

Fananga are described by the author as 'stories used to lull me to sleep'. This is the
first book of folk tales of Tonga to be written and published in the two languages,
Tongan and English, set in parallel columns. Tupou Posesi Fanua retells eleven of the
stories told her by her grandmother and adds one story of her own. The ancient stories

relate to structures and rituals which are still part of Tonga today: bygone gods and mortals, kings and people, and their loves, lives and deaths. (For details on the author's own early life, and on the grandmother who told her these stories, see item no. 135.)

379 Proverbial sayings of the Tongans.

E. E. V. Collocott, John Havea.   Honolulu, Hawai'i: Bishop Museum Press, 1922. 115p. (Occasional Papers of the Bernice Pauahi Bishop Museum of Polynesian Ethnology and Natural History, vol. VIII, no. 3).

Collocott's aim was to collect as wide a range as possible of genuine Tongan expressions. Each of his 632 proverbs has a literal English translation and a few lines of explanation. They are grouped in main subject sections: garden and farm; plants and trees; food; doing of tasks and criticism; manufactures; land creatures; birds; fish and shell fish; ships and sailing; climate and seasons; sea and coast; land features; places; distinguished people; legendary deities; religion; the person; home and compound; domestic relations; courtship and marriage; speech; disease and medicine; death and burial; wrong-doing and retribution; common people; chiefs; the Tu'i lines; kava; war; sports and games; dancing; and unclassified.

380 Tales and poems of Tonga.

E. E. V. Collocott.   Honolulu, Hawai'i: Bernice P. Bishop Museum, 1928. 169p. bibliog. (Bernice P. Bishop Museum Bulletin, no. 46).

The aim of Collocott, a missionary and teacher in Tonga, was to allow Tongans to interpret themselves through their story-telling and bards, and his collection concentrates on what he calls 'more homely pieces' which had not already been published. These he took from manuscript sources, though he does not provide specific references. He classifies the pieces that he prints under the headings of stories, poetry and songs, grouping them by such themes as places, people, work, and stages of life and death. Extensive examples are printed both in Tongan and in English translation, with explanatory notes to identify places and clarify meanings. The music of the songs is also printed.

381 Tales from the South Pacific islands.

Anne Gittings.   Owings Mill, Maryland: Stemmer House Publishers, 1977. 89p.

This simple and attractively illustrated collection of Pacific folk tales retold for young people includes four from Tonga: the fishing up of the islands by Maui; how fire came to Tonga; the love story of Toeumu and Lifotu in Vava'u; and the story of the sun-child.

382 Tales of the Tikongs.

Epeli Hau'ofa.   Auckland, New Zealand: Penguin Books, 1988. 93p.

Service in the Tongan government and at the University of the South Pacific has given Hau'ofa the background for this collection of short tales. Some display wry humour, some hilarious satire, as they gently ridicule the doings of those in political and religious power, foreign advisers and aid donors, and the conventions of society generally, in the imaginary country of Tiko. Beneath the surface they say a lot that is revealing and authentic about a Tonga that is all too recognizable.

383 **Tongan myths and tales.**
Edward Winslow Gifford. Honolulu: Bernice P. Bishop Museum,
1924. 207p. (Bernice P. Bishop Museum Bulletin, no. 8).
Gifford draws the Tongan myths and tales which he presents from the Tongan language
magazines of both the Methodist and Roman Catholic Churches which printed 'many
stories from raconteurs now long dead', and also from stories which he took down
directly from narrators when he was in Tonga in 1920-21. In an introduction, he sets
out the many parallels between the myths of Tonga and Indonesia, and the evidence of
close links with Samoa. He recounts and examines myths of creation, of the exploits
of Maui, of the sun and the moon, of gods and Pulotu (the land of the departed). There
are also tales of many of the Tu'i Tongas. He provides a corpus of material from
which many scholars since have worked.

384 **Tongan poetry.**
Futa Helu. Part 1. *Faikava*, no. 1 (1978), p. 21-25; Part 2. *Faikava*,
no. 2 (1978), p. 31-33; Part 3. *Faikava*, no. 3 (1979), p. 18-20; Part 4.
Faikava, no. 4 (1979), p. 28-31; Part 5. *Faikava*, no. 5 (1980),
p. 27-31.
This is really one paper, spread over five issues of *Faikava*. In the first part Helu
identifies the various styles of Tongan poetry. Of the ancient there are the *fakatangi*,
an ancient form of ballad which can be regarded as proto-epic; the *tangi*, an elegy
which is usually a lament on the death of a loved one; the *lave*, which is both epic and
ode; the *laulau*, a delicate propitiatory harangue; and *ta'anga*, the texts of dance
songs. Of the modern there are the *sipi*, a wooing madrigal; the *lakalaka* dance song;
the *hiva kakala*, a love lyric; the *ma'ulu'ulu* and *tau'olunga* dance songs. There is
little spoken poetry as such. Most poems were either sung or chanted, to accompany
dance. Tongan poetry, Helu notes, is essentially social poetry or collective lyricism.
Only recently have individualism and sentimentality begun to appear. He identifies a
growth of romanticism which found its highest expression in the works of Queen
Sālote. In the subsequent parts, Helu describes in detail some of the different types,
their origin, form and use, provides examples, and comments on historical references.
The fifth article states at the end 'to be continued' but no further parts were published.

Material Culture

385 Art, aesthetics, and social structure.
Adrienne L. Kaeppler. In: *Tongan culture and history.* Edited by Phyllis Herda, Jennifer Terrell, Niel Gunson. Canberra: The Journal of Pacific History, 1990, p. 59-71.

The traditional arts of Tonga reveal much about traditional Tongan society and a study of artistic products and aesthetic concepts can make it easier to understand the history, philosophy and traditional cultural values of Tonga. The creation and presentation of valuables are embedded in Tongan conceptualizations about the reproduction of society and culture. In this paper Kaeppler examines the traditional arts of Tonga: poetry with its attendant music and dance; the making of scent; bark cloths; mats; basketry and ornaments; tattooing; and wood-working. Art in the Tongan context she defines as the cultural forms that result from creative processes that use or manipulate words, sounds, movements, materials or space in order to formalize or intensify the formalization of the non-formal. The arts can best be understood as cultural forms embedded in social action. To this end she analyses the layout of space that people move in, gift giving and exchange, and how people are attached to each other. She examines Tongan concepts of skill and respect, relates them to the verbal and material arts, and sets them in their social context.

386 Art and life in Polynesia.
T. Barrow. London: Pall Mall Press, 1972. 191p. map. bibliog.

Barrow believes that the art of Polynesia is best understood and interpreted in terms of custom, religion and ethnic temperament. In Part I, he provides a comprehensive background on Polynesian origins; European discovery and settlement; social structure; daily life; food and drink; religion and symbol; the role of the craftsman; and the craftsman's tools and materials. In Part II, he examines each island group. The section on Tonga concentrates on art in wood and ivory, exquisite carved figures, few of which survived destruction by the missionaries, and war clubs with their remarkable surface decoration of figures, animals and textured patterns. He presents these through illustrations, both colour and black-and-white, with detailed captions. All these objects are now in museums and private collections, and the survey is thus totally historical.

140

There is nothing here of the art of Tonga today, for which one must refer to the new book by St. Cartmail, *The art of Tonga* (item no. 387).

387 The art of Tonga.
Keith St. Cartmail.   Honolulu, Hawai'i: University of Hawai'i Press, 1997. 152p. 3 maps. bibliog.

St. Cartmail defines art broadly in this attractively presented introduction to the art of Tonga. This is appropriate because there is no Tongan word for 'art' in the Western sense. Form and texture are governed by tradition, function and material. Thus, after a historical introduction, St. Cartmail describes and illustrates not only figures and war clubs which are perhaps the finest and best-known achievements of Tongan art but also headrests; containers such as kava bowls; food hooks and pounders; adzes; baskets; mats; *ngatu* (decorated bark cloth); necklaces and other articles of adornment; fish hooks; and canoes. He even extends his survey to include tattooing, music, dance and poetry, and the art of grave decoration today, in which articles which may seem inappropriate to the outsider, such as beer bottles, are used (item no. 401). This he sees as a unique and innovative way for Tongans of expressing their own sense of what is aesthetically appropriate. In a conclusion on Tongan art today and tomorrow, he notes that men carving in wood and bone are still active in Tonga, but largely produce pieces for the tourist market which bear little relation to traditional styles. It is women who continue to produce traditional tapa cloth, mats, necklaces, baskets and other items which still form part of the reciprocal pattern of gift and exchange within Tongan society. Appendix I lists all extant Tongan human figures and Appendix II all Tongan material in New Zealand museums.

388 'Artificial curiosities' being an exposition of native manufactures collected on the three Pacific voyages of Captain James Cook, R.N. at the Bernice Pauahi Bishop Museum January 18, 1978-August 31, 1978 on the occasion of the bicentennial of the European discovery of the Hawaiian islands by Captain Cook – January 18, 1778.
Adrienne L. Kaeppler.   Honolulu, Hawai'i: Bishop Museum Press, 1978. 293p. bibliog. (Bernice P. Bishop Museum Special Publication, no. 65).

More than 2,000 artefacts ('artificial curiosities' as they were called in the 18th century) were collected on the three voyages of Captain Cook. Kaeppler has sought to trace and record them all, establishing the history of their ownership. This book is a complete record, indicating those items shown at the 1978 exhibition. For Tonga she records about 500 items including decorations, clothing, mats, baskets, musical instruments, fishing equipment, games and weapons. For each she gives current ownership, size, evidence of authenticity and references in the literature. Many are illustrated, both in black-and-white and in colour. The Tongan section is one of the fullest and richest and Kaeppler's catalogue, in bringing these objects together, many of them remarkably well preserved, shows the changes which European contact brought to Tonga. Some items of these types are no longer made: others are still made in very similar style.

389   **Baskets in Polynesia.**
       Wendy Arbeit.   Honolulu, Hawai'i: University of Hawai'i Press,
       1990. 116p. 2 maps. bibliog.
This book examines baskets throughout central Polynesia, from the time of early
European contact to the present, observing and comparing the work of the different
countries, to each of which she devotes a chapter. Once baskets played a central part
in everyday life in Polynesia. They are still made today but their use has changed with
modern lifestyles and materials. Arbeit travelled throughout the region, and found
Tonga to be one of the most flourishing centres of basket making, which nearly died
out in the 1920s and 1930s, but was revived by Queen Sālote, who rightly saw the
potential of making baskets for tourists as a source of income for villages. Her
descriptions are accompanied by handsome photographs, fourteen of Tonga, showing
the variety of attractive styles made today, and detailed diagrams showing exactly how
they are made. She also shows how the raw materials, mostly coconut and pandanus,
are prepared.

390   **Canoes of Oceania.**
       A. C. Haddon, James Hornell.   Volume I. The Canoes of Polynesia,
       Fiji and Micronesia.   James Hornell.   Honolulu, Hawai'i: Bernice P.
       Bishop Museum 1936. 454p. 3 maps. bibliog. (Bernice P. Bishop
       Museum Special Publication, no. 27).
Hornell observes that, without the large double canoe, Polynesian migration across the
Pacific would never have attained the dimensions that it did. In this comprehensive
survey of the canoes of Oceania, based on his own research in the Pacific in 1924-25,
he focuses attention particularly on the comparative study of the outrigger attachment
and the design of the double canoe. He examines the descriptions of canoes by
European explorers, noting that their artists seldom portrayed them accurately. He
aimed to collect, correlate and arrange all known and available details of canoe
construction. In Tonga he found that only two types of smaller canoes survived. He
describes five types of outrigger canoe and two principal types of double canoe,
providing photographs where available and drawings showing details of construction.
He gives a list of technical terms, noting that many are common to Fiji and Tonga.

391   **Cook voyage artifacts in Leningrad, Berne and Florence Museum.**
       Edited by Adrienne L. Kaeppler.   Honolulu, Hawai'i: Bernice
       Museum Press, 1978. 186p. bibliog. (Bernice P. Bishop Museum
       Special Publication, no. 66).
Three lesser-known collections of artefacts collected on Cook's voyages are here
catalogued for the first time in English. Kaeppler introduces each collection, suggesting
how the objects reached them, and gives a detailed description of each piece, as
compared to the summary listing in her complete catalogue of all the Cook artefacts
(item no. 388). Leningrad has only a few pieces from Tonga. Berne and Florence each
have larger collections of over forty pieces which include bark cloth; mats; baskets;
garments; ornaments; combs; musical instruments; and weapons. There are photographs of many of the pieces. These collections are important for the study of Tongan
artefacts at the time of European contact, and this catalogue makes them accessible
and establishes their authenticity.

392 Eighteenth century Tonga: new interpretations of Tongan society and material culture at the time of Captain Cook.
Adrienne L. Kaeppler. *Man*, new series, vol. 6, no. 2 (1971), p. 204-20.
Kaeppler examines the ethnographic significance of articles collected from Tonga by Captain Cook and illustrations made by his artists, to demonstrate the relationship between social organization and material culture. She concludes that much can be learnt about the 18th-century rank-oriented social system from these specimens and illustrations, and provides examples using objects now to be seen in museums, explaining their significance in their Tongan context.

393 *Kato tu'aniu*, baskets of Tonga.
Annagrethe Ottovar. Suva: Tourism Council of the South Pacific, 1994. 36p. map.
The author describes the many types of fine and attractive baskets made in Tonga, from small lid-boxes, bowls and trays to large laundry baskets. She covers the growing, gathering and treatment of the raw materials, weaving techniques and the styles of decoration and pattern. She also advises shoppers where in Tonga to find the best baskets and provides many informative photographs.

394 Made in Tonga: manufacture of art objects from leaves, bark and wood.
Paul van der Grijp. In: *Pacific material culture: essays in honour of Dr. Simon Kooijman on the occasion of his 80th birthday.* Edited by Dirk A. M. Smidt, Pieter ter Keurs, Albert Trouwborst. Leiden, the Netherlands: Rijksmuseum voor Volkenkunde, 1985, p. 200-18.
The author examines the manufacture of tapa, mats and baskets in Tongatapu, Ha'apai and Vava'u and the role of the tourist market in affecting styles and methods. He concludes that the older inequalities which such objects indicated between commoners and chiefs has been replaced by a new inequality between the sexes. The mostly male producers of wood carvings are seen by many as artists, while the female producers of tapa, baskets and mats are not. This is ironic, given that what the men produce is 'airport art', while the women still make tapa and mats for traditional purposes.

395 Oceanic art.
Adrienne L. Kaeppler, Christian Kaufmann, Douglas Newton. New York: Harry N. Abrams, 1997. 633p. bibliog.
This large and sumptuous volume, with many colour plates, is the most recent general treatment of the art of Oceania. The section on Polynesia and Melanesia by Kaeppler treats the subjects by theme: mythology; sculptural representations of the mythological chanter; fibres, feathers and barks; and the presentation and aesthetic of the body. Within this, many Tongan objects are described and illustrated. A documentation section illustrates many objects in black-and-white. In a final section by country or principal Oceanic cultural group, the work of craftsmen is described, with further illustrations. The bibliography covers many hundreds of publications.

396   **Poetics and politics of Tongan barkcloth.**
Adrienne L. Kaeppler.   In: *Pacific material culture: essays in honour of Dr. Simon Kooijman on the occasion of his 80th birthday.*   Edited by Dirk A. M. Smidt, Pieter ter Keurs, Albert Trouwborst.   Leiden, the Netherlands: Rijksmuseum voor Volkenkunde, 1985, p. 101-21.

Kaeppler was drawn to study barkcloth, tapa, in Tonga not just as an artefact but in its ubiquitous social aspect. She had noted how drastically designs had changed from those on specimens collected by Captain Cook and in this paper she examines events, pieces of tapa, design concepts and poetry to explore an aesthetic construction of society based on a conjunction of place, genealogy and event. Understanding an aesthetic, she points out, depends on understanding an entire way of life. She shows how designs have been adapted to incorporate such motifs as the Tongan coat of arms, the lion and the eagle. She describes the tapa produced for particular special events. Pieces of tapa are about national identity, genealogical associations and the social construcion of the self.

397   **String figures from Fiji and western Polynesia.**
James Hornell.   Honolulu, Hawai'i: Bernice P. Bishop Museum Press, 1927. 88p. bibliog. (Bernice P. Bishop Museum Bulletin, no. 39).

Hornell collected and here describes string figures and string games from the southwest Pacific. Second only to Fiji was the number collected in Tonga, ten distinct figures, though he felt that many more remained to be found and recorded. Each is given its Tongan name, with a description and illustration of how it is made. Seven are common to Tonga and Fiji.

398   **Tapa in Polynesia.**
Simon Kooijman.   Honolulu, Hawai'i: Bishop Museum Press, 1972. 498p. 12 maps. bibliog. (Bernice P. Bishop Museum Bulletin, no. 234).

Tapa, decorated cloth made from the bark of trees, is found in one form or another throughout Polynesia. The author of this definitive work presents the subject in its broadest sense: the trees and shrubs which are its raw material, its manufacture and decoration, its function in society, and the design patterns and elements. In each section he brings together historical records and modern practice. The book is arranged by country rather than by process; thus in the forty-five pages on Tonga, Kooijman notes that tapa is produced from the paper mulberry tree, he describes how it is grown and harvested, how the bark is dried, peeled off the trunk, cut into strips and soaked, beaten, assembled into large sheets and decorated. He details the sources of the black, brown and red dyes used. He then examines the relief tablets made of wood or coconut husk used to apply the decoration, the motifs themselves, and the social and ceremonial as well as every-day use of the different styles of tapa. He outlines the change from the system of manufacture observed by Mariner in the early 19th century which was centred on a chief and his wife who would gather a group of women, to a more democratic system of women's guilds, usually one in each village, alongside which went the incorporation of modern motifs in the decoration. The book is fully illustrated with diagrams and photographs. Because each country is treated in the same way it is possible to compare Tongan tapa with tapa throughout Polynesia. At the end of the book, information is set out in tabular form, country by country, to facilitate comparison of sources, manufacture, decoration, dyes and dyeing, and uses.

399 **Tapa in Tonga.**
Wendy Arbeit.   Honolulu, Hawai'i: University of Hawai'i Press,
1994. 24p.

This brief booklet was written to provide visitors to Tonga with something that would
help them to understand and appreciate the tapa they saw there. Arbeit calls tapa 'the
fabric that connects Tonga's people to their culture'. She outlines its uses, no longer
for clothing as described by Captain Cook, but for gifts, for ritual dress and for
decoration. She goes through the processes for making it: the raw material, the bark of
the paper mulberry tree, the preparation of the bark and the beating of it into thin
strips joined to make large sheets, and its printing and decoration. Photographs show
every stage. There is a glossary of the main Tongan terms.

400 **To beat or not to beat, that is the question: a study on
acculturation and change in an artmaking process and its relation
to gender structures.**
Jehanne H. Teilhet-Fisk.   In: *Pacific material culture: essays in
honour of Dr. Simon Kooijman on the occasion of his 80th birthday.*
Edited by Dirk A. M. Smidt, Pieter ter Keurs, Albert Trouwborst.
Leiden, the Netherlands: Rijksmuseum voor Volkenkunde, 1985,
p. 122-48.

The introduction of a tapa-beating machine to Tonga allowed the author to analyse the
various socio-cultural actions that would be lost or radically changed if the traditional
process of beating tapa with a wooden mallet were to be superseded. But the beating
process is more than a mundane secular action. The arts can still have cultural,
symbolic and even sacred elements embedded in the process of manufacture, and the
beating of tapa aligns with gender, societal and rank-based divisions of labour.
Tensions between ideologies are exemplified in the question of whether to beat or not.

401 **Tongan grave art.**
Jehanne Teilhet-Fisk.   In: *Art and identity in Oceania.*   Edited by
Allan Hanson, Louise Hanson.   Honolulu, Hawai'i: University of
Hawai'i Press, 1990, p. 222-43.

Funerals are Tonga's most important social events in that they affirm and celebrate the
deceased's role in life and clarify how the extended family is related, as well as
offering comfort, love and a formal burial. But before the arrival of the missionaries,
only kings and chiefs had graves, sculpted from cut coral and covered with white
sand. Commoners died uncommemorated. This paper focuses on the graves of
commoners, which reflect the synthesis of neo-traditional forms with new materials
from industrial societies, applied in an innovative manner that rarely disturbs the
original meaning. The grave decorator uses bottles, cans, tinsel, fabrics, plastics or
whatever is to hand in a unique way that makes statements about attitudes to death and
is also an art form reflecting Tongan ethno-aesthetic values, surviving the critical
comments of many foreigners. Grave art, usually undertaken by women, responds
quickly to cultural change and prevailing taste, and broadcasts a new ordering of
social relationships where anyone can aspire to be noble. It transgresses the Tongan
system of rank. The author describes the conduct of funerals and the subsequent
decoration of the grave: the art is joyful and playful, the colours bright and often
gaudy. She describes and illustrates different styles of grave decoration. Recent

developments include the use of fabrics printed with religious scenes, and the adding of the person's name. Plastic flowers may now replace fresh ones. Some now prefer cement graves to sand, indicating modernity and status, and memorial stones. She sees this as part of the increased significance of the nuclear family and a rising middle class.

402   Tongan symmetries.
Donald W. Crowe.   In: *Education, language, patterns and policy.*
Edited by John Morrison, Paul Geraghty, Linda Crowl.   Suva:
Institute of Pacific Studies, 1994, p. 79-106. bibliog. (Science of
Pacific Island Peoples, Volume IV).

Crowe, a mathematician, examines geometric symmetries in Tongan decorative arts, as they appear in *ngatu*, basketry trays, rafter lashings and mats, and in old carved war clubs. He compares present-day work with that shown in old prints and finds continuity particularly in rafter lashings: those drawn by Captain Cook and other early explorers are very similar to those still done today. While he demonstrates symmetry particularly in the patterns of trays, illustrated with several photographs, he seems not to explain why symmetry is so significant, but the paper at least introduces the work to those interested in Tongan crafts generally.

403   Women's handicrafts and men's arts: the production of material culture in the Polynesian kingdom of Tonga.
Paul van der Grijp.   *Journal de la Société des Océanistes*, no. 97
(1993), p. 159-69.

This article deals with aspects of material culture which are traditionally important in Tonga. The author examines three kinds of women's work – the production of tapa cloth, mats and baskets – and two types of men's work – wood carving and the making of ornaments. The male producers are seen by many as artists, although their work is not traditional, while the women's output is a part of community production. He describes the ways in which products are made and the organization of the producers. He provides case-studies from Vava'u, Ha'apai and Tongatapu, and considers the influence of the tourist industry on what is produced. The treatment is quite brief.

404   Wrapping in images: tattooing in Polynesia.
Alfred Gell.   Oxford: Clarendon Press, 1993. 347p. bibliog.

Tattoo, with taboo, is one of the few Polynesian words to be taken into English. Tattooing was introduced into Tonga from Fiji, but it had less emphasis there than in Samoa and elsewhere in Polynesia. At the time of Cook's visit most Tongan men, but not women, were tattooed between the belly and the thighs, but it seems to have been more a matter of individual enterprise than of formal initiation or political obligation. By the mid-19th century the practice had largely died out under missionary influence. Gell sets tattooing in Western Polynesia within the context of relationships between Fiji, Tonga and Samoa and describes its practice, function and social significance in each group.

Performance Arts

405 An annotated bibliography of Oceanic music and dance.
Mervyn McLean.   Warren, Michigan: Harmonie Park Press, 1995.
Revised and enlarged second edition. 502p.

The first edition of this bibliography was published by the Polynesian Society in 1977, with a supplement in 1981. The first edition contained 2,200 entries, with over 500 in the supplement. The revised second edition adds a further 1,000 entries, and covers all the islands of the Pacific with references to books, journal articles, reviews, record sleeve notes and theses in English and other European languages. Entries are arranged in one alphabetical sequence and coded for area, with an index to the area codes. There are some 160 entries for Tonga, some of them detailed, others passing references in general accounts, ranging in time from brief mentions in the journals of Captain Cook and some of those who sailed with him, up to 1992.

406 Musical acculturation in Tonga.
R. Raven-Hart.   *Oceania*, vol. 26, no. 2 (1955), p. 110-17.

From observations made during a stay in Vava'u the author examines the way in which Western music has been adapted to Tongan taste. He gives examples of hymn tunes and popular songs to show the characteristic way in which they were adapted, in particular the importance of the bass part in their harmonization.

407 *'Otuhaka*: a Tongan dance.
Kik Velt.   Nuku'alofa: 'Atenisi University, 1991. 66p.

In the face of modern Western musical influences, the purpose of this booklet is to contribute to the preservation of one of Tonga's traditional dances, the *'Otuhaka*. It shows step-by-step how each movement is accomplished, with illustrations taken from an accompanying computer animation available on disk for Apple Macintosh. An introduction places the *'Otuhaka* among the other Tongan dances. The words sung with the dance are printed in both Tongan and English.

408 **Poetry in motion: studies of Tongan dance.**
Adrienne L. Kaeppler. Nuku'alofa: Vava'u Press, 1993. 150p. map. bibliog.

Dance is an integral part of Tongan culture, society and history. This volume reprints eight articles published between 1967 and 1978, with a new introduction. Together they offer a thorough and detailed account of all the major types of Tongan dance: not only their words, music and movement, but also their cultural and social significance. The many photographs, all taken by Kaeppler during her frequent visits to Tonga, vividly bring Tongan dance alive.

409 **Sounds of change in Tonga: dance, music and cultural dynamics in a Polynesian kingdom.**
Ad Linkels. Nuku'alofa: Friendly Islands Book Shop, 1992. 128p. 2 maps. bibliog.

Linkels sees adaptation as the key to the ability of Tongans to recover from the hardest times without losing their own identity. A Dutch musicologist, he spent several periods in Tonga exploring Tongan dance and music and the way in which it is adapting to social change today; in the process, he toured all the island groups to see performances. He describes, and illustrates with many of his own photographs, all the main types of Tongan dance and music, including the more recent developments of the brass band and pop groups. For a more scholarly treatment he refers readers to Kaeppler (item no. 408) and Moyle (item no. 411). This is a more general and personal introduction.

410 **Structured movement systems in Tonga.**
Adrienne L. Kaeppler. In: *Society and the dance: the social anthropology of process and performance.* Edited by Paul Spencer. Cambridge, England: Cambridge University Press, 1985, p. 92-118.

Broader in scope than her papers on dance published as *Poetry in motion: studies of Tongan dance* (item no. 408), this paper describes the structured movements involved in various formal activities: the ceremonial presentation of pigs; the enumeration of foodstuffs and the mixing of kava at a kava ceremony; group speeches with choreo-graphed movements; and the movements associated with the *tau'olunga* dance and its accompanying songs. All these movements visually emphasize the importance of rank and social solidarity. They are an extension of speech and gesture that add further levels of meaning to formal occasions.

411 **Tongan music.**
Richard Moyle. Auckland, New Zealand: Auckland University Press, 1987. 256p. 5 maps. bibliog.

In the first ethnomusicological study of Tongan music, Moyle analyses the accounts of Tongan music and dance provided by the early explorers and the effect of missionaries who suppressed some forms and encouraged others. He describes how songs are composed and performed; four main categories of musical instruments; the dances of the old and the new tradition; nine categories of songs; and twenty-two of game songs. He also gives space for Tongan musicians to speak for themselves. This is accom-panied by detailed technical musicological analysis and 125 musical examples. It must be said that the work has been criticized by Kaeppler for being excessively based on tapes of radio broadcasts rather than on observation of actual performances, for some inaccuracy, for lack of social context, and for being more concerned with the past than the present. An ethnomusicologist and a cultural anthropologist may have different approaches and seek the answers to different questions. Moyle's concern seems to be what the music actually consists of, set down in proper musical notation: Kaeppler's seems to be what it signifies of the nature of Tongan society. The full picture may require both approaches.

412   **Wry comments from the outback: songs of protest from the Niua Islands, Tonga.**
Wendy Pond.   In: *South Pacific oral traditions.*   Edited by Ruth Finnegan, Margaret Orbell.   Bloomington, Indiana; Indianapolis, Indiana: Indiana University Press, 1995, p. 49-63.

In Tonga, a song can convey multiple levels of meaning. Pond analyses songs from the far northern Niua islands in which, behind the obvious meaning, poets indirectly and in metaphor speak ruefully about the hardships of their lives and assert their independence of thought in the face of political and economic rule from the south. They lack leadership, while the better educated young people go to seek work and status in Tongatapu; they pay their taxes but the government does not reciprocate with aid for development. Songs, Pond concludes, give a voice to the poor and those who have no political power.

Books and Media

413 Book mart.
Nicky Harmer. *Lali*, March 1994, p. 7-9.
This magazine article surveys the bookselling scene in Tonga, noting the increasing demand for reading materials, both magazines and books. It describes the three major booksellers and examines library provision in Tonga, listing the few significant libraries that exist and deploring the lack of a national library.

414 Islands Business Pacific.
Suva: Islands Business International, 1990- . monthly.
This is a monthly news journal for the South Pacific, rather along the same lines as the older *Pacific Islands Monthly* (item no. 418) but with a stronger emphasis on politics, economics, business and trade, and associated topics such as transport and energy.

**415 Mass communication and journalism in the Pacific islands:
a bibliography.**
Compiled by Jim Richstad, Michael McMillan. Honolulu, Hawai'i:
The University of Hawai'i Press for the East-West Center, 1978. 299p.
This bibliography covers the period 1854-1975, and for each country the items are listed under broad subject headings. The seventy-eight items listed for Tonga are mainly concerned with newspapers and periodicals (12); the press (17); and radio (24). Other topics covered include cinema and the freedom of the press. Most of the items cited are news reports and articles from *The Tonga Chronicle* and *Pacific Islands Monthly*, brief indications of issues of interest at the time but not substantial.

416 Matangi Tonga: the national news magazine.
Nuku'alofa: Vava'u Press, 1985- . quarterly.
Matangi Tonga takes a firmly independent line as it reports and examines events in Tonga. It can sometimes be critical of the established order, but its coverage is thorough and well-informed, whether on proceedings in parliament, cases in the courts, the

economy, business, agriculture, education, religion or cultural events. Many issues carry extensive interviews with people in the news, such as members of the royal family or members of parliament, as well as profiles of interesting visitors to Tonga. Early issues carried material in both Tongan and English but all content is now in English only.

417 **Moving images of the Pacific islands: a guide to films and videos.**
Edited by Diane Aoki, compiled by Diane Aoki, Norman Douglas. Honolulu, Hawai'i: Center for Pacific Islands Studies, University of Hawai'i at Mānoa, 1994. 347p. bibliog. (Occasion Paper, no. 38).

This guide to over 1,000 films and videos on the islands of the Pacific and their peoples is in alphabetical order of title. Each entry gives the country or region covered, the length and technical details of format, and indicates how it may be found through a distributor, the producer or a library. There is also a brief description. The catalogue is preceded by two general essays on film in the Pacific islands. There is one combined index, covering makers, subjects and countries. Twenty-one films on Tonga in whole or in part are listed, covering many aspects of life, crafts, dance, marriages, funerals and social life as well as general travelogues.

418 **Pacific Islands Monthly.**
Suva: Fiji Times, 1930- . monthly.

For close on seventy years, *PIM* has been recording newsworthy events in the Pacific. It concentrates on political, economic and commercial aspects but cultural events, sport and even sailors' accounts of their travels are also regularly covered, in a combination of immediate news stories and background features. The correspondence columns often offer lively comment. While the larger countries such as Papua New Guinea and Fiji feature most, news from the smaller island groups, including Tonga, appears regularly. *PIM* also views Pacific issues from its largest and most involved neighbours, Australia and New Zealand.

419 **Print and broadcast media in the South Pacific.**
Romeo B. Abundo. Singapore: The Asian Mass Communication Research and Information Centre, 1985. 78p. 5 maps.

This is the report of a study commissioned by UNESCO to examine 'methods of establishing community newspapers in remote islands on the Pacific, in conjunction with other community media, notably radio'. It concludes that overall the printed media plays a lesser role and is given lower priority than radio. Only Papua New Guinea and Fiji have daily newspapers, though the difficulty of printing and distributing newspapers around a group of small, scattered islands such as Tonga is noted. In both press and radio, training and resources are inadequate. A general overview is followed by a section on each country. The few pages on Tonga outline the status and operation of the Tonga Broadcasting Commission and the *Tonga Chronicle* (item no. 422). It is incorrectly stated that the *Kalonikali* is a separate publication. *Matangi Tonga* (item no. 416) only began publication after this report was written. The report suggests that Tonga should have a daily newspaper; this has not happened and does not seem practical.

420 Publishing in Tonga.

Pesi Fonua. *Pacific Islands Communication Journal*, vol. 14, no. 1 (1985), p. 30-40.

In Tonga, as elsewhere in the Pacific, the printed word was introduced by missionaries in the early 19th century, as part of their work of evangelization and education. However, Fonua begins his brief account with *kupesi*, the wood-block printing used to decorate tapa cloth. Printing and publishing as known today began on 14 April 1811, with the production of a four-page book of bible instruction on a printing press brought by the missionaries. Most printing in the 19th century was by church and government. Fonua outlines the situation as in the early 1980s, with the largest printer being the government printing department, and the development of publishing, largely educational, in the 1970s. He describes the printing techniques then available: spirit duplicators; photocopiers; screen printing (for cards, posters and textiles); letterpress; and litho. Works locally printed and published are mostly short pamphlets and booklets, with about four books a year. Fonua identifies problems and constraints in local manufacture and distribution. There have been considerable developments since the time of writing, not least Fonua's own Vava'u Press and his news magazine *Matangi Tonga* (item no. 416), much assisted by the arrival of computers, making in-house low-cost typesetting possible.

421 Radio in Tonga.

Tavake Fusimalohi. *Pacific Islands Communication Journal*, vol. 15, no. 1 (1987), p. 63-75.

Radio Tonga began broadcasting in 1961 and immediately showed its practical value by providing warnings and instructions during a devastating hurricane. Initially a department of government, it was established as the independent Tongan Broadcasting Commission in 1975. The author describes the studios, equipment, staffing and programme schedules, which consist both of the relaying of overseas broadcasts, such as news from the BBC World Service, and locally produced material – news, religion, education, agriculture, public health and official announcements. Personal messages are also an important item. Programmes are usually financed by sponsorship and are in both Tongan and English. Broadcasting expanded from two hours a day in 1961 to sixteen in 1987. There is probably at least one radio in every household, and eighty per cent of the population listen at least once a day. Radio Tonga has had considerable effect in bringing the islands of the kingdom closer together and in encouraging communal development activities.

422 The Tonga Chronicle/Ko e Kalonikali Tonga.

Nuku'alofa: The Government of Tonga, 1963- . weekly.

The Tonga Chronicle, Tonga's only newspaper, is published weekly in two separate editions, Tongan and English. It prints local, royal, political, economic, social and sports news. While it has an official status, it can express independent views. Special events such as royal anniversaries and the annual agricultural shows are sometimes covered in colour. Some international news and features are reprinted from overseas newspapers.

423 **Who manipulates Pacific media? Influences on newspapers and television.**
Makareta Waqavonovono. *Pacific Perspective*, vol. 10, no. 1 (1981), p. 13-36.

Tonga features briefly in this general survey of Western influences on Pacific media at the time of publication. The author quotes the former editor of *The Tonga Chronicle* on the prime importance of the Tongan rather than the English version, in a discussion of the use of vernacular languages in addition to English. She identifies the kava club as an important source of communication alongside the press and radio. Discussions in the article of the foreign ownership of news media do not relate to Tonga. Waqavonovono analyses the percentage of national, Pacific, non-Pacific and sports news in *The Tonga Chronicle* and in comparable papers in Western Samoa, Fiji and Niue, finding that they do not differ greatly.

Academic Journals

424 **Archaeology in Oceania.**
Sydney: University of Sydney, 1966- . three parts a year.
This journal publishes papers and book reviews in the fields of archaeology and physical anthropology. Archaeology is considered to include both prehistoric and historic periods as well as studies of modern material behaviour. The journal covers all the islands of the Pacific Ocean, including Australia. Many reports on Lapita pottery, some relating to Tonga, were first published here.

425 **Asia Pacific Viewpoint.**
Oxford: Blackwell Publishers, 1960- . three parts a year.
Edited from the Department of Geography, Victoria University of Wellington, New Zealand, this journal publishes the research of geographers and scholars of other disciplines on the economic and social development of countries in the Asia Pacific region, paying particular attention to the interplay between development and the environment. Until 1996 it was published as *Pacific Viewpoint*, and there are more papers on Tonga and other Pacific island countries in earlier years than recently.

426 **The Contemporary Pacific: a Journal of Island Affairs.**
Honolulu, Hawai'i: Center for Pacific Islands Studies and University of Hawai'i Press, 1989- . biannual.
In its first issue the journal defined its purpose as 'to provide a scholarly vehicle for a broad-ranging exchange of ideas on contemporary developments in the Pacific Islands, expressed in the ordinary language of intelligent discourse'. Its articles, within the humanities and social sciences, include both broad surveys and detailed studies. It reviews the most significant new books. A political reviews section rounds up and comments on the most important news from each country in the region, and sections on Tonga every few issues usefully summarize key events. Regular articles on resources give details of archives and records.

427 **Faikava: a Tongan literary journal.**
Nuku'alofa: University of the South Pacific Centre, 1978-83. biannual.
The editors established *Faikava* as an outlet for creative writing in both Tongan and English, and as a forum for the exchange of ideas about literature: 'The title *Faikava* evokes the image of a group of people gathered round the kava bowl, speaking and dreaming, stretching their minds and trading old ideas and new gossip, facts and fiction'. It ceased publication after its tenth number.

428 **Journal de la Société des Océanistes.**
Paris: Musée de l'Homme, 1945- . biannual.
This journal covers the archaeology, history, anthropology, economics and overall way of life of the Pacific. While it particularly reflects French interest in its own territories, it publishes papers concerning the whole of the Pacific, both in French and in English.

429 **The Journal of Pacific History.**
Abingdon, England: Carfax Publishing Company, 1966- .
three parts a year.
This journal serves historians, prehistorians, anthropologists and others interested in the study of mankind in the Pacific islands, and is concerned generally with political, economic, religious and cultural factors affecting human presence there. Many important articles on Tonga published here have since been incorporated into the general literature. In addition to articles and book reviews, it publishes notes on source materials, comment on current affairs and a regular bibliography of theses, articles and books.

430 **The Journal of the Polynesian Society.**
Auckland, New Zealand: The Polynesian Society, 1892- . quarterly.
This is the longest-established journal in its field. It is a forum for scholarly discussion of the history, ethnology, physical anthropology, sociology, archaeology and linguistics of the peoples of the Pacific, and contains some specialist studies on Tongan society.

431 **Oceania.**
Sydney: University of Sydney, 1930- . quarterly.
Oceania is devoted to the functional study of the countries of the Oceanic region, and publishes original contributions in the field of social and cultural anthropology. Its primary regional orientation is to the indigenous peoples of Australia, Melanesia, Polynesia, Micronesia and Southeast Asia. It includes reviews of books on these areas.

432 **Oceanic Linguistics.**
Honolulu, Hawai'i: University of Hawai'i Press, 1961- . biannual.
This journal publishes current research on the languages of the Oceanic area, in their protohistorical and current forms. In the second part of each volume, there is an index of the languages covered in that volume.

433   **The Pacific Journal of Theology.**
        Suva: South Pacific Association of Theological Schools, Series II,
        1989- . biannual.

This journal seeks to stimulate theological thinking and writing by Christians living in or familiar with the South Pacific. It publishes papers on theology from a Pacific perspective and relating to Pacific cultures, as well as practical material for pastors and church workers. It also lists masters' and batchelors' theses in progress at the Pacific Theological College.

434   **Pacific Studies.**
        Honolulu, Hawai'i: The Institute for Polynesian Studies, Brigham
        Young University, 1977- . quarterly.

This publication describes itself as 'a multidisciplinary journal devoted to the study of the peoples of the Pacific Islands'. It publishes papers in the disciplines of anthropology; archaeology; art history; economics; ethnomusicology; folklore; geography; history; political science; sociolinguistics; and sociology. In addition to book reviews, some issues list recent publications on and from the Pacific islands received by a number of major academic libraries in Australia, New Zealand and the Pacific.

Encyclopaedias and
Reference Works

435 The cyclopedia of Samoa, Tonga, Tahiti and the Cook Islands.
Sydney: McCarron, Stewart & Co., 1907. 208p.

The *Cyclopedia* describes itself as 'a complete review of the history and traditions and the commercial development of the Islands, with statistics and data never before compiled in a single publication'. The sixty-six page section on Tonga describes the islands and provides statistics on population and trade; government finances; lists of people prominent in state and church; a history of Tonga; some documents relating to the fall of Shirley Baker; the address from the throne at the opening of parliament in 1906 and the reply; and information about the churches. Biographical notices follow of the most important people in Tonga, both Tongan (starting with King George Tupou II) and European – traders, church leaders, government officials and teachers. There are many photographs of people and places. The work was reprinted in facsimile in New Zealand in 1983.

436 Historical dictionary of Oceania.
Edited by Robert D. Craig, Frank P. King. Westport, Connecticut; London: Greenwood Press, 1981. 392p. 20 maps. bibliog.

The purpose of this work is to provide basic factual information on the history of the countries of the Pacific in a uniform style. Articles specifically on Tonga include: 'Atenisi Institute and University; Shirley Baker; Joel Bulu; 'Eua; William Mariner; Queen Sālote; King George Tupou I; John Thomas; Tonga; Tonga code of 1862; Tongan Constitution; Tongan oral culture; Tu'i Ha'atakalaua; Tu'i Kanokupolu; Tu'i Tonga; William Tupoulahi Tungi; Fīnau 'Ulukālala; and George Vason. Entries are introductory rather than comprehensive: each is followed by a list of sources for further study. Many other articles have references to Tonga. Appendixes list rulers, explorers, chronologies, etc. There is a select general bibliography.

437   **Oceania – a regional study.**
Edited by Frederica M. Bunge, Melinda W. Cooke.   Washington, DC:
Foreign Area Studies, The American University, 1984. 2nd ed.
572p. 22 maps. bibliog.

This is one of a series of volumes devoted to the major regions of the world. The aim
of the series is to describe and analyse economic, national security, political and social
systems and institutions in each region and to examine the interrelationship of these
systems and institutions and the way they are shaped by cultural factors. Attention is
paid to origin and tradition, dominant beliefs and values, the community of interests in
the regions and issues on which regional players are divided. The eighteen-page
section on Tonga by Stephen B. Wickman meets this brief for factual information on
Tonga in the mid-1980s, though rather less for any analysis of beliefs and attitudes.
The book also provides a general overview of the area and information on regional
organizations.

General Bibliographies

438 **Australasia and South Pacific islands bibliography.**
     John Thawley.   Lanham, Maryland; London: The Scarecrow Press,
     1997. 587p. (Scarecrow Area Bibliographies, no. 12).
This is a selective bibliography of a region about which it has been estimated that one
new book has been published daily since 1965. The majority of the 5,933 works cited
are in English and published in the last fifty years. 610 items on the South Pacific
generally are followed by sections on each country, 63 for Tonga under broad subject
headings, mostly books rather than journal articles. Bibliographical details only, with
no annotation or description, are given for the works listed. Authors only are indexed.

439 **Bibliography of Captain James Cook R.N., F.R.S.,**
     circumnavigator.
     Edited by M. K. Beddie.   Sydney: The Library of New South Wales,
     1970. 2nd ed. 894p.
The journals and printed editions of the voyages of Captain Cook are central to the
study of Tonga (item nos. 49, 50 and 53). This bibliography, based on holdings in the
Library of New South Wales (including the Mitchell Library) and other libraries in
Australia, provides the most complete listing of materials by and on Cook and his
associates. In a general section, and then for each of the three voyages, it lists
manuscripts, printed accounts, books and articles about the voyages, charts, films,
illustrations, and information about the ships. There are also sections on works by
Cook not relating to the three voyages; personal materials including portraits and
monuments; imaginative literature on the life of Cook; and material relating to his
associates. The volume of work listed demonstrates the enormous interest in Cook and
his voyages, both in his own time and since.

440 **A bibliography of Fiji, Tonga and Rotuma.**
Philip A. Snow.   Canberra: Australian National University Press,
1969. 418p. 4 maps.

Snow's book, the fruit of thirty years' work largely compiled when he was in the colonial administrative service in Fiji, is the foundation of Tongan bibliography, with 1,916 entries on the three groups generally and 1,535 specific to Tonga, and nearly 400 periodicals cited. The entries are arranged under sixty-three subject headings and there is one combined alphabetical author index. It covers papers in academic journals, articles in popular magazines, books, pieces in newspapers and even some letters and manuscript material. Full bibliographical references are provided, but there is no annotation and the significant needs to be sorted from the ephemeral. The work was completed in the mid-1960s, and thus must be supplemented for the ever-expanding output of work on Tonga in the thirty years since. H. E. Maude in his foreword describes it as 'a remarkably comprehensive and useful work which satisfies the primary practical demands made of a bibliography: the listing of published material in a form which enables its identification and therefore its eventual location'.

441 **A bibliography of Pacific island theses and dissertations.**
W. G. Coppell, S. Stratigos.   Canberra: Research School of Pacific
Studies, Australian National University, 1983. 520p.

This bibliography lists all theses and dissertations on the Pacific islands (excluding New Zealand and Hawai'i) to the end of 1980, and includes those at batchelor's and diploma level as well as master's and doctoral. The author index contains the full record. A subject and country index cross-references every entry. Under Tonga there are over 100 entries, though some theses are listed under more than one subject heading if appropriate.

442 **Dictionary catalog of the library, Bernice P. Bishop Museum,
Honolulu, Hawaii.**
Boston, Massachusetts: G. K. Hall, 1964. 9 vols. (first supplement,
1967. second supplement, 1969).

The Bishop Museum is the only American museum which confines its efforts entirely to the peoples and natural areas of the Pacific, and its library has comprehensive collections on the region. Library catalogue cards have been photographed to produce this printed catalogue. There are almost 300 entries on Tonga in the main catalogue and the two supplements, including journal and magazine articles as well as books.

443 **Dictionary catalog of printed books: The Mitchell Library.**
Boston, Massachusetts: G. K. Hall, 1968. 38 vols. (first supplement,
1970).

The massive catalogue of this major collection in Australia records over a quarter of a million items. Each entry is reproduced directly from the index card, though it is noted that many of the early entries are inadequate. Under the headings Tonga/Tongans/ Tongan language are recorded almost 600 items, many early and scarce; a search under other related headings, such as Tongatapu or Vava'u, will reveal more.

444   **Indigenous navigation and voyaging in the Pacific: a reference guide.**
Compiled by Nicholas J. Goetzfridt.   New York; Westport,
Connecticut; London: Greenwood Press, 1992. 294p. map.
(Bibliographies and Indexes in Anthropology, no. 6).

This bibliography of 694 items primarily covers journal articles and books in English, other European languages and Japanese, which concentrate on the main aspects of indigenous navigation and voyaging. Every entry is annotated, some at considerable length. Following a section of 115 entries on the Pacific in general, there are a further 398 on Polynesia. Fifty-seven entries contain references to Tonga, some central and some peripheral. Indexes are provided by author, geographical area and subject.

445   **Pacific basin and Oceania.**
Gerald W. Fry, Rufino Mauricio.   Oxford; Santa Barbara, California;
Denver, Colorado: Clio Press, 1987. 468p. map. (World
Bibliographical Series, vol. 70).

This bibliography is in the same series as the present volume and follows the same general style, selective rather than complete, and annotated. 524 items relating to the Pacific in general are listed by subject. Sections follow on Melanesia, Micronesia and Polynesia, with general works on each, and then a section on each individual country. In the inevitably brief and highly selective section on Tonga there are thirty-four entries. The comprehensive indexes direct the user to books in other sections which have some reference to Tonga, making the coverage more comprehensive.

446   **A Pacific bibliography: printed matter relating to the native
peoples of Polynesia, Melanesia and Micronesia.**
C. R. H. Taylor.   Oxford: Clarendon Press, 1965. 2nd ed. 692p. map.

The first edition of Taylor's bibliography was published in 1951. This, the second edition, is as complete as possible up to 1960. The work has four sections, covering Oceania, Polynesia, Melanesia and Micronesia, and each entry consists of bibliographical details, most without comment or annotation. General works which include reference to Tonga may be found in the Oceania section. Entries in the three regional sections are set out by country, with about 200 for Tonga under the headings of general ethnology; physical and mental characteristics; culture contact; social organization and custom; religion; music; arts; science and medicine; language; folklore; and material culture. The lack of sections on economy, trade, politics etc. is noticeable. References cover books and journals, both general and academic. This is a useful and now a classic bibliography, but in those sections which can be compared directly with Snow (item no. 440) it is less comprehensive.

447   **Pacific island studies: a survey of the literature.**
Editor-in-chief Miles M. Jackson.   New York; Westport, Connecticut;
London: Greenwood Press, 1986. 244p.

This work was planned for newcomers to Pacific studies needing a basic guide to the key social science literature, a concise synthesis of the significant literature rather than a broad-based bibliography. It is in the form of a series of bibliographic essays, allowing the writer to put into perspective a body of literature. Each group of essays is followed by an alphabetical bibliographical listing. The two-page essay on Tonga provides a very selective introduction to the most basic works on Tongan history and society.

448 **Pacific islands: a basic annotated bibliography for students, librarians and general readers.**
Roger Hughes.   London: Commonwealth Institute, 1989. 62p.
(Commonwealth Bibliographies Series).

This booklet lists, in summary form, some of the basic literature on the Pacific islands of the British Commonwealth. Entries are under the headings of general background; arts and crafts; economy; education; environment and health; history and settlement; language; literature; media; nature; people and society; politics; and religion and cults. There is an index by country. For Tonga, nineteen works are listed, one or two of the key general works in most sections. A list of major libraries in London with Pacific collections omits the School of Oriental and African Studies, which has one of the major academic collections.

449 **Pacific islands dissertations and theses from the University of Hawai'i, 1923-1996.**
Compiled by Lynette Furuhashi.   Honolulu, Hawai'i: Center for Pacific Islands Studies, University of Hawai'i at Mānoa, 1996. 116p.
(Occasional Paper, no. 39).

Theses, both masters' and doctoral, are recorded under geographical headings, by region and country. Entries give author, length, title of degree, and location number in the Hamilton Library of the University of Hawai'i. There are indexes by author, title, chronological order, degree and field of study. For Tonga, ten theses are listed, including one on Tongans in Hawai'i. The four doctoral theses are listed in the present bibliography.

450 **South Pacific bibliography.**
Suva: Pacific Information Centre, The University of the South Pacific Library, 1981- . biennial.

This bibliography continues from the *Pacific collection accession list* of the University of the South Pacific, which was published from 1975-82; it has been published annually, with a few exceptions, since 1981, and is now biennial. It aims to list as comprehensively as possible works published in the region and works published overseas relating wholly or in part to the countries of the region. It covers published and unpublished monographs; theses; government publications; serials on first appearance; maps; and other appropriate material. Monographs are listed by Dewey Decimal classification and there are indexes for author, title, series and subject. Entries and indexes are compiled by the University of the South Pacific library.

451 **South Pacific periodicals index, Volumes 14-15, 1987-1988.**
Suva: Pacific Information Centre, The University of the South Pacific, 1995. 245p.

This index began life as the *Bibliography of periodical articles relating to the South Pacific*, changing to the present title in 1984, and is based on journals held in the University of the South Pacific library. The alphabetical listing is by country and subject, followed by an author index. The work needs to be used with care, and carefully scanned. There are many entries under Tonga, with such subheadings as antiquities, foreign relations and politics. However, entries for Tonga may also be found under subject headings such as airlines or computers. Further, almost all the entries on

Tonga listed are from general periodicals, in particular *Matangi Tonga* (item no. 416). While it is very useful to have references to these, the articles are often brief. Little solid academic writing on Tonga seems to have been recorded for this period.

452 World catalogue of theses on the Pacific islands.

Compiled by Diane Dickson, Carol Dossor.   Canberra: Australian National University Press, 1970. 123p.

This catalogue is based on the microfilm library of theses held at the Australian National University, supplemented by the examination of other thesis catalogues. Besides doctoral theses, it selectively covers some at master's level. For Tonga it lists twenty-two theses, the most recent dated 1968. The six doctoral theses in English (there are also two in German) are listed in the present bibliography.

Indexes

There follow three separate indexes: authors (personal or corporate); titles; and subjects. Title entries are italicized and refer either to the main titles, or to other works cited in the annotations. The numbers refer to bibliographical entry rather than page number. Individual index entries are arranged in alphabetical sequence.

Index of Authors

DeVita, P. R. 12
Dickinson, W. R. 79
Dickson, D. 452
Donald, S. L. 107
Dossor, C. 452
Douaire-Marsaudon, F. 201
Douglas, N. 417
Duffels, J. P. 59
Düring, K. 97
Dye, T. S. 72, 79, 147, 355

E

Eckert, F. J. 16
Ellem, E. W. *see* Wood-Ellem, E.
Elliott, J. D. 267
Ernst, M. 172
Erskine, J. E. 48
Etienne, M. 210
Eustis, N. 134
Ewart, A. 28

F

Faeamani, S. 'U. 318
Fairbairn, T. I. J. 10, 290, 310
Faletau, M. 179
Fanua, T. P. 135, 378
Farmer, S. S. 115
Fawcett, J. T. 311
Feldman, H. 224
Felszer, M. 238
Ferdon, E. N. 124
Finau, M. 160
Finau, P. P. 366
Finau, S. A. 226, 235, 239, 243, 246-47
Finnegan, R. 412
Firth, S. 84
Fisher, R. L. 36
Fisk, E. K. 339
Fisk, S. J. 20
Fleming, E. M. 347-48
Fleming, S. 337
Fonua, M. 45
Fonua, P. 45, 190, 377, 420

Fonua, S. 182
Forman, C. W. 160, 164, 171
Foster, J. 330
Fox, E. 9
Fox, J. L. 99
Franco, R. W. 193
Fry, G. W. 445
Fuka, L. M. 162
Funaki, K. 326
Fungalei, L. 190
Furuhashi, L. 449
Fusimalohi, T. 421

G

Gailey, C. W. 195, 210, 215, 316
Gannicott, K. G. 363
Garrett, J. 114
Gell, A. 404
Geraghty, P. 402
Gerstle, D. 5, 17
Gifford, E. W. 18, 220, 383
Gillett, R. 361
Gittings, A. 381
Goetzfridt, N. J. 444
Gordon, T. 163, 169
Greenall, L. 3
Grijp, P. van der 104, 189, 192, 260, 338, 345, 394, 403
Groube, L. M. 82
Groves, S. A. 10
Gubler, D. J. 234
Gunson, N. 70, 75, 93, 100, 106, 109, 116, 125, 130, 176, 187, 199, 233, 262, 324, 332, 364, 385

H

Haddon, A. C. 390
Hahn, E. P. 12
Halapua, S. 308, 357
Halapua, W. 161
Hampton, N. 273
Hanson, A. 401
Hanson, L. 401

Hardaker, J. B. 347-48
Harmer, N. 413
Hau'ofa, E. 255, 285, 300, 366, 375, 377, 382
Havea, J. 379
Hayes, G. 323
Helu, H. 266
Helu, 'I. F. 177, 188, 248, 362, 369, 384
Henningham, S. 279
Herda, P. 70, 75, 93, 100, 116, 125, 176, 187, 233, 262, 324, 332, 364, 385
Hereniko, P. 190
Herr, R. 280
Hess, M. 293
Hiery, H. J. 263
Hills, R. C. 251-52
Hiroa, T. R. 158, 165
Hitchcock, J. C. 67, 234
Hoadley, S. 281
Hoffmeister, J. E. 27
Hornell, J. 390, 397
Howard, A. 183
Howe, K. R. 90
Huang, Y.-M. 67
Hughes, D. T. 159
Hughes, R. 448
Hunter, D. B. 273

I

Ikahihifo, T. 237

J

Jackson, M. M. 447
James, K. E. 184, 186-87, 204, 211, 219, 269, 321, 328, 333, 340
Jennings, J. D. 78
Jilek, W. G. 240

K

Kaeppler, A. L. 91, 183, 199, 212, 385, 388, 391-92, 395-96, 408, 410
Kaufmann, C. 395

166

Index of Titles

169

Index of Subjects

178

Map of Tonga

This map shows the more important features.

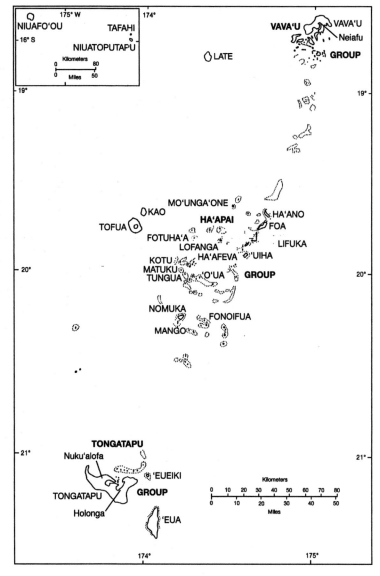

Reproduced from *Becoming Tongan* by Helen Morton with the kind permission of the University of Hawai'i Press

INTERNATIONAL ORGANIZATIONS SERIES

Each volume in the International Organizations Series is either devoted to one specific organization, or to a number of different organizations operating in a particular region, or engaged in a specific field of activity. The scope of the series is wide-ranging and includes intergovernmental organizations, international non-governmental organizations, and national bodies dealing with international issues. The series is aimed mainly at the English-speaker and each volume provides a selective, annotated, critical bibliography of the organization, or organizations, concerned. The bibliographies cover books, articles, pamphlets, directories, databases and theses and, wherever possible, attention is focused on material about the organizations rather than on the organizations' own publications. Notwithstanding this, the most important official publications, and guides to those publications, will be included. The views expressed in individual volumes, however, are not necessarily those of the publishers.

VOLUMES IN THE SERIES